FREEMASONS,
WORLD ORDER, AND
MIND WARS

FREEMASONS, WORLD ORDER, AND MIND WARS

THE GREAT REALITY OF MEMPHIS-MISRAIM MASONRY

NICOLAS LAOS

Algora Publishing
New York

Library of Congress Cataloging-in-Publication Data —

Names: Laos, Nicolas K., 1974- author.
Title: Freemasons, world order, and mind wars: the great reality of
   Memphis-Misraim masonry / Nicolas Laos.
Description: New York: Algora Publishing, [2016] | Includes bibliographical
   references.
Identifiers: LCCN 2016032065 (print) | LCCN 2016035172 (ebook) | ISBN
   9781628942194 (soft cover: alk. paper) | ISBN 9781628942200 (hard cover:
   alk. paper) | ISBN 9781628942217 (pdf)
Subjects: LCSH: Freemasonry—History. | Freemasonry—Religious aspects. |
   Freemasonry—Political aspects.
Classification: LCC HS403 .L36 2016 (print) | LCC HS403 (ebook) | DDC
   366/.1—dc23
LC record available at https://lccn.loc.gov/2016032065

Printed in the United States

"Dr Nicolas Laos's book intends to revolutionize our way of thinking by providing us with a new unconventional proposal: to transcend our Westphalian inter-state balance-of-power model, and to orient international-political thought toward a humanity-centered world order model, in the context of which power will be conceptualized and distributed according to mechanisms of self-consciousness and of communication among conscious human systems . . .

According Dr Laos's revolutionary work, humans cannot be divided into 'domestic' and 'foreign' national actors, because there are transnational cultural entities, and, more than that, humanity is ecumenical. One may also argue that Dr Laos's work is an original contribution to the idealist school of global politics. I may, indeed, argue that Dr Laos's work is a unique treatise that truly proclaims 'The End of History' by changing our way of thinking about global politics and 'world order,' and by interpreting the term 'end' as 'ultimate (transcendent) purpose' and not as the 'cease' of historical becoming."

> —Vassilis D. Kopsacheilis, Political Risk Consultant (Athens, Greece), Foreign Affairs The Hellenic Edition essayist, Author of The Geoentrepreneurs' Empire.

"Dr Laos's book . . . is not only a creative and original contribution to philosophy and esoteric research, but also a complex and grandiose noopolitical achievement."

> — Roman V. Romachev, C.I.I., CEO and Founder of the R-Techno Group (Moscow), Author of Competitive Intelligence.

"[This] book will make clear that it is natural for every Freemason to be aware of the divine spark that lives in us, and, thus, we may appreciate the Holy Grail that is in each one of us, so that we may contribute to the creation of a better world, more humane, more free, and feel proud of being builders of the Royal Art."

> — Prof. Dr Alberto Santoro (Università di Roma "La Sapienza"), Pro Grand Master of the U.M.S.O.I. (Italy).

Table of Contents

INTRODUCTION

"...I have become all things to all men,
that I may by all means save some..."

1 Corinthians 9:22

A. Esotericism

The term 'esotericism' is controversial and is often confused with the colloquial adjectival sense of something that is obscure and technical or that pertains to the minutiae of a particular area of common knowledge. The term esotericism derives from the Greek root 'eso', which means inner. Plato, in his dialogue *Alcibiades*, uses the expression "ta eso", meaning the inner things, and, in his dialogue *Theaetetus*, he uses the expression "ta exo", meaning "the outside things". The Greek adjective 'esoterikos' (esoteric) was coined by the rhetorician and satirist Lucian of Samosata (second century AD) in his book *The Auction of Lives* (paragraph 26). The term 'esoteric' first appeared in English in Thomas Stanley's *History of Philosophy*, which was published in 1701. Thomas Stanley used the term esoteric in order to describe the mystery-school of Pythagoras, since the Pythagoreans were divided into the exoteric circle (under training) and the esoteric circle (admitted into the 'inner' circle). The corresponding noun 'esotericism' was coined by the French philosopher and historian Jacques Matter in his book *Histoire Critique Du Gnosticisme* (1828), and it was popularized by the nineteenth century French occult author and ceremonial magician Eliphas Lévi (born Alphonse Louis Constant).

One of the most influential attempts to explain what unites the various currents designated by 'esotericism' in the scholarly sense is due to the prominent French scholar Antoine Faivre, who held a chair in the École Pratique des Hautes Études at the Sorbonne, he was University Professor of Germanic Studies at the University of Haute-Normandie, and also he was the director of the Cahiers de l'hermétisme and of the Bibliothèque de l'hermétisme. Faivre's definition of esotericism is based on his argument that the following four essential characteristics are present in the esoteric currents: (i) a theory of correspondences among all parts of the invisible and the visible cosmos, (ii) the conviction that nature is a living entity owing to a divine presence or life-force, (iii) the need for mediating elements (e.g., symbols, rituals, angels, visions) in order to access spiritual knowledge, and (iv) an experience of personal and spiritual transmutation when arriving at this inner knowledge.[1] However, the previous definition of esotericism is mainly descriptive, since it refers to certain behaviors, but it says nothing about the final causes of the different esoteric behaviors. Thus, Faivre's definition is not as general as Faivre and his followers assert, and it tends to limit 'esotericism' to particular esoteric behaviors (belief systems and spiritual practices) instead of offering a broad understanding of the motives that underpin the exhibition of esoteric behaviors. In this book, I shall follow a teleological approach to the concept of esotericism, in order to articulate a general definition of esotericism. My argument is that, if one wants to avoid the risks of lapsing into intellectual atavism and of fixating esotericists on particular stages of man's spiritual development, esotericism should be studied as a dynamic cultural phenomenon and particularly as an expression of man's attempt to know himself, to discern himself from the world and to impose his intentionality on the world.

In this book, I shall argue that esotericism as such, that is, the essence of esotericism (apart from the differences among particular esoteric 'schools' and currents), consists in giving witness to the reality of the human being and in particular to the autonomy of man, by focusing on the power of human consciousness's intentionality and on the outer reality's submissiveness to the intentionality of human consciousness. Additionally, the dynamic continuity between the structure of the world and the structure of human consciousness is the truth that serves as the foundation of the grand synthesis among philosophy, science and esotericism, which I propose in this book. Thus, following the previous adogmatic and teleological approach to esotericism, I understand esotericism as a program of personality creation and man's spiritual emancipation and as a Promethean erection of human

---

1 Antoine Faivre, *Access to Western Esotericism*, New York: State University of New York Press, 1994.

consciousness, which can be expressed in many different ways, such as: ceremonial magic, art, science, philosophy, religion, etc.

According to the rationale that I follow in this book, esotericism is based on the thesis that every object of consciousness exists not in itself but inextricably united to the meaning that is assigned to it by consciousness. Therefore, every manipulation of the meanings that are assigned to things and make the world meaningful is equivalent to a manipulation of the reality of the world itself by consciousness. This is, according to my rationale, the ultimate 'secret' of esotericism's power and significance. Furthermore, inherent in my previous argument is a powerful political message, since the moral autonomy that is achieved through and underpinned by my interpretation of Western esotericism implies a high level of personal and social autonomy.

B. Esotericism and the Study of History

We often have the feeling that historical 'events' provide us with cognitive security and that, due to this feeling of cognitive security, we can depend on them, because they never change, in contrast with the continually changing interpretations of them by men. But how can one intellectually legitimize his decision to treat historical events as objective (or 'crude') evidence? Isn't one's decision to depend on 'objective evidence' simply a way of interpreting what an event is? How can one define an event? When does an event begin, and when does it end? How do the initial and the final conditions of an event determine its significance and evaluation?

Until recently, historians believed that an event exists objectively, i.e. independently of human consciousness, and that, if we are not careful enough, we may stumble over it, or that it can smash up our interpretation of it. This is the position of historical positivism. However, in the twentieth century, many of the Enlightenment's certainties were destroyed; one of them was the belief in so-called cold, crude facts.[1] Thus, today, historians ask: What is an event? Historical events are not 'given,' they are not material realities buried somewhere in time. We cannot bring them back to the historical surface, clean them up and then exhibit them to our contemporaries under strong spotlights. A piece of historical research has nothing in common with a museum's showcase. Thus, today, historians have rediscovered what philosophers had been saying about history and what esotericists had been experiencing even before the Enlightenment: events are not pieces of objective evidence, and, therefore, they do not exist in some 'exoteric' record accessible by our observational skills.

---

1 Braudel, Fernand, "Histoire et sciences socials: la langue durée", Annales, Vol. 4, 1958, 725–753; Carr, Edward H., *What Is History?*, London: Penguin, 1961.

For instance, a student of the history of the Bavarian Illuminati must know that the founder of the Bavarian Illuminati was Adam Weishaupt and not Baron von Knigge and that the Order of the Bavarian Illuminati was founded in 1776. But a serious and spiritually demanding student of the history of the Bavarian Illuminati will search behind the previous facts in order to analyze the motives that guided Weishaupt's historical action, and he will seek to understand the existential purpose and the ethos of the Bavarian Illuminati. In general, the most spiritually fruitful approach to history is focused on the analysis of people's and societies' systems of fundamental significations, or values.

In the Bible, the above truth was stressed by Simeon when he prophesied that Jesus Christ would have a paradoxical effect on Israel and on people in general and that he would be "a sign which shall be spoken against" (Luke 2:34). Indeed, Christ being a person and a Mystery, and not an archaeological object, is open to several, different interpretations, according to each person's way of relating to the Christ Mystery and according to each person's ethos. After all, Jesus Christ himself said that men can know God the Father through God the Son and that the knowledge of God the Son presupposes a mystical participation and progress in God the Holy Spirit: "the Comforter [Paraclete] the Holy Ghost, whom the Father will send in my name, he shall teach you all things, and bring all things to your remembrance, whatsoever I have said unto you" (John 14:26). In other words, according to the Bible, orthodox Christology depends on a peculiar cultural attitude (participation in the Holy Spirit and psychological openness toward Christ's Gospel), and, therefore, the institution of the 'Church of Christ' is nothing more and nothing less than the community of people who participate in a common experiential knowledge of God through His Incarnate Logos, Jesus Christ.

Hence, in order to understand the Mystery of Christ, we must bear in mind Gabriel Marcel's distinction between 'problem' and 'mystery'. The distinction between 'problem' and 'mystery' hinges on the notion of participation. Marcel explains the distinction between problem and mystery as follows: a problem is something that one meets, and it is clearly differentiated from the intentionality of the observer's consciousness, whereas a mystery is something in which a person's intentionality is embedded.[1] A mystery is a peculiar problem that feeds back into its own structure. Thus, the initiates of the Christ Mystery understand Jesus Christ as the Archetype of the Divinized Man, whereas those who approach Jesus Christ as if he were merely an archaeological problem articulate a totally different Christology, e.g., they use fragmented and controversial

---

1 Marcel, Gabriel, *Being and Having*, trans. K. Farrer, Westminister: Dacre Press, 1949, 117.

archaeological information in order to challenge orthodox Christology by formulating intriguing speculations about Jesus' family and personal life, and sometimes they write 'masterpieces' of "pop pseudohistory," as Laura Miller characterized Michael Baigent's book *Holy Blood, Holy Grail* in a book review published in *The New York Times* on February 22, 2004. Furthermore, many Christian Church authorities, in their attempt to defend their doctrines against heretics and to impose their doctrines in an intellectually coercive manner, try to transform theological beliefs into coercive 'objective' truths, and, therefore, they repeat the heretics' errant Christological methodology, since they degrade Christology into an archaeological problem.

C. Esotericism, Culture, and Civilization

In order to place the study of esotericism within a philosophically and scientifically rigorous framework and in order to avoid charlatanism and spiritually sterile speculation, we must study esotericism as a cultural phenomenon. Hence, we must clarify two more concepts, namely, civilization and culture. From a broad perspective, the concept of civilization includes the concept of culture, but, from a narrower perspective, 'civilization' can be differentiated from 'culture' on the basis of the argument that 'civilization' is simultaneously the means and the result of the collective consciousness's attempt to achieve for itself better terms for its adaptation to the world, whereas 'culture' is the result of man's reflection on his life. Civilization is a structure that consists of technology and institutions. On the other hand, culture is a reflective attitude toward institutions and an attempt to transcend institutions through myth, whose complex structure reflects the structure of institutions. In fact, 'myth' is the spiritual core of the elements of civilization, and, therefore, it should be clearly distinguished from the notion of 'tale,' or 'fiction.'[1] The creation of tales is an unsuccessful attempt to satisfy humans' quest for an inspiring and spiritually life-giving myth. In other words, tales are unsuccessful substitutes for myth. Myth is the most important manifestation and the core of culture. Myth translates experienced reality into a symbolic language, and in this way it leads toward the experiential participation of the collective consciousness in the same experience of reality, since myth allows the partaking of all areas of the conscious and the unconscious mind into the same experience of reality.

The primary purpose of civilization is to exert control over untamed forces and hence to transform them into forces that are controlled by human

---

1 Jung, Carl G., "The Relations Between the Ego and the Unconscious", in *The Portable Jung*, edited by J. Campbell, New York: Penguin Books, 1971; Lévi-Strauss, Claude, The Raw and the Cooked, trans. John and Doreen Weightman, Chicago: The University of Chicago Press, 1969

consciousness in order, ultimately, to harmonize all controlled forces with each other and with human reason. Human reason, under its different manifestations (namely, technical, scientific, and moral ones) oversees the successive phases of civilization and evaluates them according to its own dispositions. The dispositions of human reason are subject to change according to the manner in which each society understands its needs. In general, irrespective of whether a civilization gives priority to materialistic pursuits or to more spiritual pursuits, the essence of 'civilization' primarily consists in the objectivation of the intentionality of consciousness through the construction of technological systems (e.g., machines, tools, etc.) and through institutions, whereas the essence of 'culture' primarily consists in the objectivation of the intentionality of consciousness through artistic creation, philosophy and scientific theories and models. However, civilization and culture are neither contradictory nor incompatible to each other. Even though civilization corresponds to 'technical construction' and culture corresponds to 'spiritual creation,' culture is embodied in civilization and underpins civilization, and, additionally, civilization underpins the integration of culture into history.

Hence, there is a dialectical relation between civilization and culture, both at the level of their essences and at the level of their manifestations. Civilization seems to be founded on a concrete set of knowledge,[1] whereas culture seems to be founded on a concrete set of experiences. In terms of civilization, the progress of humanity consists in the technological and institutional progress of society. On the other hand, in terms of culture, the progress of humanity is evaluated according to the spiritual deepening of the human being. Thus, as Christopher Bamford has pointed out in his inspiring book An Endless Trace: The Passionate Pursuit of Wisdom in the West, two powerful motives weave beneath the surface of the West's spiritual history: the desire to understand and the desire to love.[2]

D. A Remark about Religion, Spirituality, and Secularism

Given that, in the present book, I shall use many of the methodological and stylistic characteristics of 'philosophical anthropology' (as the latter has been formed and delineated by such philosophers as Max Scheler, Ernst

---

1 'Knowledge' is an intellectual function according to which one constantly considers that an object corresponds to reality. Knowledge presupposes a correspondence between thing and intellect. This argument has been put forward by Aristotle in his Metaphysics, 1011b25, as follows: "To say of what is that it is not, or of what is not that it is, is false, while to say of what is that it is, and of what is not that it is not, is true", and virtually identical assertions can be found in Plato (Cratylus, 385b2; Sophist, 263b).
2 Bamford, Christopher, *An Endless Trace: The Passionate Pursuit of Wisdom in the West*, New York: Codhill Press, 2003.

Cassirer, Martin Heidegger, Hans-Georg Gadamer, Hans Jonas, Maurice Merleau-Ponty, Paul Ricoeur, etc.), I shall put emphasis on the study of the human being as a "symbolic animal," according to Ernst Cassirer's terminology,[1] as well as on methodic studies in "symbolic anthropology" and the "imaginary", according to Gilbert Durand's terminology.[2] When I refer to the imaginary, I mean the set of values, institutions, laws and symbols common to a particular social group.

Therefore, due to the fact that my work is focused on the creative and symbolic dimension of the social world, I dare to challenge and, in fact, cross borders among different 'camps' of cultures and mentalities in order to elucidate what happens in the inner ('eso') cosmos of the Western man and society, that is, in that spiritual locus from where religion, spirituality, art and science emerge, and to study how the creativity of the human spirit is objectivated in historical becoming. Hence, the present book presupposes that its readers are familiar with 'symbolic thought,' or at least they intend to employ symbolic thought, and that they are ready to cross borders among different intellectual 'camps.'

E. Acting on the Square

I started my Masonic journey in 1997, when I was initiated into the Craft in the "Honor Per Onus" Lodge No. 6586 of the United Grand Lodge of England, having been 'proposed' by the late W. Bro. Theodore Frangos, who was a Grand Officer of the United Grand Lodge of England and a prominent member of the Cypriot-British community of London. Within six months of my initiation, I was raised to the sublime degree of a Master Mason. During 1997–9, at Lodge meetings, which took place at the Freemasons' Hall, the headquarters of the United Grand Lodge of England, which has been at 60 Great Queen St, London, since 1775, I had several opportunities of meeting interesting and well-intended people and of reading many authoritative Masonic books and historical documents at the Grand Library.

Even though the United Grand Lodge of England (UGLE) is an internationally respected institution, to which I personally owe a debt of gratitude, the fact that the UGLE strictly prohibits political and religious discussion in its Lodges and the fact that it cultivates a ritualistic and bureaucratic attitude toward Freemasonry have made me realize that what the UGLE regards as "regular Freemasonry" is only an exoteric aspect of

1 Cassirer, Ernst, *The Philosophy of Symbolic Forms*, Volume One: Language, Volume Two: Mythical Thought, trans. R. Manheim, New Haven: Yale University Press, 1955.
2 Durand, Gilbert, *Les Structures Anthropologiques de l'Imaginaire: Introduction à l'Archétypologie Générale*, Paris: P.U.F., 1963.

Freemasonry and that the UGLE deprives the average Lodge of the right to discuss the most significant issues of humanity, namely, ontology, religion, politics, and economics. Moreover, in the 2000s, I was deeply disillusioned with the decision of the UGLE to use the Freemasons' Hall (which is the headquarters of the UGLE and the principal meeting place for Masonic Lodges in London) for product launches, fashion shows, conferences, drink receptions, and dinner dances; for instance, in 2005, it hosted events for London Fashion Week and the Lancôme Design Awards, and, in 2006, it hosted the Julien MacDonald Fashion Show and the Alternative Hair Show! The previous policy of the UGLE reminded me of those irreverent persons in Jesus Christ's time who would transform the Temple of Jerusalem into a marketplace and who were thus fiercely and publicly repudiated by Jesus Christ.[1]

In 1999, I left London, and I continued my Masonic journey in some Greek Lodges that were sympathetic and interesting, such as the "Greek-Speaking Hotel" Lodge No. 67 of the National Grand Lodge of Greece and the "Etairia ton Filikon" Lodge No. 116 of the Grand Lodge of Greece, where I socialized with engaging persons, and I participated in several Masonic Orders beyond the Craft. However, to my despair, most so-called 'regular' Greek Lodges (specifically, those Lodges that operate under the auspices of the Grand Lodge of Greece and of the National Grand Lodge of Greece[2]) are Masonic replicas of the UGLE system combined with malicious local intrigues and stunningly superficial discussions. After all, given that the modern Greek State was founded in the 1830s as a geopolitical and geoeconomic pivot of Western Europe's Great Powers in the Eastern Mediterranean and the Balkans, most modern Greek cultural and political institutions, including Greek Freemasonic Grand Lodges, are not only spiritually alienated from the authentic traditions of ancient and medieval Hellenism, but they also serve Western Great Powers' strategic goals and neocolonialist policy. Especially in the twentieth century, as regards culture, the modern Greek State degraded into a poor colony of its Western geostrategic and economic 'patrons.'[3]

---

1 Matthew 21:12–14; Mark 11:15; Luke 19:45.
2 The National Grand Lodge of Greece was founded in 1986 by Lodges that split from the Grand Lodge of Greece.
3 During the twentieth century, Greece was governed by a politically outer-directed and spiritually incompetent bourgeois elite (whose paradigmatic representatives were such Prime Ministers as Eleftherios K. Venizelos, Konstantinos G. Karamanlis, Andreas G. Papandreou, and Konstantinos Simits as well as a group of merchants associated with ARAMCO, SIEMENS, Lockheed Martin, Dassault Group, Goldman Sachs, Deutsche Bank, and other Western multinational corporations), and the majority of its people gradually lapsed into a petty-bourgeois mentality. It is worth pointing out that, until 1964, the American CIA (and not the Greek State) had been directly and exclusively

Thus, ultimately, I chose to follow a different personal Masonic path in the context of the U.S. Obedience of the Ancient and Primitive Rite Memphis–Misraim ("Sons and Daughters of Aaron" Lodge, Atlanta, Georgia), which, at least, allowed me to develop and pursue an alternative Freemasonic strategic vision. Finally, in 2015, I was awarded the 97th and *ne plus ultra* Degree of this Rite (at the "Misir" Lodge, in Vršac, Serbia), and, in the same year, the Grand Commander of the Supreme Council of the Regular Grand Orient of Rites for Greece, W. Bro. Angelos Bavellas—who is a regular 33rd Degree Mason (having direct initiatory lineage to the Supreme Council that was founded in Greece on July 24, 1872, by Demetrios Rhodocanakis, as a thirty-third-degree member of the Supreme Council of Scotland) and Past Master of the "Ionia" Lodge No. 7 of the National Grand Lodge of Greece—bestowed upon me the 33rd Degree Diploma on behalf of his Obedience's Scottish Rite Supreme Council. When I first contrasted the esoteric content of Freemasonry with Victorian ethics, Puritanism, Papal despotism, and with the ethos of U.S. Evangelical fundamentalists and Zionists, I realized that, in the modern Western world, esoteric Freemasonry is an 'island' of benevolent spirituality in an ocean of distorted Christianity and repulsive systems of morality.

As a young postgraduate researcher, back in 1997, I was eager to acquire knowledge, not only in order to fascinate and feed my hungry brain cells, but also in order to spiritually develop myself. I was bored of the most popular extracurricular activities in which my coevals' were indulging (such as watching sports and entertaining themselves in noisy clubs drinking large quantities of alcohol and listening to stunningly low quality music), and I was seeking experiences of mental fulfillment and justice, while encountering several phenomena of spiritual insignificance and moral nihilism. Moreover, since my early youth, I have had a Christocentric libertarian ideology, a strong interest in philosophical anthropology, and, with regard to international politics, I lean toward Hedley Bull's world society theory enriched with the concept of 'great political hypostasis,' which I have developed and explain in this book.

As regards my libertarian ideological orientation, I should stress that, in contrast to the U.S. approach to Libertarianism, which is essentially equated with laissez-faire economics, 'libertarian,' throughout modern European history, meant socialist anarchist, that is, an anti-statist, anti-Bolshevik socialist. My approach to Libertarianism stems from a metaphysically grounded theory of social unity. Furthermore, I understand and endorse 'anarchism' not as a theory of social chaos, but as the thesis that there is no self-justified authority and that the ultimate source of authority is God;

---

paying all employees of Greece's State Intelligence Service (currently called National Intelligence Service) their wages.

hence, the ultimate source of authority transcends any historical or physical necessity and cannot be manipulated by any historical actor. Thus, even though I believe that Liberalism is the lesser evil among the three basic political theories of modernity (namely, Liberalism, Communism, and Fascism), and, therefore, I salute Liberalism's victories over Communism and Fascism, I am not an advocate of Liberalism, and I counter-propose a metaphysically grounded type of Libertarianism.

Libertarianism is neither libertinism nor hedonism. On the contrary, from my perspective, Libertarianism gives rise to a society of maximum personal and socio-economic freedom in which individuals are not psychically plebeian, that is, selfish or morally irresponsible, but they are psychically noble, that is, their psychic space is big enough to encompass the entire humanity, and they organize their social life on the basis of free and voluntary agreements among free and morally responsible individuals. Thus, even though I strongly oppose Ayn Rand's theory of individualism[1]— which degrades human beings into selfishly behaving microeconomic robots—I do not hesitate to support many of David Friedman's laissez-faire economic arguments,[2] since I believe that social unity should be founded on esoteric principles (specifically, on personal moral responsibility, psychic transparency, and spiritual freedom), and not on statism. However, in contrast to David Friedman's indiscriminately anti-statist arguments, I believe that a free economic market should operate within the context of a strong political regime—precisely, what I call a 'great political hypostasis'— whose strategic purpose should be to protect and promote the corresponding people's cultural identity and be primarily accountable to eternal values and principles that transcend history. In addition, as it has been pointedly argued by the libertarian author and blogger Sean Gabb, "there is no reason to believe that most people want to be free in the sense demanded by libertarians."[3] After all, God himself permits people to choose the road to

---

1 Having been raised and trained as a Soviet subject, and having turned into a zealous and superficial advocate of the United States' system of market capitalism, Ayn Rand never managed to appreciate or understand the wealth and the complexity of humanity's spiritual life. Thus, the 'capitalist heroes' of Ayn Rand's novels and political essays are neurotic, spiritually shallow, and superficial men who, in essence, are no more free than the members of the Soviet Union's system of state capitalism (or bureaucratic socialism). In other words, Ayn Rand substituted a one-dimensional man molded by a textbook of American microeconomics for an one-dimensional man molded by a textbook of Leninism, and she thought that, in that way, she had discovered the elixir of freedom.
2 Friedman, David D., *The Machinery of Freedom*, La Salle, Illinois: Open Court, 1995.
3 Gabb, Sean, "Must Libertarians Believe in Open Borders?", 12 August 2015; see: http://thelibertarianalliance.com/2015/08/12/must-libertarians-believe-in-open-borders/

serfdom, known as the path of Satan, over the road to freedom, known as the path of God, if they so wish.

For the aforementioned reasons and with the aforementioned mentality, I decided to join Freemasonry. Since my first steps in Freemasonry, I have been appreciating the elitist tradition of Freemasonry and its traditional orientation toward principles of spiritual nobility. Having said that, it is also true that many contemporary Freemasonic Obediences are in a deep crisis, having been tragically infected by the flaws of modernity and postmodernism, and many Freemasons disgrace their initiation by treating Freemasonry as if it were a dining club and/or a shelter for deficient personalities struggling for profane seniority and prone to every kind of intellectual fallacy. Additionally, from the eighteenth century onward, several Western ruling elites have been using Freemasonic and other esoteric institutions in order to manipulate the 'middle class' in the West and in order to create and manipulate ruling elites in the Western colonies and the Third World.

As a person who has deep knowledge of history and big files of historical documents, I am well aware that, on several occasions, the fields of intelligence services, Freemasonry, and politics overlap. For instance, the disaffected ex-MI6 officer Richard Tomlinson, author of the controversial book *The Big Breach*, has provided researchers with important information about the significant yet elusive and clandestine interplay among British intelligence agents, Soviet/Russian intelligence agents, Freemasonry, and key policy-makers in both the UK and the Soviet Union/Russian Federation.[1] Therefore—since my personal sense of 'patriotism' does not refer primarily to any particular historical subject *per se* (e.g., a nation-state, a Sovereign, a Statesman, etc.), but it primarily refers to my sense of devotion to my spiritual principles, which constitute my real homeland and the criterion by which I choose my political affiliations and loyalties at each time—I have decided to act in the realm of Freemasonry according to my own patriotic agenda.

Finally, regarding my personal approach to esotericism, in general, and to Freemasonry, in particular, I should mention that I defend a type of esotericism that helps man to become psychically deeper and a partaker of God, while simultaneously affirming the material world and history and undertaking one's historical responsibilities in a creative way. Therefore, my approach to esoteric studies is substantially different from Gnosticism,

---

1 Tomlinson, Richard, *The Big Breach: From Top Secret to Maximum Security*, Moscow: Narodny Variant Publishers, 2001; Tomlinson's book was subsequently serialized by *The Sunday Times*. See also: Warren, Marcus, "Tomlinson Spy Memoir Plot Thickens," *The Telegraph*, January 24, 2001; see: http://www.telegraph.co.uk/news/worldnews/1319316/Tomlinson-spy-memoir-plot-thickens.html

which is very popular among modern Western esotericists.[1] Gnosticism (from Greek 'gnosis,' which means knowledge) refers to a set of religious beliefs and spiritual practices based on the doctrine of salvation by a peculiar esoteric knowledge that promises to 'liberate' the soul from the material world.[2]

The roots of Gnosticism can be traced to non-Christian and pre-Christian Asian religious communities. In his Epistle to the Colossians, the Apostle Paul combated Gnostic teachings that had infiltrated the Colossian Church and were undermining Christianity. The Gnostics taught that spirit is good, whereas matter is evil (Colossians 1:15–20), thus keeping the human being in a state of inner existential conflict. The Apostle Paul's answer was that both heaven and earth are actualizations of God's will, and, hence, as we read in Genesis 1:31, they have been crated "very good." Moreover, in my philosophical research work, I have elucidated and defended the Hesychasts' thesis about the psychosomatic nexus and unity of the human being, as opposed to the Gnostics' dualistic arguments.[3]

Neoplatonism provided several Gnostic schools with the idea of a continuum of degrees of being that lie between the extreme ontological poles of being and non-being. Thus, Gnostics developed various hierarchies of ontological emanations, or divine beings, known as 'Aeons.' However, in contrast to Neoplatonism, various Gnostic schools adopted radically dualistic Asian religious traditions, and they converged to the idea of the essential evil of this present existence. Gnostics developed various ritualistic systems through which they attempted to liberate their members from what they believed to be a corrupt sensuous world. On the other hand, Neoplatonism followed the Greek philosophical tradition, which was characterized by the joyful acknowledgment of and homage to the beautiful and the noble in the sensuous world. Thus, for instance, in the third century AD, all the major Neoplatonists, such as Plotinus, Porphyry, and Amelius, attacked the Sethian Gnostics.

In contrast to classical Greek aesthetics, to Neoplatonism, and to Orthodox Christianity, the Gnostics endorsed a radical dualistic attitude, and, thus, they argued that Christ could not be both human and divine (Colossians 1:15–20, 2:2–3). For instance, Cerinthus (ca. AD 100), the founder of a Gnostic school in the Roman Province of Asia, depicted Christ as a heavenly spirit separate from the man Jesus. The Apostle Paul's answer

---

1 By 2008, there were three dedicated university chairs in the subject of Western esotericism, at the University of Sorbonne, the University of Amsterdam, and the University of Exeter, with the latter two institutions also having developed Master's Degree programs in it.

2 Bauer, Walter, *Orthodoxy and Heresy in Earliest Christianity*, Philadelphia: Fortress Press, 1971.

3 Laos, Nicolas, *Methexiology: Philosophical Theology and Theological Philosophy for the Deification of Humanity*, Eugene, Oregon: Wipf and Stock Publishers, 2016.

was that Christ was the divine Logos in the flesh. In general, in presenting Christ as the Archetype of the new human being, and of Adam and Eve restored to the divine course appointed by God, there is a clear soteriological leitmotif present everywhere in the writings of the early Greek Fathers: that the Divine Logos, namely, Jesus Christ, became man, so that man could achieve deification by grace. In his "Discourse on the incarnation of the Word" (Patrologia Graeca, Vol. 25, 192B), Athanasius the Great (a fourth century Orthodox Christian Bishop of Alexandria) argues that Christ "was made man, that we might be made God."

F. In search for the meaning of Freemasonry

I do not regret my participation in Freemasonry, because I have known Freemasonry, and I have been practicing it in the proper way, and because, by being engaged in an organization whose declared goals are, in principle, irrelevant to selfish pursuits and the petty-bourgeois mentality, I have gradually cultivated the principle of esoteric exaltation as the ultimate criterion of my choices. The pursuit of esoteric exaltation has given me what I have not found in exoteric educational processes and in conventional values, and it has been keeping me vigilant, in the sense that I have developed a sharp sense of truth. Moreover, in the context of no Masonic organization, have I ever compromised my spiritual and political convictions for whatever reason.

In 1846, the English cleric, schoolmaster, topographer, and writer Reverend Dr. George Oliver—who was elected Deputy Provincial Grand Master of Masons for Lincolnshire in 1832, and who was appointed an honorary member of the Grand Lodge of Massachusetts, with the rank of Deputy Grand Master, in 1840—wrote a booklet entitled *An Apology for the Freemasons*, which is one of my primary sources of inspiration for writing this book. In his *Apology for the Freemasons*, the Reverend Dr. George Oliver confuted the following objections against Freemasonry:

First objection against Freemasonry: a true Christian cannot or ought not to join Freemasonry, because particular Masonic prayers to God, especially in the context of the first degrees, to which non-Christians may be admitted, do not refer to the mediation of Christ. With regard to this objection, the Reverend Dr. George Oliver has argued as follows: "although prayer is undoubtedly of much greater efficacy when used in the Redeemer's name, yet it will not be difficult to prove that the offering up of such prayers is not without precedent, even amongst the formularies of devotion which have been prescribed for the observance of Christians." In particular, the Liturgical Rites of all traditional Christian Churches contain several prayers that do not explicitly refer to the mediation of Christ. Furthermore, in the context of inter-religious dialogues and meetings, many Christian clerics publicly pray together with officers of other religions.

Many Masonic prayers are short addresses to the Great Architect of the Universe for a blessing on our labors, but the Great Architect of the Universe is not a particular divine Being, that is, the Great Architect of the Universe is neither a distinct Masonic God nor any distinctly Masonic perception of the deity. The term 'Great Architect of the Universe' is merely a name by which Masons call and invoke God in accordance with the symbolic system of Symbolic Masonry. However, Symbolic Masonry is not singular in this interpretation. For instance, in Hebrews 1:10, the Apostle Paul writes the following: "You, Lord, in the beginning, laid the foundation of the earth. The heavens are the works of your hands," thus glorifying God as the Great Architect of the Universe. In his *Apology for the Freemasons*, the Reverend Dr. George Oliver points out that "Jews, Turks, and Hindus, may join in the [Masonic] prayers, and apply them to the Supreme object of their respective adoration," but "every Christian Mason in appealing to the Grand Architect of the Universe, ought to be fully impressed with the salutary truth, that his prayer is directed to God through the mediation of Christ."

However, given that believers in the heresy of Judeochristianity, to which I referred earlier, and advocates of religious syncretism, whose ethos and imperialist agenda I also clarified earlier, have penetrated Freemasonry and systematically attempt to use Freemasonry as an instrument in order to promote their belief systems and implement their agendas, those Freemasons who defend the traditional, Christian, European Freemasonry should be vigilant against these distortive forces, which aim at transforming naïve Freemasons into pawns in the hands of corrupt elites. In order to understand the seriousness of the previous distortive forces, it is useful to mention, for instance, a certain "Jerusalem" Lodge, which was established in December 1995, adjacent to the Temple Mount, in the Grotto of King Solomon; this Freemasonic Lodge's goal is to work for the physical rebuilding of King Solomon's Temple. This "Jerusalem" Lodge cooperates with networks of Jewish and 'Christian' (precisely, Judaizing Christian) extremists,[1] and its official founder is Giuliano di Bernardo, who served as the Grand Master of the Grand Orient of Italy from 1990 until 1993. In 1993, di Bernardo resigned from the Grand Orient of Italy, and, with the support of the United Grand Lodge of England, he founded the "Regular Grand Lodge of Italy" on the model of English Freemasonry; in December 1993, he obtained the

---

1 The declared goal of the "The Temple Mount and Land of Israel Faithful Movement," which was founded in 1967 by Gershon Salomon, is to rebuild King Solomon's Temple and remove the Dome of the Rock and the Al Aqsa mosque, which it characterizes as "pagan shrines"; see: http://templemountfaithful.org/objectives.php

official recognition of the United Grand Lodge of England. Moreover, di Bernardo was the right-hand man of the Seventh Marquess of Northampton (Spencer Douglas David Compton) on the "Temple Mount Project," which is an attempt to rebuild King Solomon's Temple as the material seat of a new utopia founded on Jewish mysticism. In fact, Giuliano di Bernardo has written a book on his vision of rebuilding King Solomon's Temple, which is entitled *La ricostruzione del Tempio: Il progetto massonico per una nuova utopia*, and it was published in 1996 by Marsilio Editori (Venice, Italy). The Seventh Marquess of Northampton served as the Pro Grand Master of the United Grand Lodge of England from 2001 until 2009.

Second objection against Freemasonry: Freemasonry inculcates the principles of brotherly love and charity as peculiarly incumbent on Freemasons, whereas charity, to be acceptable to God, should proceed from a love of God through Jesus Christ. With regard to this objection, the Reverend Dr. George Oliver has argued that, first of all, participation in a fraternity cultivates special bonds of mutual trust founded on deep mutual knowledge and appreciation, as it is acknowledged even by the Apostle Paul in Galatians 6:10, and, secondly, in many parts of Masonic lectures, the precepts of Masonry regarding charity are general and unrestricted. Thus, according to the Emulation Ritual (Explanation of the First Degree Tracing Board), one of the most widely practiced rituals of English Masonry, "a Mason's charity should know no bounds save those of prudence."

Third objection against Freemasonry: the mention of the Lord's name in the Lodge is a contravention of the third commandment. With regard to this objection, the Reverend Dr. George Oliver has argued as follows: "there are three ways of using the holy Name of God, which have been pronounced sinful. 1, By wilful perjury; 2, By rash and profane swearing; 3, By an irreverent use of it in common conversation. It does not appear, however, that either of these is included in the objection." The use of the name of the Lord in serious discourse is neither sinful nor improper. Moreover, the Apostle James says that, when instructing the Christian converts on the correct method of performing their worldly duties, the Lord's name can be used in ordinary discourse, too (James 4:13–15).

Fourth objection against Freemasonry: several persons who are unfriendly to Freemasonry claim that the Christian Church has insufficient knowledge of Freemasonry, since the latter is a secret society, and that, therefore, the Christian Church cannot and should not trust Freemasonry. First of all, Freemasonry is not a secret society, but a society with secrets, in the sense that the existence, the values, and the rituals of Freemasonry are publicly known. Secondly, as the Reverend Dr. George Oliver argues in his *Apology for the Freemasons*, the traditional medieval Masonic organizations were explicitly serving both the Church and the State, and many Masonic degrees are Christian, and only Christian Masons espousing the Christian Trinitarian doctrine can be admitted to them. Moreover, on several occasions, in England, the Grand Masters of Masonry were selected from among the highest dignitaries of the Church, such as the following:[1]

AD 597, Austin the Monk.
AD 680, Bennet, Abbot of Wirral.
AD 856, St. Swithin.
AD 957, St. Dunstan, Archbishop of Canterbury.
AD 1066, Gondulph, Bishop of Rochester.
AD 1155, The Grand Master of the Templars.
AD 1216, Peter de Rupibus, Bishop of Winchester.
AD 1272, Walter Giffard, Archbishop of York.
AD 1307, Walter Stapleton, Bishop of Exeter.
AD 1357, William of Wykeham, Bishop of Winchester.
AD 1375, Simon Langham, Abbot of Westminster.
AD 1413, Henry Chichely, Archbishop of Canterbury.
AD 1443, William Waynfleet, Bishop of Winchester.
AD 1471, Richard Beauchamp, Bishop of Salisbury.
AD 1515, Cardinal Wolsey.
AD 1552, John Poynet, Bishop of Winchester.

As I explain in this book, gradually, Freemasons, especially the most cultivated among them, started realizing the difference between basic religion, on the one hand, and spirituality and illumination, on the other. Like any other fantasy, basic religion is caused by a peculiar intellectual confusion, whose cure is the purpose of the mystics' path; the mystics seek the illumination of the heart, the seat of the mind, through mystical prayer, that is, through an unceasing unity between man and God, as distinguished from intellectual prayer, which is based on created images and sentiments, and from religious formalism.

The spiritual sickness of man, that is, the essence of what we call spiritual sickness, consists in the weakening of the heart's communion with the glory of God (Romans 3:23), by its being swamped by extraneous thoughts (Romans 1:21–24, 2:5). In such a state, one imagines God to be in the image of one's sick self or even of animals (Romans 1:22). The inner person (esoteric man) suffers spiritual death, because of which all have sinned (Romans 5:12) by becoming enslaved to the instincts, which deform love by subjugating it to the self-centered search for security and happiness. The cure of the previous sickness begins by understanding that, whereas the

---

1 Oliver, Rev. George, *The Antiquities of Free-Masonry*, new edition, London: Richard Spencer, 1843, pp. xiv, xv.

intellect, as a distinct power of the soul, is the seat of reason, that is, the psychic faculty of cognition, the mind (in Greek, *nous*), whose essence is the heart, is the repository of God's uncreated energies in man, and, therefore, the mind must be purified from all thoughts and images (Romans 2:29), both 'good' and 'bad,' which must be restricted to the intellect. One thus becomes free from slavery to everything extraneous, such as self-indulgence, wealth, property, and even one's parents and relatives (Matthew 10:37; Luke 14:26), in order for his mind to be divinely illuminated, without any thoughts or images impeding the process of divine illumination. This is the essence of what I call 'transcendental mysticism' in this book. In particular, by the term 'transcendental mysticism,' I mean the merging of philosophy and theology within a truth that ontologically transcends man, and, yet, it can be accessed by man through mystical experience, in accordance with my general philosophical orientation, which I have called methexiology.[1]

In contrast to the aforementioned mystical culture, in the Middle Ages, the dominant administrative Church authorities had the tendency to transform the Christ Mystery into a formalist basic religion, and the Papacy, in particular, was struggling to establish itself as the absolute overlord of the human reason and fantasies. In this context, and for the previous reasons, during the Middle Ages and the Renaissance, several administrative Church authorities turned against mysticism, in general, and their persecutions of mysticism culminated in the Papal prohibition on Freemasonry. In 1738, Pope Clement XII issued a Papal bull entitled *In eminenti apostolatus specula*, with which he prohibited Roman Catholics from becoming Freemasons.[2] On November 26, 1983, Joseph Ratzinger, the then Cardinal-Prefect of the Vatican's Sacred Congregation for the Doctrine of the Faith (known in the sixteenth century AD as the Holy Inquisition), issued a statement approved by Pope John Paul II according to which "the faithful who enroll in Masonic associations are in a state of grave sin and may not receive Holy Communion," and "membership in them (Masonic associations) remains forbidden."

The attacks that have been unleashed by the Vatican against Freemasonry constitute an integral part of the Vatican's policy to persecute mysticism and transform the Christ Mystery into an exoteric, formalist, and authoritarian religious system. In fact, in the context of their exoteric and selfish religious strategies, both Eastern and Western administrative Church authorities tend to transform their Churches into corrals for the management of their

1 Laos, Nicolas, *Methexiology: Philosophical Theology and Theological Philosophy for the Deification of Humanity*, Eugene, Oregon: Wipf and Stock Publishers, 2016.
2 After the Papal bull *In eminenti*, the Papal prohibition of Freemasonry was reiterated and expanded upon by Benedict XIV (1751), Pius VII (1821), Leo XII (1826), Pius VIII (1829), Gregory XVI (1832), Pius IX (1846, 1849, 1864, 1865, 1869, 1873), and notably Pope Leo XIII in the encyclical *Humanum genus* (1884). Additionally, in 1917, the Vatican's Code of Canon Law forbade books promoting Freemasonry.

followers, and, thus, they tend to be trapped in a distorted way of thinking about the 'catholicity,' or universality, of the Church. Being a true 'catholic' does not consist in being in communion with any particular episcopal See. The true and genuine 'catholicity,' that is, 'universality,' consists in being in ontologically grounded communion with the deity, or the Absolute. This esoteric interpretation of 'catholicity' implies enables one to transcend the dilemma 'holism versus individualism' by proposing a type of person whose psychic space is infinite. Holism suppresses one's existential otherness (individuality), and individualism shrinks one's psychic space due to egoism. My interpretation of 'catholicity' gives rise to and underpins an individual whose inner space is as big as the Holy Virgin Mary's womb, and, thus, capable of encompassing the Whole.

In the eighteenth, the nineteenth, and the twentieth centuries, as several administrative Church authorities were distancing themselves from Freemasonry, for their own selfish reasons, and as the Vatican in particular was demonizing and subverting Freemasonry, Freemasonry became vulnerable and susceptible to the spiritual influence of several non-Christian communities and esoteric 'schools' which started infiltrating Freemasonry in order to take advantage of Freemasonic networks and solidarity, thus creating several 'Masonries' within traditional Masonry. Moreover, in the eighteenth, the nineteenth, and the twentieth centuries, on several occasions, national intelligence agencies, various political movements, and even members of organized crime attempted to utilize Freemasonry, each one of them for the sake of one's own strategic goals. Therefore, the elucidation of the history and the identity of Freemasonry is a complicated and arduous task, which I shall try to accomplish in this book. In addition, another scope of the present book is to inform my readers about the "United Traditionalist Grand Sanctuaries of the Ancient and Primitive Rite Memphis–Misraim," which is a new international Freemasonic movement that I have founded on the basis of what I call 'transcendental mysticism,' which I elucidate in the present book.

THE DECLARATION OF
THE UNITED TRADITIONALIST GRAND SANCTUARIES OF
THE ANCIENT AND PRIMITIVE RITE MEMPHIS–MISRAIM

"The vision of Christ that thou dost see is my vision's greatest enemy.
Both read the Bible day and night, but thou read'st black where I read white.
His seventy disciples sent against religion and government."[1]

As the Founder and President ('Grand Hierophant-General') of the international Freemasonic fraternity that is called the *United Traditionalist*

---

1 Blake, William, *The Everlasting Gospel*, ca. 1818; the "seventy disciples" to whom Blake refers were emissaries of Jesus Christ mentioned in Luke 10:1–24.

Grand Sanctuaries of the Ancient and Primitive Rite Memphis–Misraim, I am herewith elucidating its structure, values, and strategy, which pertain to the great existential and ethical problems of humanity.

Each Freemasonic system is a symbolic technology or, in other words, an economy of signs (significations) that underpins an anthropological and social architecture. Just as each technology can be used by different historical actors and serve different purposes, the 'symbolic technology' of Freemasonry can be used by different forces and for different reasons. Thus, there are several mutually different and distinct Freemasonic systems. We reject every claim that any particular Freemasonic entity, whichever it may be, has a monopoly on defining and/or administering 'regular Freemasonry'; we perceive each and every Freemasonic organization as a symbolic construction company based on its own architectural plans; we have exerted the right of each sovereign Grand Masonic Body to modify and interpret Masonic rituals according to its own strategy, maintaining, however, the fixed structure and the fixed plot of the established Freemasonic myths and degrees; and, thus, we have articulated and herewith, honestly and courageously, propose our own architectural plan for a *Traditionalist, Activist, and Interventionist Freemasonry*. In other words, the United Traditionalist Grand Sanctuaries of the Ancient and Primitive Rite Memphis–Misraim is a Freemasonic organization that has its own ethos, and it has created and uses its own version of the Ancient and Primitive Rite Memphis–Misraim, which it proposes to the world, in general, and to Freemasons, in particular.

Our own Masonic Order's motto is "hypostatically we are initiated, fraternally we rise," meaning that each of us has sought initiation and experiences the real truth according to one's own free will and existential otherness, yet, by being transparent to the real truth, we are transparent to each other, too, and we thus build an expanding Holy Empire of true Gnosis, or divine Knowledge.

According to our traditionalist, activist, and interventionist ethos and ritual, in the United Traditionalist Grand Sanctuaries of the Ancient and Primitive Rite Memphis–Misraim:

We are concerned with the study of comparative mythology and symbology and with broad cultural identity issues. As regards religion, in particular, we study comparative religion and, especially, the itinerary of the human spirit from the beginning of civilization until the historical disclosure of the Incarnate Logos of God, namely, Jesus Christ, who gave humanity the perfect religion.

By the term 'tradition,' we refer to the supratemporal and transtemporal Truth, which is being transferred from the past to the future through the present, thus making the present meaningful and referring time to eternity.

Due to its traditionalist ethos, the United Traditionalist Grand Sanctuaries of the Ancient and Primitive Rite Memphis–Misraim promotes *Unity in Truth*, that is, spiritual unity in the context of the traditional principle of the real good (the good-in-itself), and, from this perspective, it rejects the Hegelian principle 'thesis-antithesis-synthesis.' The Hegelian principle 'thesis-antithesis-synthesis,' originally coined by the German philosopher Georg W. H. Hegel, is a process that seeks to establish a world monologue through the Hegelian dialectic, which deifies history and, ultimately, leads to the deification of a particular historical subject that historically embodies the final 'synthesis' (and manipulates both the 'thesis' and the 'antithesis' according to one's own selfish interests). Hence, the Hegelian principle 'thesis-antithesis-synthesis' is a sacrilege against the uncreated Great Architect of the Universe, whom it degrades into a historical world order. But, as the Apostle Paul asks, "what fellowship do righteousness and iniquity have? Or what fellowship does light have with darkness?" (2 Corinthians 6:14).

We maintain that the truth of 'tradition' is identical with the 'sacred,' and, hence, traditionalism consists in a peculiar sacerdotal system, precisely, in a system founded and focused on man's initiation in the real good (the good-in-itself). In the context of traditionalism, as we understand it, every historical form of authority and hierarchy stems from tradition and refers to tradition. Furthermore, from our perspective, tradition consists in a human community's belief in the real good, as proclaimed by the ancient mystery schools, Plato's philosophy, and the great religious traditions of humanity, in contradistinction to the civilizations that are dominated by the social classes of the merchants and the moneylenders, in contradistinction to Marxism (irrespectively of the particular differences among the various Marxist currents), and in contradistinction to Fascism (in all its forms and varieties).

We agree with the French traditionalist scholar and Freemason René Guénon that, gradually, in the context of secularization, the dominant Western Christian communities, namely, the Vatican, the Puritans, and the Evangelicals, lost the deep initiatory character and the esoteric underpinnings of Christianity (the Christ Mystery), and they degraded into exoteric religious systems.[1] However, we highlight something of which René Guénon was ignorant, specifically, the mystical Christianity of the Orthodox East. The mystical Christianity of the Orthodox East, as it was formed by Greek and Slavic Church fathers during the Middle Ages, preserved the initiatory and esoteric character of genuine Christianity, and, therefore, it belongs to traditionalism; in particular, according to the

---

1 For an introduction into René Guénon's life and thought, see Waterfield, Robin, *René Guénon and the Future of the West*, 2nd edition, Hillsdale, NY: Sophia Perennis, 2002.

United Traditionalist Grand Sanctuaries of the Ancient and Primitive Rite Memphis–Misraim, the mystical Christianity of the Orthodox East, being centered on the deification of humanity, is the most perfect traditionalist path. Unfortunately, however, gradually, the institutional administrative authorities of several Eastern Orthodox Churches failed to adhere to the mystical tradition of Hesychasm,[1] they compromised with the spirit of secularization, and they formed bureaucratic, superstitious, and formalist structures.

Following the traditionalist thought of René Guénon, we discard every type of spiritualism (such as necromancy, mediumism, the New Age movement, etc.), because, from the perspective of traditionalism, spiritualism is a phenomenon of counter-initiation, precisely, it consists in a restructuring of pseudo-traditions originated in modernity, and it is damnable because it seeks to intercept the real tradition, and it is manifestly characterized by populism and by lack of spiritual coherence.

The assemblies (that is, the Lodges, the Colleges, the Chapters, the Senates, the Areopaguses, the Tribunals, the Consistories, the Supreme Councils, and the Grand Tribunals) of our Order have an activist ethos, in the sense that we act, precisely, revolt, against everything that, according to our principles, is deprived of moral legitimacy, or fraudulent, or sacrilegious. Each time that we fight against a force, we act in this way because we discard its legitimacy, and because we resort to another source of legitimacy, specifically, to that source of legitimacy that is called soul or spirit. In this context, our activist ethos is inspired by Antigone, the heroine of Sophocles's homonym tragedy, and by John the Baptist. Antigone despises King Creon's edicts due to her reverence to tradition and to the divine Law, which Creon offends. For similar reasons, John the Baptist exerts severe and public criticism against King Herod and Princess Herodias.

With regard to politics, our Order is primarily focused and founded on Plato's political philosophy and on Orthodox Christian mysticism (known also as Hesychasm or Neptic theology). Additionally, our Order creatively and selectively utilizes political and philosophical essays written by British High Tories (e.g., the poet T. S. Eliot, the Member of Parliament, classical philologist and poet John Enoch Powell, the Member of Parliament and historian Alan K. M. Clark, the philosopher Roger Scruton, etc.), by the U.S. libertarian scholars David D. Friedman, Noam Chomsky, and Murray Rothbard, by the Russian novelist Fyodor M. Dostoyevsky, by the Russian geopolitician and politologist Alexander Dugin, by the French social anthropologists Gilbert Durand and Michel Maffesoli, by the French

---

1 For a thorough study of Hesychasm, see: Laos, Nicolas, *Methexiology: Philosophical Theology and Theological Philosophy for the Deification of Humanity*, Eugene, Oregon: Wipf and Stock Publishers, 2016.

Christian anarchist philosopher Jacques Ellul, by the Austrian-American Christian anarchist polymath and polemicist Ivan Illich, and by the British Christian anarchist scholar Gilbert K. Chesterton.

The task and the supreme responsibility of the ruling elite, which must be the spiritual nobility of society, are to safeguard the truth of the transcendent moral principle and to cultivate people's relationship with the transcendent moral principle as the foundation of man's socialization and individuation. From his personal relationship with the transcendent moral principle, man derives his particular, individual value, being an individual partaker of the transcendent moral principle, and, by participating in the same transcendent moral principle, individuals constitute an authentic society, founded exactly on the event on their participation in the same transcendent moral principle. Therefore, we vehemently reject nationalism, racialism, and autocracy.

Furthermore, we reject any theory of radical ecology, biocentrism, 'sacred geography,' and geopolitical determinism, and instead we counter-propose a metaphysically grounded theory of anthropocentrism that stems from the Holy Bible. In particular, the book of Genesis teaches that the human being is the crown of God's creation, and that man was created in the image of God.[1] In the same spirit, the Apostle Paul writes, in Hebrews 2:6–8, that God "crowned" man "with glory and honor" and has put "all things in subjection under his feet."

The United Traditionalist Grand Sanctuaries of the Ancient and Primitive Rite Memphis–Misraim is systematically concerned with comparative religion and history of philosophy, but, it is neither adogmatic nor syncretistic, because it maintains that the faith in Jesus Christ and his blood give rise to a new Israel of Grace, namely, a global, transnational community of true believers. In Galatians 3:26–29, the Apostle Paul explains that racism and nationalism contradict Christianity, and that the incarnation of the divine Logos, that is, the perfect self-disclosure of God within history, through Jesus Christ, underpins a peculiar kind of global society:

> For you are all children of God, through faith in Christ Jesus; for as many of you as were baptized into Christ have put on Christ. There is neither Jew nor Greek, there is neither slave nor free man, there is neither male nor female; for you are all one in Christ Jesus. If you are Christ's, then you are Abraham's offspring and heirs according to promise.

In Hebrews 11:8, the Apostle Paul explains that Abraham was chosen by God because of his faith. Abraham was not chosen because of his biological race or his national culture, but because of only one reason, namely, his faith. Moreover, in the book of the Acts 17:26, we read that God "made from one

---

1 Genesis 1:27.

blood every nation of men to dwell on all the surface of the earth." Jesus Christ founded the true Israel of Grace, that is, the spiritual nation of the true believers, as the Apostle Peter wrote in 1 Peter 2:9–10:

But you are a chosen race, a royal priesthood, a holy nation, a people for God's own possession, that you may proclaim the excellence of him who called you out of darkness into his marvelous light. In the past, you were not a people, but now are God's people, who had not obtained mercy, but now have obtained mercy.

In the same spirit, in Ephesians 2:14–16, the Apostle Paul refers to the genuine, global Israel of Grace, which was founded by Jesus Christ, and to the Christians' metaphysical vision of *Pax Christiana* as follows:

For he [Jesus Christ] is our peace, who made both [the Jews and the Gentiles] one, and broke down the middle wall of separation, having abolished in his flesh the hostility, the law of commandments contained in ordinances, that he might create in himself one new man of the two, making peace, and might reconcile them both in one body to God through the cross, having killed the hostility through it.

In this sense, we are Christian libertarian globalists, and we proclaim "one Lord, one faith, one baptism."[1]

The United Traditionalist Grand Sanctuaries of the Ancient and Primitive Rite Memphis–Misraim, in general, and its Inner Circle, in particular, promote the aforementioned metaphysical, globalist vision of *Pax Christiana*. The Inner Circle of the UTGS is called the "Venerable Order of the Illuminati Princes, Knights of the Hellenic Gnosis, York, Constantinople, the Kievan Realm, and Moscow" (for simplicity often referred to as the Venerable Order of the Illuminati Princes), and its members are the spiritual and political soldiers of the UTGS. This Order is concerned with the study and the promotion of the idea of the Constantinian Arc, specifically, of a geocultural space whose strategic pivots are the historical Greek space in the Haemus Peninsula (known also as the Balkan Peninsula), the cradle of the Greek culture (which was also the cultural underpinning of the Roman Empire), the English city of York (whose Roman name was Eboracum), where Constantine the Great was proclaimed Roman Emperor in 306 AD, Constantinople (known also as the New Rome), the over-millenary capital of the Eastern Roman Empire (from 330 AD until 1453), the Kievan Realm, where Vladimir Sviatoslavich the Great converted to Byzantine Christianity in 988 and Christianized the Kievan Rus, and Moscow (known also as the Third Rome), which became the administrative center of the Russian Orthodox Church in 1589, when the See of Moscow was elevated to a Patriarchate.

---

1 Ephesians 4:5.

The Venerable Order of the Illuminati Princes is an Orthodox Christian fraternity and think-tank within the broader fraternal organization of the United Traditionalist Grand Sanctuaries of the Ancient and Primitive Rite Memphis–Misraim, and its conception of Symbolic Masonry is founded on and stems from *The Shepherd of Hermas*.[1]

The founding Grand Sanctuary of the United Traditionalist Grand Sanctuaries of the Ancient and Primitive Rite Memphis–Misraim is the Sovereign Grand Sanctuary of Greece of the Ancient and Primitive Rite Memphis–Misraim, which I founded in 2015 on the basis of a relevant Charter issued by the Sovereign Grand Sanctuaries of Serbia (Orient of Vršak) and of the State of Georgia, U.S.A. (Orient of Atlanta) of the Ancient and Primitive Rite Memphis–Misraim (see Appendix, Document 1) and on the basis of a Masonic Treaty of mutual recognition and friendship signed in 2015 between the Sovereign Grand Sanctuary of Greece of the Ancient and Primitive Rite Memphis–Misraim and the Italian Freemasonic organization that is called Unione Massonica di Stretta Osservanza Iniziatica (U.M.S.O.I.), which, in 1998, was officially recognized by the Southern Jurisdiction of the Ancient and Accepted Scottish Rite for the U.S.A., which is internationally acknowledged as the Mother Scottish Rite Supreme Council of the world. Additionally, the Sovereign Grand Sanctuary of Greece of the Ancient and Primitive Rite Memphis–Misraim has signed several Masonic Treaties of mutual recognition and friendship with other Masonic Bodies that follow the Ancient and Primitive Rite Memphis–Misraim and/or other Masonic Rites.

The United Traditionalist Grand Sanctuaries of the Ancient and Primitive Rite Memphis–Misraim accepts both men and women on equal terms (with regard to both ritual and administration) and deals with the entire spectrum of philosophy (ontology, epistemology, ethics, philosophical psychology, political philosophy, philosophy of history, and philosophy of religion) and with the entire spectrum of politics and world affairs. Members of other Freemasonic Obediences are welcome to apply in order to participate in the works of the United Traditionalist Grand Sanctuaries of the Ancient and Primitive Rite Memphis–Misraim as visitors or as regular members, under terms and conditions set forth by the Grand Hierophant-General of it.

The work of the United Traditionalist Grand Sanctuaries of the Ancient and Primitive Rite Memphis–Misraim is addressed neither to lukewarm persons nor to persons who seek to be passively and selfishly

---

1 *The Shepherd of Hermas* is a Christian literary work of the second century. The allegorical visions that are included in the *Shepherd of Hermas* are strongly Masonic in tone, in the sense that, in Hermas's visions, the different types of people are symbolized by different stones, and Christ's Church is symbolized by "a great tower, built upon the waters, of splendid square stones." See, for instance: http://www.earlychristianwritings.com/text/shepherd.html

accommodated in a solid, formalized certitude, but, instead, the work of the United Traditionalist Grand Sanctuaries of the Ancient and Primitive Rite Memphis–Misraim is befitting philosophical minds that are fixed on eternal realities and have no leisure to turn their eyes downward upon petty affairs. The United Traditionalist Grand Sanctuaries of the Ancient and Primitive Rite Memphis–Misraim declares that, in one way or another, we will all burn: others will burn in the infernal fires of their selfishly trained 'egos,' and others will burn in the alchemical purification process that is called 'albedo.' In the United Traditionalist Grand Sanctuaries of the Ancient and Primitive Rite Memphis–Misraim, we choose to be transparent to the transcendent in order to successfully accomplish the Great Work.

Glory be to God!

Athens, Greece Most Ill∴ Bro∴ Dr. Nicolas Laos, 33°, 97°
February, 2016. Founder and Grand Hierophant-General
United Traditionalist Grand Sanctuaries of the
Ancient and Primitive Rite Memphis–Misraim

1. The Rosicrucian Enlightenment

A. Alchemy and the goal of transmutation

The term 'transmutation' is an alchemical concept that means an attempt to understand the logoi of beings in order, ultimately, to purify and ontologically perfect material objects and man himself. First, alchemy is related to the practices that were used in the Greco-Roman Egypt by goldsmiths and other artificers in metals, who had developed techniques for painting metals so as to make them look like gold. Secondly, alchemy is related to the theory of the unity of matter (originated by Greek pre-Socratic philosophers), according to which all those things we are accustomed to call different kinds of matter were primordially derived from one primary kind of matter (*prima materia*), whose alchemical symbol is the Ouroboros, a serpent-dragon eating its own tail. Thirdly, alchemy is related to the Aristotelian principle that every art is and must be "mimesis," in the sense that, according to Aristotle's *Poetics*, 50a15, art 'enmatters' species, and mimesis is "the constitution of things" (in Greek, *he ton pragmāton systasis*). Fourthly, alchemy is related to the ancient Greek concept of "cosmic sympathy," also symbolized by the Ouroboros. In the context of ancient Greek medicine, according to the *Hippocratic corpus* (*De alim.*, 23:1), sympathy refers to the relationship among different parts of the body, particularly, it refers to the fact that, when a part of the human body somehow suffers, another part may be affected, too. In the context of ancient Greek sociology, according to Aristotle's *Politics*, 1340a13, sympathy refers to the fact that people may share the feelings of their fellow-citizens. Moreover, during the Hellenistic period, Stoic philosophers such as Chrysippus and Posidonius developed the concept of "cosmic sympathy" in order to describe the interconnectedness among the different parts of the universe.

In the study of alchemy, practice and experiment are necessary, thus paving the road to modern natural science, but these need to be preceded by theoretical knowledge, which constitutes the philosophical or spiritual aspect of alchemy. In general, alchemy has two aspects: the material and the spiritual. The argument that alchemy was merely a primitive form of chemistry is untenable by anyone who is familiar with works written by its chief adepts. Additionally, the argument that alchemy is only a set of philosophico-theological teachings and that the alchemists' chemical references are only allegories is equally untenable by anyone who is familiar with the history of alchemy, since many of alchemy's most prominent adepts have made significant contributions to chemistry, and they have not been notable as teachers either of philosophy or of theology.

The most ancient known alchemist is the Greek alchemist Zosimos of Panopolis, who flourished in the Greco-Roman Egypt in the late third century AD and in the early fourth century AD. The tenth century AD Byzantine encyclopedic dictionary *Souda* writes that *chemeia*, from which alchemy (in Greek, *alchemeia*) is derived, is the art of making silver and gold (the two so-called perfect metals), thus emphasizing the practical aspect of alchemy.[1] Additionally, according to the *Souda*'s lemma *chemeia*, the Roman Emperor Diocletian (AD 284–305) burned several alchemical books that existed in Egypt and contained information about the art of making silver and gold, because he didn't want the Egyptians to accumulate wealth through the practice of alchemy, and because he was afraid that the Egyptians would be empowered and emboldened by the practice of alchemy.

However, Byzantine scholars maintain that alchemy has two aspects: the material and the spiritual. For instance, the Byzantine rhetorician Aineias Gazaios (fifth/sixth century AD), in his philosophical dialogue entitled *Theophrastus*, tries to explain the resurrection of bodies on the Judgment Day through the divine Creator's art, according to which the body and the soul are united integrally, and, for this purpose, Aineias Gazaios draws examples from the practice of alchemy.[2] In particular, in his Theophrastus, Aineias Gazaios refers to the art of transmutation, by which it was sought to produce silver and gold from other, less precious metals, while, with regard to spiritual alchemy, Aineias Gazaios conceives of transmutation as an art that leads to the spiritualization of matter and the salvation of the psychosomatic nexus of the human being. It is important to mention that, in contrast to radically dualistic approaches to spiritual alchemy, which reflect

---

1 Hunger, Herbert, *Die Hochsprachliche Profane Literatur der Byzantiner*, Vol. 2, München: Beck, 1978.
2 Gaza, Enea di, *Teofrasto*, Napoli: Salvatore Iodice, 1958.

an Asian world-negating mentality and crave for the liberation of spirit from the material world, the Byzantine approach to spiritual alchemy seeks to lead man as an integral union of mind and body (matter) to the actualization of his divine potential.

In the Middle Ages and in the Renaissance, both material and spiritual alchemy expanded throughout the Islamic world and Western Europe, and various alchemical 'schools' were developed by Arab, Persian, and Western European alchemists, such as: Al-Farabi (born in Damascus, in the ninth century AD), Ibn Umayl (a tenth century AD Arab alchemist who synthesized Greek alchemy and Islamic spirituality), Al-Tughra'i (a Persian alchemist born in Isfahan, in the eleventh century AD; his alchemical texts incorporated extensive extracts from earlier Arabic alchemical writings and Arabic translations of Zosimos of Panopolis's Greek alchemical treatises), Roger Bacon (a thirteenth century English philosopher and Franciscan friar), Paracelsus (1493–1541), etc. Ethan Allen Hitchcock's *Remarks upon Alchemy and the Alchemists* (1857) is one of the most important Western sources for the study of the history and the meaning of alchemy.

From the perspective of modern chemistry, an 'element' is defined as a body that is substantially different from all others, while having constant character itself, and that it is indivisible except into parts of itself. However, the alchemists' elements, namely, Fire, Air, Earth, and Water, are types of four modes of force or matter, and they represent states that are mutually related and dependent, in accordance with the aforementioned ancient Greek concept of "cosmic sympathy." In particular, in the context of alchemy, the following correspondences hold:

Fire–Heat–Dryness
Air–Heat–Moistness
Earth–Cold–Dryness
Water–Cold–Moistness

The aforementioned alchemical correspondences are based on Aristotle's natural philosophy, according to which matter, simple or combined with its developments, may exist in each of these states.

Apart from the aforementioned four elementary states, the alchemists refer to minerals and seven metals, as forms of matter that are essentially stable, except in the hands of an adept alchemist, who might accomplish the Great Work, that is, the transmutation of one of them into another. For the alchemical process of transmutation, one substance was requisite, precisely, the Philosopher's Stone, known also as the Quintessence and as the Son of the Sun. This was to be derived from the Philosophical Mercury, the Philosophical Salt, and the Philosophical Sulphur, which by putrefaction or calcination, became Black, and then by further processes White, and finally the Redness of Perfection was achieved. In the medieval alchemical texts, the sublimation or volatilization of a substance is called the White

Eagle, whereas the Black Eagle refers to putrefaction, by which is meant conversion by heat of dissolved substances or liquids into a form of sediment or precipitate, or of melted substances into slag or a form of ashes. Thus, one of the most well-known alchemical principles is "Solve et Coagula," meaning either dissolve and precipitate from solution, or melt and solidify. The aforementioned Philosopher's Stone was the Key to Transmutation, since, according to the Alchemists, by the power of the Philosopher's Stone, one form of matter could be changed into another: Lead could be transmuted into Silver, called by them the Moon (in Latin, Luna) or the Queen, while Silver could be transmuted into Gold, called by them the Sun (in Latin, Sol) or the King.

On the symbolical and philosophical planes, the alchemical principle "Solve et Coagula," that is, "volatilize and fix," can be interpreted as follows: the fallen soul becomes fixed in matter, and, particularly, the mind that is coagulated and fettered by the world of the senses suffers the consequent loss of the power of direct spiritual communion with God; by mystical death, precisely by being dead for the world of the senses, and by casting off the body's animal passions, the mind is released from its bondage and becomes a partaker of God's uncreated energies. The alchemical principles Sun and Moon, which, in chemistry, correspond to Gold and Silver, respectively, symbolize the soul and the body of man, respectively. The alchemical principles of Mercury, Salt, and Sulphur symbolize the active principle, the passive principle, and their synthesis, respectively. Furthermore, when alchemists maintain that, by time and force, the Black Dragon of putrefaction can become fashioned into the White Swan of purity, they refer to a mental change (in Greek, *metanoia*), precisely, to the return of the mind to the heart and the liberation of the mind from bodily sensation.

Western alchemy is intimately related to the resurgence of Hermeticism and Neoplatonic varieties of ceremonial magic in the fifteenth and the sixteenth centuries AD. According to Hermeticism, namely, the cult of Hermes Trismegistus,[1] the classical elements (earth, air, fire, water) make up the physical world, while the spiritual world (God, the One, the All) created the physical world by an act of will.[2] In particular, according to Hermetic cosmology, there is a reciprocal relationship between the physical world (the physical 'microcosm') and the spiritual world (the spiritual 'macrocosm'): the world is a beautiful whole, and creation can be understood by understanding that earthly realities imperfectly mirror supernatural realities, in accordance with the Hermetic maxim "as above, so below."

---

1 The *Hermetica* are Egyptian-Greek wisdom texts from the second and the third centuries AD that are mostly presented as dialogues in which a teacher, generally identified as Hermes Trismegistus ('thrice-greatest Hermes'), enlightens a disciple. These texts form the basis of Hermeticism.
2 Barnstone, Willis, ed., *The Other Bible: Jewish Pseudepigrapha, Christian Apocrypha, Gnostic Scriptures, Kabbalah, Dead Sea Scrolls*, San Francisco: Harper, 2005.

Sir Isaac Newton has translated the Emerald Tablet—one of the most important pieces of *Hermetica* reputed to contain the secret of the prima materia and its transmutation—as follows:

'Tis true without lying, certain most true. That which is below is like that which is above that which is above is like that which is below to do the miracles of one only thing. And as all things have been arose from one by the mediation of one: so all things have their birth from this one thing by adaptation. The Sun is its father, the moon its mother, the wind hath carried it in its belly, the earth its nurse. The father of all perfection in the whole world is here. Its force or power is entire if it be converted into earth. Separate thou the earth from the fire, the subtle from the gross sweetly with great industry. It ascends from the earth to the heaven again it descends to the earth and receives the force of things superior and inferior. By this means ye shall have the glory of the whole world thereby all obscurity shall fly from you. Its force is above all force. For it vanquishes every subtle thing and penetrates every solid thing. So was the world created. From this are and do come admirable adaptations whereof the means (Or process) is here in this. Hence I am called Hermes Trismegist, having the three parts of the philosophy of the whole world. That which I have said of the operation of the Sun is accomplished and ended.[1]

In the fifteenth and the sixteenth centuries AD, the students of magic were highly learned persons seeking to understand the reality of nature on the basis of the writings of ancient authorities, such as Plato, Pythagoras, and Hermes Trismegistus, and they believed that human reason was insufficient to provide man with the knowledge of the divine mysteries.[2]

B. The Kabbalistic Tree of Life

In Hebrew, 'Kabbalah' means a primordial tradition, or an oral tradition. The spiritual core of the Kabbalah is more ancient than Christianity, older than the Mosaic traditions, end even older than the Egyptian or any other system of religion or philosophy now known, because the origin, or the spiritual core, of the Kabbalah is man's quest for divine illumination and union with God. The spirituality of the Kabbalah is a synthesis of Pythagoreanism, Neoplatonism, and Biblical mysticism.

The primary Kabbalistic treatises are the *Wisdom of Solomon*, the *Zohar* (or *Book of Light*), and the *Sefer Yetsira* (or *Book of the Creation*). The treatise

---

1 See Dobbs, B. J. T., "Newton's Commentary on the Emerald Tablet of Hermes Trismegistus," in *Hermeticism and the Renaissance*, edited by I. Merkel and A. G. Debus, Washington: Folger Shakespeare Library; London : Associated University Presses, 1988, p. 183.
2 Purver, Margery, *The Royal Society: Concept and Creation*, Cambridge: M.I.T Press, 1967.

Wisdom of Solomon is said to have been written in Hellenistic Alexandria, and it is attributed to Philo of Alexandria (ca. 25 BC–ca. 50 AD), a Hellenistic Jewish philosopher, whose purpose was to harmonize Greek philosophy with Jewish spirituality. Philo's allegorical and symbolical treatises and his concept of the Logos as God's creative principle were important for several Christian Church fathers, and they influenced early Christology. The *Zohar* was written by Simeon ben Yochai and first printed in Mantua in 1558. The author of the *Sefer Yetsira* is unknown and scholars place its origin at sometime between 100 BC and 800 AD, but it was originally published in Provence, in the thirteenth century AD, by Rabbi Isaac ben Abraham.

The uncreated divine light is the foundation of the Kabbalistic system. Light was the first manifestation of God in nature. No man can really know God, except as He manifests Himself in His own light, which is neither the sensible light of the physical Sun nor the light of human technology, but it is the uncreated light of god's glory, that is, a spiritual light, which is apparent only to the inner vision of those illuminated by that light. The Bible, in both the Jewish and the Christian parts, emphasizes the Kabbalistic distinction between the exoteric or sensible light and the esoteric or mystical light; in fact, the previous distinction is the foundation upon which rests the superstructure of the Byzantine Christian mystics', namely, the Hesychasts', theological superstructure.

The most important Kabbalistic symbol is the Tree of Life, through which one can understand the universe in connection with the Bible, and, in particular, one can understand that the one God produces all and sustains all, by tracing the gradual and orderly process of creation and its inner harmony. The Kabbalistic Tree of Life consists of ten Sefirot (singular, Sefira), that is, emanations, or levels of reality, through which the *Ein Sof* (the Infinite and Unknowable One) reveals Himself and continuously creates and sustains both the physical realm and the chain of higher intelligible realms;[1] these ten Sefirot are connected together by twenty-two paths corresponding to the Hebrew letters. The *Zohar* emphasizes that the *Ohr Ein Sof*, that is, the uncreated divine light, is the vital dynamic force in Nature, and that, by the study of this uncreated light, one is enabled to acquire knowledge of the unknowable reality. In the Old Testament, this light corresponds to Jacob's Ladder, by which one ascends to celestial knowledge,[2] and, in the New Testament, this light corresponds to Christ's Transfiguration.[3] Additionally, the same uncreated light is symbolized by the upward point of the upward Pentagram (five-pointed star), which is also one of the most important Pythagorean symbols.

---

1 *Ein Sof* literally means no boundary, and, generally, it means total fulfillment.
2 Genesis 28:10–19.
3 Matthew 17:1–9; Mark 9:2–8; Luke 9:28–36; 2 Peter 1:16–18.

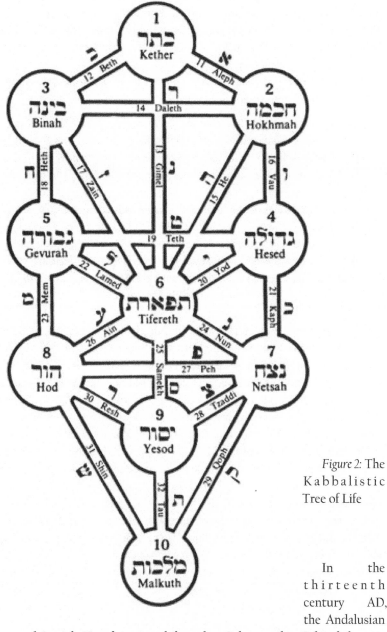

Figure 2: The Kabbalistic Tree of Life

In the thirteenth century AD, the Andalusian poet and Jewish Neoplatonist philosopher Solomon ibn Gabirol, known also as Avicebron, wrote a book entitled *Liber de Causis*, in which he argues that God is wise, and that, from His own wisdom, He has seen fit to make His Will manifest in Light, whereby all existences and substances in the created world are created and sustained by God through God's light. God's will, God's essence, God's unity, and God's eternal existence are mysteries, and we can know God only through His manifestations of Himself in divine light. Hokhmah: Wisdom; major esoteric emblems: the uplifted rod of power, the straight line, *and the tower.*

The ten Sefirot of the Kabbalistic Tree of Life are the following (listed in order from the Beginning to the End):

> *Kether: Crown; major esoteric emblems: the crown, the point, and the swastika.*
> *Binah: Understanding; major esoteric emblem: the chalice.*
> *Hesed: Mercy; major esoteric emblems: the pyramid, the tetrahedron, and the scepter.*
> *Gevurah: Power; major esoteric emblems: the pentagon, the sword, the spear, and the chain.*
> *Tifereth: Beauty; major esoteric emblems: the cube and the rosy cross.*
> *Netsah: Victory; major esoteric emblems: the lamp, the rose, and the seven veils.*
> *Hod: Splendor; major esoteric emblem: the apron.*
> *Yesod: Foundation; major esoteric emblems: the perfumes and the sandals.*
> *Malkuth: Kingdom; major esoteric emblems: the Equal Armed Cross, the double cubed altar, the circle, and the triangle.*

The supernal triad of the Tree of Life, consisting of Kether, Binah, and Hokhmah, is known as the Spiritual, Super-Celestial World, and it corresponds to the supernal alchemical triad, which consists of Salt, Sulfur, and Mercury. In terms of ontology, Kether is pure Being, Binah is Form, and Hokhmah is Energy. Tifereth is the Law of Harmony and the channel of God's Love in the world. Tifereth corresponds to the Son through Whom one can know the Father. Tifereth, Hesed, and Gevurah constitute the second triad of the Kabbalistic Tree of Life, while Yesod, Netsah, and Hod constitute the third one; these two triads combined constitute the Hexad, known also as the Seal of Solomon. Moreover, the second triad (i.e., Tifereth, Hesed, and Gevurah) is often mentioned as the subjective principle, and, from this perspective, it refers to the realm of culture, while the third triad (i.e., Yesod, Netsah, and Hod) is often mentioned as the objective principle, and, from this perspective, it refers to the realm of historical objectification.

With regard to the human being (often called the Microcosm), the ten Sefirot correspond to the following spiritual experiences:

1. Kether: union with God

2. Hokhmah: the personal vision of God, face to face,

3. Binah: vision of Sorrow and Struggle

4. Hesed: vision of Providence

5. Gevurah: vision of Strength, Power

6. Tifereth: vision of Love and Harmony
7. Netsah: vision of Beauty Triumphant
8. Hod: Truthfulness
9. Yesod: the awareness of the True Will
10. Malkuth: vision of the Holy Guardian Angel.

In summary, according to the Kabbalah, there is an upper, transcendent force in which all human beings live. This force is entirely good, bestowing, and giving. We, as human beings, exist hypostatically. Due to our hypostatic way of being, we can choose to live egoistically and, thus, opposite to the transcendent force, or, alternatively, we may choose to care for connection with the 'Other,' and, thus, we may decide to be transparent to the deity, since the connection with the 'Other,' that is, one's psychic transparency, is the essence of one's spiritually. Finally, according to the diagram of the Kabbalistic Tree of Life, we may attain unification with God.

C. The Fraternity of the Rose and Cross: Rosicrucian Enlightenment versus the European Enlightenment

The history of the Rosicrucians goes back to medieval Germany. The earliest public notice of the Fratres of the Rose and Cross appeared in 1614 in a pamphlet printed at Kassel in Germany and entitled *Fama fraternitatis Rosae Crucis* (The Fame of the Fraternity of the Rose and Cross). In 1615, a new edition of the previous pamphlet appeared, to which was added another one, entitled *Confessio Fraternitatis* (The Confession of the Fraternity), giving great promises about future revelations. In 1652, the Welsh mystical philosopher and naturalist Thomas Vaughan, who was writing under the pseudonym of Eugenius Philalethes, translated the work into English.

The *Fama Fraternitatis* starts as follows:
Seeing the only Wise and Merciful God in these latter days hath poured out so richly his mercy and goodness to Mankind, whereby we do attain more and more to the perfect knowledge of his Son Jesus Christ and Nature, that justly we may boast of the happy time, wherein there is not only discovered unto us the half part of the World, which was heretofore unknown and hidden, but he hath also made manifest unto us many wonderful, and never heretofore seen, Works and Creatures of Nature, and moreover hath raised men endued with great Wisdom, which might partly renew and reduce all Arts (in this our Age spotted and imperfect) to perfection; so that finally Man might thereby understand his own Nobleness and Worth, and why he is called *Microcosmus*, and how far his knowledge extendeth in Nature.

The *Fama Fraternitatis* announced the existence of a discrete fraternity founded in the late Middle Ages by a German nobleman, the "pious, spiritual, and highly-illuminated Father" Fr. C.R. (Christian Rosenkreutz). According to the *Fama*, dissatisfied with monastic life, the young C.R. travelled with a Father P.A.L. to the East in search of knowledge, and he reached Cyprus, where his friend died in 1393. Brother C.R. then went on to Damascus, where he conducted further studies, and subsequently he went to Egypt, where he remained for a long time. He journeyed along the Mediterranean Sea and visited Fez, where he studied the accumulated scientific and philosophical knowledge as well as the magic, that is, the alchemical treatises, of the Arabs. In fact, by the late Middle Ages, the Arabs and the Persians had already created big libraries, and they had collected and translated many ancient Greek philosophical and scientific books. During the reign of the Abbasid caliphs al-Mansur (AD 754–75) and Harun ar-Rashid (AD 786–809), many works of ancient Greek philosophers and scientists, such as Aristotle, Hippocrates, Galen of Pergamon, Ptolemy, and Euclid were translated into Arabic by such prominent translators and scholars as Ibn Bakhtishu, Theodore Abu Qurrah, al-Bitriq and his son Yahya, etc. The Abbasid caliph al-Mamun (AD 813–33), son of Harun al-Rashid, supported the study of ancient Greek philosophy and science, and he was an advocate of philosophical free thinking. Moreover, in Baghdad, caliph Harun ar-Rashid founded an intellectual center called the "House of Wisdom" (in Arabic, Bayt al-Hikma), which was generously sponsored and developed further by caliph al-Mamun. Finally, Brother C.R. crossed over into Spain, where he learned the Jewish Kabbalah and the philosophy of the Moors. It is worth pointing out that the Moors were the first great improvers of natural sciences in medieval Western Europe, since they had acquired their sciences from the Greeks through the Byzantine Empire, and they created renowned universities in Spain, such as those of Seville, Cordova, and Granada; "and such was the reputation which they had acquired, that crowds of learned men from various countries resorted to Spain to study those sciences."[1] During his journey in search of wisdom, Brother C.R. observed how the Eastern sages shared their knowledge without jealousy, hypocrisy, or egoism.

In 1402, Brother C.R. returned to Germany, and he settled down to codify the vast amount of knowledge that he had collected. However, in Germany, he found only hostility and indifference. Thus, in Germany, in a place now unknown, Brother C.R. established a fraternity of sympathetic brethren, namely, the Fratres R.C., who met annually in secret in the "House of the Holy Spirit," as they called their assembly, with the aim to advance science

---

1 *The Edinburgh Encyclopedia*, Vol. 17, Philadelphia: Joseph Parker, 1832, p. 388.

and an esoteric approach to religion and to further a deep reformation of knowledge.

Six ordinances were laid down to govern the original members of the Rosicrucian Fraternity in the conduct of their lives, namely:

1. None of them should profess any great powers, knowledge, or authority to the outer world, but they should do good and heal the poor freely.

2. No peculiar habit should be worn when out in the world to make them conspicuous or liable to persecution.

3. On one day at least in every year all Fratres should assemble to record their work and communicate to each other their gains of knowledge.

4. Every Frater should seek one or more suitable persons to succeed him.

5. "R.C." or "C.R." should be their seal, mark and character.

6. The Fraternity should remain a secret or private one, at least for a hundred years, if not longer.

Around 1450, the eldest Fratres or Magistri designed and executed a funeral Chamber in which Brother C.R. should be buried when his end came. Brother C.R. died in 1484, and he was entombed. On the door of the vault the inscription "Post centum viginti annos patebo" was engraved on a brazen plate, meaning that the vault should be opened after 120 years. This long period passed by, and, even though Roman Catholicism had been fiercely attacked by the Religious Reformation, the work of the Rosicrucians had continued in peace and secrecy. In 1604, the Fratres then forming the central group of the Rosicrucian Fraternity disclosed the door of the secret chamber and entered the vault, where the Founder's body was lying in perfect condition, clothed in the symbolic robe and the insignia of his office of Magus (i.e., Head) of the Fraternity, and there were found stored the original books and achievements of the earliest members.

Through symbols and in allegorical language, the original Rosicrucian manifestos, namely, the *Fama* and the *Confessio*, are concerned with the following goal: the union of religion and science in the context of a spiritual quest for the real truth of both the visible and the invisible things. This is the context in which Rosicrucians study systems of Eastern mysticism, such Hermetic philosophy, Alchemy (i.e., the Hermetic Art), and the Kabbalah, they delve into natural sciences, they promote the development of science, in general, and, simultaneously, they cultivate an esoteric approach to religion. The unifying principle that pervades the entire spectrum of the Rosicrucians' endeavors is their longing for communion with the one, ultimate source of the meaning of all beings and things, visible and invisible. Therefore, genuine Rosicrucianism simultaneously opposes the Papacy's spiritual despotism, formalist religiosity, and the dryly reasonable scientism of the European Enlightenment.

The European Enlightenment is also known as the Age of Reason, and it spans a period of time from the 1620s to the 1780s. During that period of time, the dominant cultural and scholarly forces in Western Europe emphasized reason, analysis, and individualism rather than tradition. However, it should be mentioned that, by the early seventeenth century, the major traditional institutions in Western Europe, such as the Papacy, the Puritans, and several mainstream scholarly communities, had degraded tradition into an authoritarian formalist system incapable of existentially satisfying the human being. Faced with the crisis and the corruption of all their available traditional institutions and authorities, the scholars of the European Enlightenment hastened to the resort of reason and individualism, thus exchanging one evil for another.

Beyond the appearances of the European Enlightenment's creative and free-thinking intellectuals, inherent in the European Enlightenment is a system that is invisible to the materialist eye, and it consists of mental mills used by 'Satan' as the lord of fatalism and spatio-temporal necessity to crash and destroy those who cannot see through it. The world of the European Enlightenment is enthralled by a false god who works through the closed world of the selfhood, the self-centered ego, and, particularly, through clanging rationalism. This is the world of quantification, scientific formalism, and finitude, whereas the inner world is, at least potentially, infinite and free. The kingdom of God is within us.[1]

The most extreme form of the European Enlightenment's rationalism is fundamentalist materialism. Fundamentalist materialists oppose all forms of mysticism, advocate dogmatic positivism, and they religiously believe in the principle of arbitrary coincidence. Thus, fundamentalist materialism quiets existential anxieties, makes the restless mind inert, ends the perpetual enquiring and wondering, and, eventually, it stops free thought entirely.

Moreover, in the sphere of politics, the European Enlightenment's political and economic thought has given rise to the industrial society. The industrial society is focused on machines and mechanistically organized systems, because it thinks like a machine, and its god is mechanistic. In other words, the most distinctive characteristic of the industrial society is neither technology *per se* nor the mechanization of production *per se*, but the subservience of human consciousness to the logic of the machine. Thus, the dominant mentality of the industrial society is worse than plebeian, it is mechanistic.

---

1 Luke 17:21.

D. The esoteric reality of advanced science: geometry as successful magic

The essence of magic consists in man's attempt to impose his intentionality on his existential conditions and, generally, on the world. In other words, magic is the most primitive, yet methodical and systematic, attempt of humanity to restructure the world, or the external reality, according to humanity's will. Put simply, magic consists in setting a goal and going about accomplishing it. Therefore, through magic, man started realizing that the reality of his existential conditions and, generally, of the world is susceptible to change and, particularly, to the restructuring intervention of the intentionality of human consciousness in the world. Intimately related to this awareness is the awareness that there is a structural continuity between the reality of the world and the reality of consciousness.

The reality of the world (the 'exoteric' realm) and the reality of consciousness (the 'esoteric' realm) are not one, but they are (structurally) united. If the reality of the world were merely an extension or a projection of the reality of consciousness, then self-knowledge would be equivalent to and essentially synonymous with cosmology, which is not true, and the human mind would not need to try so hard in order to understand and explain the reality of the world. On the other hand, if the reality of the world were totally distinct from the reality of consciousness, then the human mind would be unable to achieve even partial knowledge of the world.

The aforementioned fundamental awarenesses of magical thought underpin advanced science, and they have been scientifically corroborated. The prominent French mathematician René Thom, the father of Catastrophe Theory, has argued that "geometry is successful magic."[1] In scientifically rigorous geometrical language, by the term 'system,' we should understand the content of a domain D of the space-time. We remind that a 'domain' of an n-dimensional Euclidean space is a connected open subset of ; a space is said to be 'connected' if it cannot be represented as the union of two or more disjoint nonempty open subsets. The inputs of a system are, at least partially, controlled by the observer/manager of the given system, and the outputs of a system are, at least partially, analyzable and/or understandable by the observer/manager of the given system. Thus, a 'system' can be understood as an entity that responds to every input $u \in U$ with an output $v \in V$, where u is a vector of the k-dimensional Euclidean space U, and v is a vector of the m-dimensional Euclidean space V.

Action aims at solving local problems, whereas understanding is aimed at the universal and, hence, the global. As a consequence, there are two

---

1 Quoted in Ziegler, Günter M., *Do I Count?: Stories from Mathematics*, Boca Raton, FL: CRC Press/Taylor & Francis Group, 2014, p. 186.

scientific poles: one pole seeks pure knowledge, and, therefore, it maintains that the fundamental end of science is the understanding of reality, whereas another pole is primarily concerned with action. However, in an apparently odd way, the solution of local problems requires non-local means, and the explanation of global phenomena requires their reduction to formal local situations. Always man's goal remains the same, namely, to obliterate the compulsions of space-time, wherefore humanity utilizes every easily controlled mode of non-local action (e.g., in the fields of transportation, communication, medicine, warfare, etc.).

Magic aims at solving individual and local problems, and it is focused on action at a distance. In accord with the magical world-conception, Einstein's general theory of relativity studies gravitation as a force taking place at each mathematical point (i.e., locally) and, thus, the resulting curvature of space as a localized event, Maxwell's equations explain electromagnetism as a local phenomenon, and, in quantum mechanics, Bell's theorem entails actions at a distance, which Einstein has called "spooky."

The first scientific theory of space is due to ancient Greek geometricians, whose results have been methodically expounded by Euclid. According to Euclidean geometry, space is three-dimensional and isotropic (i.e., invariant with respect to direction). The Euclidean perception of space, modified by the fact that it was associated with the concept of gravity, was enriched and completed by Isaac Newton. However, in contradistinction to Newton's realism, Kant endorses an idealist approach to space (and time), in the sense that he argues that space is an a priori schema of consciousness, and that, through this schema, the intellect can articulate synthetic statements about the sensible world, whereas sense-perception is fragmented.

In 1854, in his seminal research paper "On the Hypotheses which Lie at the Foundations of Geometry,"[1] the German mathematician Bernhard Riemann introduced the idea of "a multiply extended magnitude out of general notions of quantity," and he showed that "a multiply extended magnitude is susceptible of various metric relations," where, by the term 'metric,' mathematicians mean a rule for measuring distance; Riemann, in particular, studied n-dimensional spaces whose intrinsic geometry is determined by a quadratic formula ('metric') for the infinitesimal change in distance dx. Such a structure is now called a Riemannian manifold. Different manifolds yield different geometries, depending on their dimensions and on their metric (a function that defines a distance between each pair of

---

1 Riemann read this research paper on June 10, 1854 for the purpose of his "Habilitation" with the philosophical faculty of Göttingen; Riemann, Bernhard, "On the Hypotheses which Lie at the Foundations of Geometry" (translated by Henry S. White), in *A Source Book in Mathematics*, edited by David E. Smith, 411–425, New York: Dover, 1959.

elements of a set). In other words, Riemann proved that mathematicians can define infinitely many different geometries, thus showing that the classical Euclidean–Newtonian geometry is not the only possible geometry and that, contra Kant, the Euclidean space is not an *a priori* schema of consciousness.

2. Chivalry

A. The essence of chivalry

The term chivalry is derived from the image of a warrior on the horseback. The literal meaning is horsemanship, from Latin *caballus* (*cheval* in French). Chivalry, referring to the medieval institution of Knighthood, has three aspects, or dimensions: the military, the social, and the religious.

The military aspect of chivalry: With regard to its military dimension, chivalry was the heavy cavalry of the Middle Ages, constituting the chief and most effective warlike force. The knight, or chevalier, was the professional soldier of the Middle Ages. The peculiar characteristics of the knight were the following: (i) His weapons: the only offensive weapons were the lance for the encounter and the sword for the close fight, that is, the weapons common to both light-armed and heavy cavalry, but the characteristic distinction of the knights lay in their defensive weapons, which varied with different periods (these weapons were always costly to acquire and heavy to bear, such as the coat of mail, which prevailed during the Crusades, and the plate armor introduced in the fourteenth century AD). (ii) His horses: the knight was equipped with at least three horses, specifically, the battle horse, which was led by hand and used only for the onset, a second horse for the route, and the pack-horse for the luggage. (iii) His attendants: the knight required one attendant to conduct the horses, another to bear the heaviest weapons, especially the shield, or escutcheon (*scutum*, hence *scutarius*, squire), still another to aid his master to mount his battle horse or to raise him if dismounted, and a fourth to guard prisoners, primarily those of quality, for whom a high ransom was expected (from the thirteenth century AD, the squires also went armed and mounted and, passing from one grade to the other, were raised finally to knighthood). (iv) His flag: banners attached to and carried on the lance were a distinctive mark of chivalry.

The social aspect of chivalry: The career of a knight was costly, and, in fact, it required personal means in keeping with the station, since a knight had to defray his own expenses in periods during which the sovereign had neither treasury nor war budget at his disposal. In those areas where land was the major factor of production and, hence, the major source of wealth, each ruler who intended to raise an army divided his domain into military fiefs, and the tenant was held to military service at his own personal expense for a fixed number of days (e.g., forty in France and in England during the Norman period). The previous fees, like other feudal grants, became hereditary and, thus, gave rise to a noble class, for whom the knightly profession was the only career. However, knighthood was not hereditary, though only the sons of a knight were eligible to its ranks. In boyhood, they were sent to the court of some noble, where they were trained in the use of horses and weapons, and they were taught lessons of courtesy. From the thirteenth century AD, the candidates, after they had attained the rank of squire, were allowed to take part in battles, but they could be admitted to the rank of a knight (by means of a peculiar ceremonial called "dubbing") only when they had come of age, commonly twenty-one years. Every knight was qualified to confer knighthood to aspirants who fulfilled the requisite conditions of birth, age, and training; where the condition of birth was lacking in the aspirant, the sovereign alone could create a knight, as part of his royal prerogative.

The religious aspect of chivalry: The participation of the Church in the ceremonial of conferring knighthood, particularly, the blessing of the Knight's sword by the clergy, gave to chivalry a religious character. Initially, the form of this ritual was very simple, but, gradually, it developed into an elaborate ceremony. Before the blessing of the sword on the altar, many preliminaries were required of the aspirant, such as confession, a vigil of prayer, fasting, a symbolical death, and investiture with a white robe, for the purpose of impressing on the candidate the purity of soul with which he was to enter upon such a noble career. Kneeling, in the presence of the clergy, he pronounced the solemn vow of chivalry, at the same time often renewing the baptismal vow, and then the one chosen as godfather struck him lightly on the head and/or the shoulders with a sword (the "dubbing") in the name of God and (often) the patron saint of the particular chivalric order.

Many different codes of chivalry have been set down; most contain the following eight issues: (i) You shall defend the Church. (ii) You shall respect all weaknesses and shall constitute yourself the defender of them. (iii) You shall love the country in which you were born. (iv) You shall not recoil before your enemy. (v) You shall scrupulously perform your feudal duties, if they be not contrary to the laws of God. (vi) You shall never lie and shall remain faithful to your pledged word. (vii) You shall be generous and give largess to everyone. (viii) You shall be everywhere and always the champion of the Right and the Good against Injustice and Evil.

B. The historical phases of the chivalric institution

First period: The Roots of Chivalry: Historical evidence corroborates the argument that Christian Chivalry began with the Emperor Constantine the Great in the fourth century AD, and it is particularly related to a miraculous incident that occurred in the life of the Roman Emperor Constantine the Great after the battle of Saxa Rubra in the year of our Lord 312 in which he finally defeated his rival Emperor Maxentius. The manner of his conversion to Christianity is thus related: upon an evening, during the march of his army on Rome, Constantine was meditating on the fate of sublunary things and the dangers of his expedition, and, sensible of his own inability to succeed without divine assistance, he supplicated heaven to grant him inspiration and wisdom to choose the right path. Thus, he had the following vision: suddenly there appeared in the heavens a pillar of light in the shape of a cross, with the inscription "In hoc signo vinces" (i.e., "in this sign you will conquer"). Recognizing the power of this symbol and understanding that a great idea has the potential to change the world, the Emperor caused a Royal Standard to be made bearing as a device a Cross like that which he had seen in the heavens, and he ordered that it should always be carried before him in his wars as an ensign of victory and celestial protection. The tradition then relates that, thereupon, several Christians among the soldiers came forward and openly avowed their faith, and that the Emperor, to commemorate the event, directed them to wear a Red Cross with sixteen stars denoting the sixteen letters of the mystical words on their armor. On reaching the Capital, Constantine, with the assistance of Eusebius, is said to have opened a Conclave of Knights of the Red Cross, and, thereafter, these valiant and illustrious men formed the personal bodyguard of their Sovereign. Among the other acts of Constantine, his encouragement of learning is conspicuous. He also ordered that the Scriptures should be carefully kept and frequently read in all Churches, and he undertook effective actions for the relief of the poor and for other pious purposes.

Second period: The Crusades: The Crusades introduced the golden age of chivalry, yet the Crusaders themselves were remnants from the feudal age, and the era of the Crusades was a period of significant social and cultural change for Western Europe. In the late eleventh century AD, socially wrecked people—who were useless to the new emerging ruling elites of Western Europe—were 'exported' to the East in order to be killed or, if they won, to create new fiefs in the East.

In the eleventh century AD, in Western Europe, the bourgeoisie emerged as a historical and political subject when the market towns (the "bourgs") of Central and Western Europe developed into cities founded and focused on trade. The previous urban expansion was made possible due to a process of organized economic concentration that derived from the organization of individual businessmen (craftsmen, artisans, merchants, etc.) into guilds, which resisted against ethically degraded rent-seeking feudal landlords whenever the latter were following an arbitrary and extremely greedy economic policy. Moreover, gradually, the bourgeoisie created its own civilization, and, by the end of the Middle Ages, the bourgeoisie politically allied with the king or the queen against the power of the feudal lords, thus paving the way to the modern monarchy and the modern nation-state.[1]

During the period of the Crusades, the rescue of the Holy Land, in Palestine, from Moslem domination and the defense of pilgrims became the new object of the knight's vow. In this context, Pope Urban II called the First Crusade (1096–9) for a number of religious and political reasons. His temporal authority was weakened by the recent sacking of Rome by the German King Henry IV and the Normans, and it was threatened by the strategic alliances among the various kings and princes of the Western and the Eastern Christendom.

In particular, in 1075, Pope Gregory VII threatened to excommunicate the German King Henry IV in order to impose the decisions of the councils of 1074–5, which, among others, denied secular rulers the right to place members of the clergy in office. As a consequence of the previous canonical decision, the bishops of the local Church of Germany, who were often powerful feudatories, could claim their freedom from imperial authority, whereas King Henry IV wanted to enhance and centralize his authority. King Henry IV extracted revenge on Pope Gregory VII by getting rid of those disloyal to him, strengthening his army, and then invading the Italian peninsula and laying siege to Rome. Pope Gregory VII fled to Hadrian's mausoleum, which had been transformed into the Papal fortress of Castel Sant'Angelo, and he was then rescued by the Normans under Robert Guiscard, who, in the

---

1 Pirenne, Henri, *Medieval Cities: Their Origins and the Revival of Trade*, updated edition, Princeton, NJ: Princeton University Press, 2014.

meantime, burnt and pillaged Rome. The Normans took Pope Gregory VII south, to Salerno, where he lived in exile until his death in 1085. King Henry IV then had an irregular council appoint a Pope of his choosing, namely, Archbishop Guibert of Ravenna, who took the Papal name of Clement III. However, the cardinals who were still loyal to Pope Gregory VII elected the abbot of the Benedictine abbey of Monte Cassino as Pope Victor III. Thus, now, the Roman Catholic Church had a Pope and an anti-Pope. In 1088, the cardinals managed to agree upon the election of a new Pope; he was Ode de Lagery, Cardinal of Ostia, who took the name of Urban II.

Thus, when Pope Urban II ascended to the Papal throne, the political power and the temporal authority of the Papacy had been seriously injured, the strongest ruler in Christendom, specifically, the Eastern Roman ("Byzantine") Emperor, and the Eastern Orthodox Church were, respectively, the strongest temporal and spiritual opponents of the Papacy, the revenues of the Roman Catholic Church had dropped dramatically, and Western European Christians were embroiled in several fights among themselves. Thus, in 1095, when the Eastern Roman Emperor Alexios I Komnenos appealed to Pope Urban II, requesting that Western volunteers come to his aid and help to repel the invading Seljuk Turks from Anatolia, Pope Urban II seized that great historical opportunity in order to enhance the power of the Papacy. In 1095, in March at the Piacenza Council and then in November at the Council of Clermont, Pope Urban II orchestrated the call for Holy War, changing, however, the goal-posts, and asking for a Crusade to liberate the Holy Land.

The siege of Jerusalem by the Crusaders took place from June 7 to July 15, 1099. The Crusaders seized Jerusalem from the Fatimid Caliphate and laid the foundations for the Crusader Kingdom of Jerusalem after a series of fierce battles. Many Muslims sought shelter in the Al-Aqsa Mosque, the Dome of the Rock, and the Temple Mount area, in general. With regard to the fights that took place in the Temple Mount, the *Gesta Francorum* (a Latin chronicle of the First Crusade written in circa 1100–1 by an anonymous author) mentions the following: "[the Crusaders] were killing and slaying even to the Temple of Solomon, where the slaughter was so great that our men waded in blood up to their ankles." Jews fought side-by-side with Muslim soldiers to defend Jerusalem against the Crusaders, and, according to the Muslim chronicle of Ibn al-Qalanisi, "the Jews assembled in their synagogue, and the Franks burned it over their heads."[1] In 1099, Godfrey of Bouillon, a Frankish knight who was one of the leaders of the First Crusade, took the title "Advocatus

---

1 Gibb, H. A. R., *The Damascus Chronicle of the Crusades: Extracted and Translated from the Chronicle of Ibn Al-Qalanisi*, New York: Dover, 2003, p. 48.

Sancti Sepulchri" (Protector of the Holy Sepulcher), and he was inaugurated as ruler of Jerusalem.

Third period: The Military Orders: After the conquest of Jerusalem by the Crusaders, the necessity of a standing army became peremptory, in order to prevent the loss of the Holy City to surrounding hostile nations. Out of this necessity, arose the military orders for perpetual warfare against the "infidels," which was adopted as a fourth monastic vow. The Order of Saint John of Jerusalem, of Rhodes, and of Malta (often referred to simply as the Knights of Malta) began as an Amalfitan hospital founded in Jerusalem around 1070 to provide care for poor and sick pilgrims to the Holy Land. After the foundation of the Crusader Kingdom of Jerusalem in 1099, it became a religious and military order under its own charter, and it was charged with the care and defense of pilgrims to the Holy Land. Following the loss of the Christian territory in the Holy Land, the order operated from Rhodes, over which it was sovereign, and later from Malta, where it administered a vassal state under the Spanish viceroy of Sicily. The Maltese Cross is identified as the symbol of Christian warriors known as the Knights Hospitaller or Knights of Malta: this cross is eight-pointed and has the shape of four "V" shaped arms joined together at their bases, so that each arm has two points. The eight points are said to symbolize the following eight chivalric virtues: loyalty, piety, frankness, bravery, glory/honor, contempt of death, helpfulness toward the poor and sick, and respect for the Church.

The Hospitaller Order of Saint Lazarus of Jerusalem originated from a hospital for lepers that had been built in Palestine by a group of Armenian monks working under the rule of St. Basil in the years preceding 1100.[1] Whereas the inmates of the Hospitaller Order of Saint John were merely visitors and changed constantly, "the lepers of the Hospitaller Order of Saint Lazarus were condemned to perpetual seclusion," and "they were regarded as brothers or sisters of the house which sheltered and cared for them."[2]

The Poor Fellow-Soldiers of Christ and of the Temple of Solomon (in Latin, *Pauperes commilitones Christi Templique Salomonici*), commonly known as the Knights Templar, the Order of Solomon's Temple (in French, *Ordre du Temple* or *Templiers*), or simply as Templars, were among the most wealthy and powerful Christian military orders of the Crusade Kingdom of Jerusalem. In 1119, the French Knight Hugues de Payens approached King Baldwin II of Jerusalem and proposed creating a monastic order for the protection of these pilgrims. King Baldwin and Warmund, the Latin Patriarch of Jerusalem, agreed to the request, probably at the Council of Nablus in January 1120, and the king granted the Templars a headquarters in a wing of the royal

---

1 Ellul, Max Joseph, *The Green Eight Pointed Cross*, Malta: Watermelon/Saint Lazarus Hospice Foundation, 2004, p. 24
2 Ibid., p. 25.

palace on the Temple Mount in the captured Al-Aqsa Mosque. The Temple Mount had a mystique, because it was above what was believed to be the ruins of King Solomon's Temple. Hence, the Crusaders referred to the Al Aqsa Mosque as King Solomon's Temple, and, from this location, the new order took the name of Poor Knights of Christ and the Temple of Solomon, or Knights Templar.

The Order of the Knights Templar, gradually, established financial networks across the whole of Christendom. If a nobleman wanted to participate in the Crusades, and, in general, if a person wanted to travel to the Holy Land, he could place his assets under Templar management while he was away. Having thus accumulated wealth throughout Christendom, the Order of the Knights Templar, around 1150, began generating letters of credit for pilgrims journeying to the Holy Land. In other words, the Order of the Knights Templar, gradually, developed an innovative and powerful banking system capable of supporting the use of cheques. The Order of the Knights Templar accumulated great wealth through donations and banking activities, it acquired large tracts of land, both in Europe and the Middle East, it built Churches and castles, it was involved in manufacturing, import and export, it had its own fleet of ships, and, from the fall of Acre in 1291 until the dissolution of the Order of the Knights Templar, the island of Cyprus was one of the major centers of the Knights Templar.[1]

In 1306, King Philip IV of France (called "the Fair"; in French, *Philippe le Bel*) expelled the Jews from France, and, in 1307, he launched a pogrom against the Order of the Knights Templar, because he was deeply in debt to both Jewish usurers and the Templar Order, and he saw them as a "state within the state." On Friday, October 13, 1307, Jacques de Molay, the 23rd and last Grand Master of the Knights Templar, and several other Knights Templar in France were arrested. King Philip IV had the Templars charged with several trumped-up charges, most of which were identical to the charges that had previously been leveled by Philip's propaganda agents against Pope Boniface VIII.[2] Under pressure from King Philip, Pope Clement V disbanded the Order in 1312. Jacques de Molay was burned at the stake in Paris in 1314 by order of King Philip IV.

Fourth period: Humanist Chivalry: After the Crusades, chivalry gradually lost its religious aspect, and it focused on the principle of honor *per se*. In this context, in the nineteenth and the twentieth centuries, many chivalric orders were, in essence, transformed into chivalric humanitarian organizations. For

1 Ralls, Karen, *Knights Templar Encyclopedia*, Franklin Lakes, NJ: Career, 2007.
2 The conflict between Pope Boniface VIII and King Philip IV of France was a consequence of the rising power of the 'nation-state' and of the general tendency of the increasingly powerful monarchs, including King Philip IV of France, to consolidate their power vis-à-vis other institutions.

instance, the United Grand Priories of the Hospitaller Order of Saint Lazarus of Jerusalem, formed on May 13, 1999 by its founding Master-General Frà John Baron Dudley von Sydow von Hoff, is an international confraternity of hospitallers who apply themselves to the relief of those in need of hospice care, and it models itself upon the traditions and ideals of the medieval, chivalric, and hospitaller Order of Saint Lazarus of Jerusalem.

Fifth period: Court Chivalry: In its last stages, chivalry became a mere court service. For instance, the Order of the Garter, founded in 1348 by King Edward III of England, the Order of the Golden Fleece, founded in 1430 by the Duke of Burgundy (known as Philip the Good), and the Order of Saint Michael, founded in 1469 by King Louis XI of France (in competitive response to the Burgundian Order of the Golden Fleece), were brotherhoods not of crusaders but of courtiers, whose only aim was to contribute to the splendor of the sovereign.

Sixth period: Symbolic or Esoteric Chivalry: Intimately related to the humanist period of chivalry is the gradual emergence of an understanding of chivalry that emphasizes the true, internal, nobility of a person. Symbolic or esoteric chivalry is reached through the true nobility of a person. For instance, this is the manner in which Freemasonry and several other esoteric societies use the concept of chivalry.

3. Freemasonry

A. Esoteric and Exoteric Freemasonry

Ḥuram 'abi, known also among Freemasons as Hiram Abiff, was the son of a widow of the tribe of Naphtali and of a man of Tyre who was a worker in bronze, and "he was filled with wisdom and understanding and skill, to work all works in bronze."[1] Hiram Abiff "came to King Solomon, and performed all his work," since he fashioned and set up the two bronze pillars at the porch of the Temple of Jerusalem: "he set up the right pillar, and called its name Jachin; and he set up the left pillar, and called its name Boaz."[2] Similarly, the Masonic Art, an art *par excellence*, has two aspects: an Esoteric one and an Exoteric one.

The Esoteric aspect of the Masonic Art constitutes the spirit of the Craft, and the Exoteric aspect of the Masonic Art constitutes the structure of the Craft. Whereas the Exoteric aspect of the Masonic Art can be learned, taught, and given, the Esoteric aspect of the Masonic Art can only partially be learned, taught, and given, because, beyond a certain point, it emerges in the Freemason's consciousness from the outside as a personal experience of illumination.

---

1 1 Kings 7:14.
2 Ibid., 7:21.

B. The origins of Freemasonry

Myth, as we have inherited it from Plato's philosophy and the ancient Mysteries, gives life to ideas. In the context of the activity of mythologizing consciousness, knowledge is not derived from static representation, but it constitutes an itinerary of the entire human being toward truth. Thus, in his dialogues *Gorgias* and *Republic*, Plato argues that *paideia* (i.e., classical Greek education) consists in a transition from *doxa* (i.e., a belief, unrelated to reason, that resides in the unreasoning, lower-parts of the soul) to the real being. A philosophical myth is not merely an intellectual method of teaching, because it elucidates the significance of its subject-matter and not only the content of its mythological subject-matter. Thus, a myth is not an allegory, but it is a symbol: in contrast to an allegory, a myth does not simply refer to something else, but also it discloses the significance of that 'else,' to which it refers. Additionally, in contrast to the analytical method, the mythological method of seeking truth consists in entering into the thing, that is, in knowing its significance, rather than going around it from the outside.

In the context of Freemasonic dramas (as in every theatrical play and myth), the significance of each symbol is embodied, and, thus, it is not an unsubstantial abstraction. The content of a symbol discloses the author's intention, while the material entity that substantiates a symbol (e.g., a person who substantiates a symbol in the context of a ritual or a theatrical play, ritualistic objects, etc.) is imprinted by the life of the author's intention. The recognition of the previous two levels on which a symbol can be approached and studied (namely, at the level of a symbol's content and at the level of the material entity that substantiates a symbol) allows us to interpret mysticism in a creative way, just like an artefact.

The exact origin of the term Freemasonry is not known. In 1391, at Oxford, there is reference to a "master of free stones," and there are also Masons called "mason layers." The term Freemason is known to have been in use in 1374. The prefix 'free' was used to describe those who worked in and sculptured and carved free stone, which was a fine grained sandstone or limestone lending itself to easy carving and sculpturing and suitable for window and door frames, vaultings, capitals, and other ornamentation used largely in Gothic Architecture. Moreover, the prefix 'free' was used to indicate a free man, especially in Scotland. This was meant to refer to a man who had completed his indentures and was free to work on his own. The first recorded use of the word Lodge in a Masonic context can be traced back to the building of a Cistercian Monastery at Vale Royal near Chester in 1278. In that period of the history of Masonry, the Lodge was a hut in which Masons conversed, organized their work, took their midday meals, and, on certain occasions, they could even sleep. By the mid-fourteenth century AD, there were elaborate rules governing the behavior of Masons of the Lodge attached to York Minster.

In ancient times, Masonry became a true science and art by the Greeks. In 1940, C. F. C. Hawkes, assistant Keeper of Antiquities in the British Museum, published his seminal book entitled *The Prehistoric Foundations of Europe to the Mycenaean Age*, in which he argued that the megalithic architecture, the use of copper, the building of walls around cities, and the erection of ancient edifices are gifts of the Aegean civilizations to the rest of the European peoples. The distinguished Freemason, researcher, and historiographer Manly P. Hall (1901–90), in his seminal book entitled *The Secret Teachings of All Ages: An Encyclopedic Outline of Masonic, Hermetic, Qabbalistic and Rosicrucian Symbolical Philosophy*, using the language of myth and symbology, argues that the "Dionysian Architects" constituted an ancient secret society whose principles and doctrines were similar to those of modern Freemasonry. According to Hall, the Dionysian Architects constituted an organization of builders bound together by their secret knowledge of the relationship between the exoteric and the esoteric aspects of architecture, and they were supposedly employed by King Solomon in the building of the Temple of Jerusalem, although they were not Jews, and they were followers of Bacchus and Dionysus. Moreover, according to Hall, the Dionysian Architects erected many of the great monuments of antiquity, they possessed a secret code for communicating among themselves and for marking their stones, they had special convocations and sacred feasts, and Hiram Abiff was an initiate of this society. The motif that is known as the Seal of Solomon, or hexalpha (two interlaced equilateral triangles), was also one of the Dionysian Architects' symbols.[1] With regard to the ancient Roman Colleges, Manly P. Hall, in his aforementioned book, argues that the Roman *Collegia* of skilled architects were a subdivision of the greater Ionian body, and that it is most likely that the Dionysian Architects exerted profound influence on early Islamic culture, too. Indeed, it is a historical fact that ancient Roman art was derived from and relied heavily on ancient Greek art. According to M. P. Hall (Ibid), during their expeditions in the East, the Knights Templar contacted the architectural heritage of the Dionysian Artificers and introduced many of their symbols and doctrines into medieval Europe.

Sir David Brewster, in his book *The History of Freemasonry*, published in 1804, argues that the Masons sent to King Solomon from Tyre were members of the Dionysian fraternity. In the eleventh century BC, the inhabitants of

---

1 The hexalpha probably emerged as a symbol of harmonious duality and, particularly, of the ten primary contrasting qualities of Pythagoras, namely: the limited and unlimited, odd and even, male and female, one and the many, right and left, rest and motion, straight and curved, light and darkness, good and bad, and the square and the oblong. In the context of Pythagorean philosophy, the hexalpha and the icosahedron represent the union of complementary forces.

the area of the ancient Greek city of Athens thought that their country was too small and the soil of poor quality. They sailed to Asia Minor and drove out the inhabitants of a piece of land that they called Ionia where they built many towns. They took with them their knowledge of the sciences and arts and they introduced the original Mysteries of Pallas and Dionysus, the Roman Bacchus, into Ionia.

John A. Weisse, M.D., in his book *The Obelisk and Freemasonry*, published in 1880, argues that the Dionysian Artificers made their appearance not later than 1000 BC, they enjoyed particular privileges and immunities, they possessed secret means of recognition, and they were bound together by special secret ties. In his previous book, Weisse argues that it has been claimed that King Solomon of Israel, at the instance of King Hiram of Tyre, employed the Dionysian Artificers at the Jerusalem temple and palace, and that they were also employed at the construction of the Temple of Diana at Ephesus. Additionally, according to Weisse (ibid.), from the Dionysian Artificers, sprang the guilds of the traveling Masons known in the Middle Ages.

In medieval times, Freemasonry was a closed Trade Guild. In those years, the Masters of the Craft were in possession of secret knowledge about the weights of various types of stone per solid cubit, their capacity, the effects of grains, the methods used to raise stones to their required setting, the construction of machines to achieve this, and many other matters connected with the Craft of Masonry. Thus, in the Middle Ages, a Master of the Craft was justified in claiming that he was a Master of Arts and Sciences. With the decay of the Guilds, this knowledge ceased to retain its secret nature, and it became more generally available through the textbooks and tables of the Architectural and Engineering Professions, which have now taken the place of the Guild of Masons. However, the journey of the stones has provided a symbolism of the advance of the men who wrought the stones. In the context of Symbolic Masonry, the stone and its worker became identified in the Lodge symbolic ceremonies. In all the different rites of Symbolic Masonry, the Candidate represents a "living stone" that is being wrought from the rough, in which it is received from the Quarry, to a state of perfection. Thus, even though there are various different Freemasonic Rites practiced around the world, the most general definition of Symbolic Masonry is that it is a system of spiritual development based on the symbolic use of Operative Masons' tools, habits, methods of work, and structures of organization.

In an enumeration of the guilds entitled to representation in the Common Council of London in 1370, guild No. 17 was the "Company of Freemasons," and guild No. 34 was the "Company of Masons." The Company of Masons appears to have been of greater numerical strength than the Company of

Freemasons, since it had four representatives as against two for the other. Albert Mackey's *History of Freemasonry* suggests that the Freemasons formed a smaller and more select society, but this is pure speculation, because there are no historical facts about the special social status of Freemasons. However, the previous list establishes the existence of two separate guilds. Ultimately, these two guilds were merged, taking a coat of arms which displayed three white castles with black doors and windows on a black field, together with a silver or scalloped chevron and on it a black set of compasses. Furthermore, town mason guilds frequently united with, or formed parts of, guilds of other workers employed in the building trades, and the rules laid down for practical guidance of members of the Craft corresponded in the main with similar rules laid down in other craft guilds of that period.

In the British Museum, there is an old document of about 1390 AD that gives some rules and regulations, or, as they are known among Freemasons, "Charges.' This document is called the *Regius Poem*, and it is admitted to be the oldest genuine record of the Craft of Masonry known.[1] The prominent Masonic researcher Silas H. Shepherd, who was Chairman of the Wisconsin Grand Lodge Committee on Masonic Research between 1916 and 1936, in his book entitled *Landmarks of Freemasonry*, has transcribed the previous Charges as follows:

The Fifteen Articles

1. The Master Mason must be steadfast, trusty and true, and render perfect justice to both his workmen and his employer.

2. The Master Mason shall be punctual in his attendance at the general congregation or assembly.

3. The Master Mason must take no apprentice for less than seven years.

4. The Master Mason must take no apprentices who are bondmen, but only such as are free and well-born.

5. The Master shall not employ a thief, or maimed man for an apprentice, but only those who are physically fit.

6. The Master must not take a craftsman's wages for apprentices' labor.

7. The Master shall not employ an immoral person.

8. The Master must maintain a standard of efficiency by not permitting incompetent workmen to be employed.

9. The Master must not undertake to do work which he cannot complete.

---

1 For the complete original text, see *Constituciones Artis Geometriae Secundum Euclydem*, with introductory remarks by H. J. Whymper, London: Spencer & Co., Great Queen Street, 1889. The modern English translation was made by Roderick H. Baxter, Past Master of Quatuor Coronoti Lodge, No. 2076, under the auspices of the United Grand Lodge of England, and it is reproduced by A. G. Mackey, *Encyclopedia of Freemasonry*, new and revised edition, New York and London: The Masonic History Company, 1914.

10. No Master shall supplant another in the work undertaken.

11. The Master shall not require Masons to work at night except in the pursuit of knowledge.

12. No Mason shall speak evil of his fellows' work.

13. The Master must instruct his apprentices in everything they are capable of learning.

14. The Master shall take no apprentice for whom he has not sufficient labor.

15. The Master is not to make false representation nor compromise any one of his fellows.

The Fifteen Points

1. Those who would be Masons and practise the Masonic Art are required to Love God and His Holy Church, the Master for whom they labor and their brethren, for this is the true spirit of Masonry.

2. The Mason must work diligently in working hours, that he may lawfully refresh himself in the hours of rest.

3. The Mason must keep the secrets of his Master, his Brethren and his Lodge.

4. No Mason shall be false to the craft but maintain all its rules and regulations.

5. The Mason shall not murmur at fair compensation.

6. The Mason shall not turn a working-day into a holiday.

7. The Mason shall restrain his lust.

8. The Mason must be just and true to his brethren in every way.

9. The Mason shall treat his brethren with equity and in the spirit of brotherly love.

10. Contention and strife shall not exist among the brethren.

11. The Mason shall caution his brother kindly about any error into which he may be about to fall.

12. The Mason must maintain every ordinance of the Assembly.

13. The Mason must not steal nor protect one who does.

14. The Mason must be true to the Laws of Masonry and the Laws of his own country.

15. The Mason must submit to the lawful penalty for any offence he may commit.

The aforementioned Charges indicate that Freemasonry was not only a technical activity, but simultaneously it was organized in such a manner that it safeguarded and promoted a specific ethos. Thus, from the outset, Freemasonry has also been a cultural institution. The fact that Freemasonry has a cultural core, which transcends the technical activities of Operative

Masons, allowed and encouraged the survival of Freemasonry as a symbolic system, namely as a cultural phenomenon, after the decay of the guild system. The presiding officer of a Symbolic Lodge is called the Worshipful Master. The term 'worshipful' is derived from the Old English 'worchyppe' or 'worchyp,' and it means 'greatly respected.'

In Scotland, historians have found undeniable evidence of the existence of Lodges of stonemasons (i.e., Operative Masons). Lodges were geographically-defined units controlling the operative trade on the basis of their statute law. In 2008, the Freemasonic researcher Philippa Faulks and the Scottish Freemason Robert L. D. Cooper, curator of the Scottish Masonic Museum and Library, published a book entitled *The Masonic Magician*, in which they argue that the oldest written records of stonemasons' Lodges exist in Scotland and belong to Lodge Aitcheson's Haven commended on January 9, 1599. However, that Lodge ceased to exist in the mid-nineteenth century, and, thus, the oldest records of a Lodge that remain in existence are those of the Lodge of Edinburgh (Mary's Chapel), No. 1; the first entry in the minute book is dated July 31, 1599.[1]

On December 28, 1598 and on December 28, 1599, William Schaw (1550–1602) —who, in 1583, was appointed the King's Master of Works[2] (by King James VI of Scotland) —drew up the documents that today are known as the First and the Second Schaw Statutes, and they include instructions to Scottish stonemasons' Lodges on practical matters concerning Operative Masonry. However, the Schaw Statues also include instructions that have a cultural and particularly moral character; for example: "that they be true to one another, live charitably together as become sworn brethren and companions of Craft"; and: "that they observe and keep all the good ordinances set down before concerning the privileges of their craft as set down by their predecessors of fond memory." In Vitruvius's era, many Scottish noblemen were interested in Hermeticism, and King James VI of Scotland, himself, offered financial support to the Italian alchemist John Damian. Hermetic and Neoplatonic studies, including alchemy, were significantly encouraged and expanded after the wedding of King James's daughter Elizabeth Stuart to Frederick V, Elector Palatine and King of Bohemia, and, gradually, Rosicrucianism prevailed in the Scottish academic life.

---

1 Faulks, Ph., and Cooper, R. L. D., *The Masonic Magician: The Life and Death of Count Cagliostro and His Egyptian Rite*, London: Watkins, 2008, p. 131.
2 On December 21, 1583, King James VI appointed William Schaw principal Master of Works in Scotland for life, with responsibility for all royal castles and palaces. By the terms of his appointment, Schaw, for the rest of his life, was to be: "Great master of work of all and sundry his highness's palaces, building works and repairs, and great overseer, director, and commander of whatsoever policy devised or to be devised for our sovereign lord's behalf and pleasure" (see *Register of the Privy Seal of Scotland, 1581–1584*, Vol. 8, No. 1676, 1982, 276–277).

Furthermore, historians have found undeniable evidence that Scottish operative Lodges began, in the seventeenth century, to admit non-operative members as "Accepted," that is, honorary or gentlemen, Masons, and that, by the early eighteenth century, the Accepted Masons had gained the ascendancy.[1] The Lodges in which the Accepted Masons had gained the ascendancy became symbolic, or 'speculative,' Lodges, while others continued practicing Operative Masonry. The speculative, or symbolic, Scottish Lodges eventually combined to form the Grand Lodge of Scotland in 1736. In addition, historical research has discovered references to the Scottish stonemasons' Lodges having a Mason's Word and secret modes of recognition, thus establishing a system of mutual trust among travelling Operative Masons: through their secret Word and secret modes of recognition, Operative Masons could gain work or sustenance whenever they were visiting the area of another Lodge.[2]

The above historical facts corroborate the hypothesis that there has been a gradual transition from Operative Masonry to Symbolic (or Speculative) Masonry, and, therefore, that modern Freemasonry (Symbolic Masonry) is a direct descendant of the medieval guilds of Operative Masons. This hypothesis has been strongly defended by Harry Carr, a prominent Freemason and historian of Freemasonry.[3] On the other hand, the previous hypothesis has the following weak points: (i) The institutional framework within which and the exact manner in which the operative Masons' Lodges have been transformed into symbolic Lodges are not known exactly. Moreover, especially in England, by the 1600s, the guild system, with the exception of the London Livery Companies, was virtually moribund, but, suddenly, in 1717, four symbolic Lodges decided to create the Grand Lodge of London and Westminster. Thus, in the history of English Freemasonry, there is a 'black-out' period between the decay of the guild system in the early seventeenth century and the creation of the symbolic London Grand Lodge in 1717. (ii) The first symbolic, or speculative, English Freemason is Elias Ashmole (1617–92), a natural scientist and alchemist, who joined a Lodge in Warrington, Cheshire, in 1646. However, the actual records of the Lodge, and, therefore, his initiation into the Craft, are lost, if there ever were such records, and the only relevant information we have is a short entry in his personal diary.

---

1 Hamill, John, *The Craft: History of English Freemasonry*, London: Aquarian Press, 1986.
2 Ibid.
3 In his research paper entitled "600 Years of Craft Ritual" (*Ars Quatuor Coronatorum*, Vol. 81, 1968), Carr wrote: "I do insist, however, that our present-day speculative Freemasonry is directly descended from the operative masonry whose beginnings we can trace back to the earliest record of organization among masons in 1356." Moreover, see Carr, Harry, *The Freemason at Work: The Definitive Guide to Craft*, 7th edition, revised by Frederick Smyth, London: Ian Allen, 2007.

Ashmole mentions the names of the persons who were present during his initiation into the Craft, in 1646. None of those persons was an operative member of the Craft. Thus, Ashmole's diary does not help us to understand the institutional and spiritual framework within which operative members of the Craft co-existed with symbolic (gentlemen) members of the Craft in the same Lodges. Nor does Ashmole's diary explain the nature of the Lodge into which he was initiated. Furthermore, Ashmole does not even clarify his motives for joining Freemasonry.

Therefore, in order to understand the transition from Operative Masonry to Symbolic Masonry, we need to shift our attention from the history of Freemasonic institutions as such to the motives and the historical environment of the originators of those institutions, thus endorsing a so-called "indirect approach," in John Hamill's terminology.[1] In other words, we have to focus our attention and research on the motives of the originators and the leaders of Freemasonic organizations and on the historical framework within which they act. Moreover, in order to understand the historical development of Freemasonry, we need to bear in mind the following facts: (i) the Neoplatonic spirit that prevailed in seventeenth century Western Europe, in the context of which the work of the first century BC Roman architect Marcus Pollio Vitruvius occupied a conspicuous position;[2] (ii) the cultural developments that took place in Western Europe during the Renaissance, whose history is identified with artists, engineers, and inventors such as Filippo Brunelleschi (1377–1446), Donato Donatello (ca. 1386–1466), Sandro Botticelli (1445–1510) και Leonardo Da Vinci (1452–1519), as well as with mystical philosophers and scientists such as Giordano Bruno (1548–1600), Henry C. Agrippa (1486–1535), Jakob Böhme (1575–1624), Robert Boyle (1627–1691), John Dee (1527–1608), Paracelsus (ca. 1494–1541) και Sir Walter Raleigh (ca. 1554–1618); (iii) the Freemasonic and political turmoil of the eighteenth century Europe.

---

1 Hamill, *Craft: A History of English Freemasonry*, chapter 1.
2 Vitruvius is the author of the treatise *De Architectura*, known today as *The Ten Books on Architecture*. In his *De Architectura*, Vitruvius argues that a structure must exhibit the three qualities of *firmitas*, *utilitas*, and *venustas*, that is, it must be solid, useful, and beautiful. By analogy, modern Freemasons maintain that a Symbolic Lodge is founded on the following three symbolic pillars (principles): wisdom, strength, and beauty. The Italian architect Andrea Palladio (1508–80) and the Italian polymath Leonardo da Vinci (1452–1519) were particularly fond of Vitruvius's work, and around 1490 da Vinci drew the "Vitruvian Man," based on the correlations of ideal human proportions with geometry described by Vitruvius in Book III of his treatise *De Architectura*. In particular, according to Vitruvius's *De Architectura* 3, 1:2–3, the length of the outspread arms is equal to the height of a man, from the hairline to the bottom of the chin is one-tenth of the height of a man, and the central point of the human body is the navel, because, "if a man be placed flat on his back, with his hands and feet extended, and a pair of compasses centered at his navel, the fingers and toes of his two hands and feet will touch the circumference of a circle described therefrom."

In the 1650s, Oliver Cromwell—an English Parliamentarian, military leader, and Puritan who was elected Member of Parliament for Huntingdon in 1628 and for Cambridge in the Short (1640) and Long (1640–9) Parliaments—established the most radical dictatorship in Europe.[1] Cromwell was one of the signatories of King Charles I's death warrant in 1649. Cromwell was a fervent Puritan and an advocate of a model of liberal oligarchy. In particular, the civil unrest that was led by Oliver Cromwell in England, in 1643, prevented England from consolidating and developing further a traditional Christian society binding the Monarchy, the Church, the State, the nobles, and the people into one solemn bond. In traditional societies, the source and the foundation of authority is tradition as a system of eternal values, whereas, in liberal oligarchies, the source and the foundation of authority is economic power. Thus, for instance, Antonio Fernandez Carvajal, a Portuguese-Jewish merchant and contractor of Cromwell's Army, together with a group of Amsterdam usurers exploited the civil unrest that was led by Cromwell in 1643 in order to promote their interests in England.[2]

On June 4, 1647, Cornet Joyce, acting on secret orders from Cromwell, seized King Charles I, and, simultaneously, a new radical party sprung up in the English Army styled by themselves "Rationalists," since they argued that they possessed no knowledge or talents, but simply the reason that God had given them to be their guide.[3] In December 1648, those Members of Parliament who wished to continue negotiations with King Charles I were prevented from sitting for parliament by a troop of radical soldiers headed by Colonel Thomas Pride (that episode soon came to be known as Pride's Purge). The remaining body of MPs, known as the Rump, agreed that King Charles I should be tried on a charge of treason. Finally, King Charles I was executed on January 30, 1649. As a member of the Rump Parliament, Cromwell dominated the short-lived Commonwealth of England, but, on April 20, 1653, he dismissed the Rump Parliament by force, setting up a short-lived nominated assembly known as Barebone's Parliament, and, on December 16, 1653, he was invited by his fellow leaders to rule as Lord Protector of England, Wales, Scotland, and Ireland.

---

1 Sharp, David, *Oliver Cromwell*, Oxford: Heinemann, 2003, p. 60.

2 In the 1650s, Carvajal was not only advancing money to Cromwell's camp, but also he was of service to Cromwell in obtaining information as to the Royalists' activities in Holland. One of Carvajal's servants, Somers, alias Butler, and one of Carvajal's relatives, Alonzo di Fonseca Meza, acted as intelligencers for Cromwell in Holland, and they reported about Royalist levies, finances, and spies, as well as about the relations between Charles II and Spain. See also Ramsay, Captain A. H. M., *The Nameless War*, Britons, 1952, Chapter 1.

3 "They, soon, however, acquired the more expressive title of 'Levellers,' as their reason showed them that all distinctions between man and man should be levelled" (Keightley, Thomas, *The History of England*, 2nd edition, London: Longman, 1842, Vol. 2, p. 170).

Not only did Cromwell impose a fierce dictatorial regime on the British Isles, but also he attempted to substitute his Puritan doctrine for the Anglican Church and to control the British intellectual life. Thus, in 1650, Cromwell proclaimed and appointed himself Chancellor of the University of Oxford. However, in 1648, at Oxford, Dr. John Wilkins, who was an Anglican priest, the author of *Mathematical Magic*, a student of alchemy, and the Warden of Wadham College, assembled a group of prominent scientific researchers, such as chemist Robert Boyle, physicist and astronomer Robert Hooke, anatomist William Petty, and young future architect Christopher Wren. Cromwell and his Puritan regime were not sympathetic toward esoteric studies, astronomy, and mathematics. Thus, Wilkin's group became a secret scholarly society known as the "Invisible College."

After Cromwell's death, in 1658, the monarchy was gradually restored. King Charles II, the eldest surviving son of Charles I, ascended to the British throne on May 29, 1660. He was a keen supporter of the new generation of English scientists. In 1659, Christopher Wren was appointed Professor of Astronomy at Gresham College in Bishopsgate, and his rooms became the principal meeting place of the Invisible College. In 1660, several members of the Invisible College, including Wilkins, Wren, Boyle, and Ashmole, participated in the formation of the Royal Society for the advancement of science. In 1662, King Charles II granted a royal charter to the Royal Society.

The eighteenth century was an era of major changes in Freemasonry and of major political changes and revolutions in Europe and America, since, in 1707, following the Treaty of Union that had been agreed on July 22, 1706 by the Kingdom of England and the Kingdom of Scotland, the Scottish Parliament and the English Parliament united to form the Parliament of Great Britain, based in the Palace of Westminster in London, the home of the English Parliament, the American Revolution broke out in 1776, and the French Revolution broke out in 1789.

After the death of Queen Anne of Great Britain, in 1714, King George I of Great Britain (George Louis; German: Georg Ludwig) ascended the British throne as the first monarch of the House of Hanover (a German royal dynasty that has ruled the Duchy of Brunswick-Lüneburg). Even though more than fifty Roman Catholics bore closer blood relationships to Anne, the Act of Settlement, passed by the Parliament of England in 1701, prohibited Roman Catholics from inheriting the British throne, and George was Anne's closest living Protestant relative. However, Jacobites attempted to depose George and replace him with Anne's Roman Catholic half-brother, James Francis Edward Stuart, who was the son of the deposed James II of England and Ireland, but their attempts failed.

In 1685, King Charles II of England, Scotland, and Ireland died without leaving an heir, and, thus, he was succeeded by his brother, who became James II of England and Ireland and James VII of Scotland. Charles II was Anglican. Charles's English parliament enacted the Clarendon Code, which consisted in a series of laws that sought to uphold the establishment of the Church of England against Roman Catholicism and Protestant nonconformists. However, Charles II favored a policy of religious toleration. In 1672, Charles II issued the Royal Declaration of Indulgence, in which he purported to suspend all penal laws against Roman Catholics and other religious dissenters. Additionally, in 1672, he forged an alliance with Roman Catholic France and started the Third Anglo-Dutch War (England's Royal Navy joined France in its attack against the Dutch Republic). Charles's brother, King James II of England and Ireland was Roman Catholic. He was the last Roman Catholic monarch to reign over the Kingdoms of England, Scotland and Ireland, and he was deposed in the Glorious Revolution of 1688.

Throughout the reign of James II, members of Great Britain's Protestant political elite were suspecting him of being pro-French and pro-Roman Catholic and of secretly planning to become an absolute monarch. However, King James II's clash with the English Parliament was due to the following reasons: on the hand, James II was promoting a centralized royal authority over Great Britain, and, simultaneously, he was attempting to establish a regime of religious liberty, which would safeguard the freedoms of English Roman Catholics and Protestant nonconformists (e.g., the Quakers), but, on the other hand, the English Parliament, being concerned about the growth of absolutism that was occurring in other European countries and about the loss of the legal supremacy of the Church of England, saw their opposition to King James II's policy as a way to preserve what they regarded as traditional English liberties.

When James II produced a Roman Catholic heir, namely, James Francis Edward Stuart, Prince of Wales (born on June 10, 1688), the tension between James II and the English Parliament (particularly the Anglican elite) exploded, and leading nobles called on James II's Protestant son-in-law and nephew William of Orange, to land an invasion army from the Netherlands, which he did in the Glorious Revolution of 1688. William of Orange was sovereign Prince of Orange from birth, Stadtholder of Holland, Zeeland, Utrecht, Gelderland, and Overijssel in the Dutch Republic from 1672, and King of England, Ireland, and Scotland from 1689 until his death (1702). In 1677, he married his mother's niece and his first cousin, Mary, the daughter of his maternal uncle King James II of England. On November 5, 1688, William landed at the southern English port of Brixham, and, ultimately, James II was deposed; in particular, James II fled England, and, thus, he was held to have abdicated. In February 1689, William and Mary became co-regents over the Kingdoms of England, Scotland, and Ireland after they were offered the throne by the Convention Parliament irregularly summoned by William after his successful invasion of England. William and Mary reigned together until her death in 1694, after which William ruled as sole monarch. William and Mary left no heir, and they were ultimately succeeded by Mary's younger sister, Anne. In 1689, James II landed in Ireland, and he made a serious attempt to recover his throne from William and Mary. After the defeat of the Jacobite forces by the Williamites at the Battle of the Boyne, in July 1690, James II returned to France, where he lived out the rest of his life as a pretender at a court sponsored by his cousin and ally, King Louis XIV of France. To end the Glorious Revolution, William and Mary signed the English Bill of Rights of 1689, which signaled the end of several centuries of tension and conflict between the crown and the parliament, and it consolidated the institutional supremacy of the Church of England in Great Britain. Moreover, the Bill of Rights inspired English colonists in Massachusetts, New York, and Maryland to revolt against the rule of King James II and his proposed changes in colonial governance.

With regard to William of Orange, it is worth pointing out that, in 2002, the Italian journalist and writer Rita Monaldi and her husband, Francesco Sorti, who is also an Italian journalist, published a book entitled *Imprimatur* based on a number of new historical sources discovered by the authors in the Vatican Archive and the Public Record Office of Rome. In the previous book, Monaldi and Sorti maintain that there was a secret agreement between William of Orange and Pope Innocent XI. In particular, Pope Innocent XI had effectively financed the overthrow of the Roman Catholic King James II by the Protestant claimant William of Orange in the Glorious Revolution of 1688, because of the following reasons: (i) Pope Innocent XI's family, the Odescalchi (based in Como), were an important banking dynasty that had lent money to William of Orange and sought a financial return;[1] (ii) Pope Innocent XI wanted to prevent Great Britain and France from establishing an alliance that could change the European system of balance of power and adversely affect the influence of the Papacy in European affairs; (iii) James II was Roman Catholic in a broad traditionalist metaphysical sense, and, thus, he was an advocate of religious toleration and freedom, which contradicted

---

1 In the ledgers of Carlo Odescalchi, brother of Pope Innocent XI and administrator of the family's vast patrimony until his death in 1673, Monaldi and Sorti found the testimonies of loans of the Odescalchi to Dutch merchants, members of the Dutch Admiralty, and William of Orange's counsellors. These loans were sent to Amsterdam through a company that was called Cernezzi & Rezzonico, and it was officially run from Venice by two merchants, namely, Pietro Martire Cernezzi and Aurelio Rezzonico, but it was secretly belonging to the Odescalchi.

the Papacy's spiritual despotism. Moreover, the Stuarts were traditionally supporters of the Scottish Hermetic tradition and of alchemy, thus cultivating an esoteric approach to Christianity and a mystical synthesis between religion and science, which clash with the Papacy's rationalism and with the Protestants' literalism, fundamentalism, and moralism.

James II, being primarily supported by the Tories (British conservatives), was a protector of science and of the Royal Society (i.e., the most important academic institution in Great Britain), whereas the Whigs (British liberals), advocating the regimes of William of Orange and of Oliver Cromwell, wanted to manage the masses through Puritanism, lack of philosophical education, and superstition, and to transfer political power from the aristocrats, the scientists, and the philosophers to the bankers and the merchants. In 1701, under the reign of William of Orange, the English Parliament passed the Act of Settlement, according to which anyone who becomes a Roman Catholic, or who marries one, becomes disqualified to inherit the British throne. Additionally, the Act of Settlement placed limits on both the role of foreigners in the British government and the power of the monarch with respect to the Parliament of England. In 1713, the Parliament of Westminster invited George, the Electorate of Hanover, to be crowned King George I of Great Britain and Ireland. Thus, King George I became the first British monarch of the House of Hanover, which succeeded the House of Stuart and the House of Orange.

George I was keen to eliminate every Jacobite element from British Freemasonry. In the context of the previous policy of Masonic 'purity,' the Premier Grand Lodge of Georgian England forbade all religious and political discussions within Masonic Lodges, and it proclaimed that "pure Ancient Masonry" consists only of the three Craft degrees—namely, those of the Entered Apprentice, the Fellow Craft, and the Master Mason—and the Holy Order of the Royal Arch of Jerusalem, being considered as the completion and perfection of the third Craft degree. Under the Hanoverian dynasty, every element that sustained prior (i.e., pre-Hanoverian) forms of Freemasonic activity is declining or is deep down: traditional Christianity, chivalric values, spiritual nobility, mysticism, and the centralized royal authority are declining, and the only way in which Hanoverian Freemasonry ever approaches these issues is the other way around, in the sense that it tries to accommodate minorities, it tries to suggest that majority should be more liberal-minded, thus, indirectly yet significantly cultivating and promoting religious syncretism, the oligarchical mentality of particular groups of the nobility, and bourgeois principles, and it maintains that the keystone of the Freemasonic system is the principle of toleration.

Even though Freemasonry already existed before the eighteenth century, the year 1717 marks the commencement of a new system of Freemasonic organization and government, namely, the 'Grand Lodge' system. In particular, the "Grand Lodge of London and Westminster," known also as the "Premier Grand Lodge of England," was conceived and established on St. John the Baptist's day, June 24, 1717, by the following four Symbolic Lodges:

1. The Goose and Gridiron, St Paul's Churchyard, established 1691,

2. Crown Ale House Lodge, Lincoln's Inn Fields, established 1712,

3. The Apple Tree Tavern, Covent Garden, now known as the Lodge of Fortitude and Old Cumberland No. 12 (under the auspices of the United Grand Lodge of England), and

4. The Rummer and Grapes, Channel Row, Westminster, later known as Horn Lodge.

The first three Grand Masters of the Grand Lodge of London and Westminster were the following: Anthony Sayer, "a Gentleman," who was elected in 1717; George Payne, who was elected in 1718 (he was appointed Secretary to the Tax Office in 1732 and Head Secretary in 1743); and the Rev. Dr. John Theophilus Desaguliers, who was elected in 1719, and who was later three times Deputy Grand Master (he was a French-born British natural philosopher, Protestant clergyman, and engineer who was elected to the Royal Society in 1714 as experimental assistant to Sir Isaac Newton).

Under the leadership of the Rev. Dr. John Theophilus Desaguliers, and, in 1721, when Grand Lodge of London and Westminster secured John Montagu, Second Duke of Montagu, as their first noble Grand Master, the Grand Lodge of London and Westminster acquired new rituals, and it experienced rapid development. The Rev. Dr. John Theophilus Desaguliers was a French-born Huguenot clergyman. When King Louis XIV of France revoked the Edict of Nantes in 1685, John (in French, Jean) Desaguliers and his two-year old son John Theophilus fled France and settled in Hanoverian England. The Edict of Nantes of 1598, which was issued by King Henry IV of France, had granted the Huguenots (i.e., French Protestants, mainly inspired by John Calvin) the right to practice their religion without persecution from the state. However, gradually, the Huguenots started becoming a state within the state by implementing a plan for virtual provincial independence and by pushing France to develop in a bourgeois direction.

In general, Calvinism was directed much more against the centralized authority of the King than against the Papacy. Huguenots, in particular, means confederates, and it is the French translation of the German term *Eidgenossen*, which was an appellation of the Geneva Calvinists, who were in conflict with the Roman Catholic Duke of Savoy. The Huguenots' ideology promoted the empowerment of the French feudal barons, who had been subdued by King Louis XI, but they had been fighting the central monarchy for centuries, and now they had a new ideology to rationalize their struggle for a redistribution of power. Thus, in 1685, by the Edict of Fontainebleau, Louis XIV revoked the Edict of Nantes. As a result of the revocation of the Edict of Nantes, thousands of French Calvinists were driven into exile; among them was the Rev. John Desaguliers, the father of John Theophilus Desaguliers. The Rev. John Desaguliers was ordained as an Anglican by Bishop Henry Compton of London, and, in 1694, with the assistance of his young son, he founded a school in Islington. He died in 1699. After the death of his father, the Rev. Dr. John Theophilus Desaguliers decided to pursue further studies at Christ Church College, Oxford, where he followed the usual classical curriculum, and he graduated with a Bachelor's degree in 1709. Additionally, he attended lectures by the mathematician John Keill in Natural Philosophy. In 1712, he obtained a Master's degree from Hart Hall, the forerunner of Hertford College, Oxford. In 1719, Oxford University awarded him an honorary Doctorate of Civil Law, and his doctorate was incorporated by Cambridge University in 1726. John Theophilus Desaguliers was ordained as a deacon in 1710, at Fulham Palace, and as a priest in 1717, at Ely Palace in London. He became one of the most prominent pedagogues of Hanoverian England.

In the eighteenth century, the Grand Lodge of London and Westminster was formed under the direction of the Rev. Dr. John Theophilus Desaguliers. According to the official history of the Grand Lodge of London and Westminster, the Third Degree of Freemasonry, namely, that of a Master Mason, first appeared in London, about ten years after the formation of the first grand lodge. In particular, the Third Degree was first conferred in 1726, in London, in the Society for Music and Architecture. However, the "Five Points of Fellowship," which constitute a significant element of the Third Degree, first appeared in Scottish Masonic catechisms before 1717. In particular, the Edinburgh Register House Manuscript (1696), the Airlie Manuscript (1705), and the Chetwode Crawley Manuscript (ca. 1710), all include catechisms that give the Five Points of Fellowship. The Five Points of Fellowship are intimately related to the Five Points of Entrance, and the Rev. Dr. George Oliver defined them in his *Landmarks* as follows: "Assisting a brother in his distress, supporting him in his virtuous undertakings, praying for his welfare, keeping inviolate his secrets and vindicating his reputation as well in his absence as in his presence." Additionally, Samuel Cole, who was at one time the Grand Secretary of the Grand Lodge of Maryland, in his book entitled *The Freemason's Library* (originally published in 1817; second edition in 1826), argues that the Five Points were symbolized by hand, foot, knee, breast, and back.

In the 1720s, the Rev. Dr. John Theophilus Desaguliers invented the myth of Hiram Abiff, which soon became the main theme of the Third Degree in the context of the Grand Lodge of London and Westminster. Thus, according to the Grand Lodge of London and Westminster, Hiram Abiff is the major Masonic archetype of the 'Architect.' In 1730, we find the first reference to the Hiramic legend, which is the mythological framework of the Third Degree. The first record we have of the Hiramic legend being introduced in Freemasonry occurs in 1730, when Samuel Prichard published his book entitled *Masonry Dissected*, and he referred to Hiram as Grand Master Hiram. In 1 Kings 7:1-21, in the Old Testament, we can find details about King Solomon's Temple, and, we read the following about Hiram: "King Solomon sent and brought Hiram out of Tyre. He was the son of a widow of the tribe of Naphtali, and his father was a man of Tyre, a worker in bronze; and he was filled with wisdom and understanding and skill, to work all works in bronze. He came to King Solomon, and performed all his work. For he fashioned the two pillars of bronze, eighteen cubits high apiece; and a line of twelve cubits encircled either of them. He made two capitals of molten bronze, to set on the tops of the pillars. The height of the one capital was five cubits, and the height of the other capital was five cubits. There were nets of checker work, and wreaths of chain work, for the capitals which were on the top of the pillars; seven for the one capital, and seven for the other capital. So he made the pillars; and there were two rows around on the one network, to cover the capitals that were on the top of the pillars: and he did so for the other capital. The capitals that were on the top of the pillars in the porch were of lily work, four cubits. There were capitals above also on the two pillars, close by the belly which was beside the network. There were two hundred pomegranates in rows around the other capital. He set up the pillars at the porch of the temple. He set up the right pillar, and called its name Jachin; and he set up the left pillar, and called its name Boaz."

Based on the aforementioned Biblical references, Desaguliers articulated the following didactic myth in order to be taught in the Third Degree ceremony, in the context of which the candidate impersonates Hiram Abiff: Being knowledgeable in architecture and in metallurgy, Hiram Abiff was sent by Hiram King of Tyre, to Solomon King of Israel, to direct the construction of the Temple at Jerusalem, which the Israelites intended to erect to the glory of the Great Architect of the Universe. Hiram Abiff divided his workmen into three groups: Apprentices, Companions, and Masters. To be able to distinguish and recognize each group, he gave it its own set of secrets, precisely, a Word, a Sign, and a Grip. The works drawing to their close, three evil Companions, having been unable to obtain the secrets of a Master, decided to extract the Sign, the Word, and the Grip of a Master from Hiram Abiff by any means. When Hiram Abiff finished his devotions, he moved toward the South entrance of the Temple, where he was opposed by the first evil Companion, who was armed with a heavy Plumb Rule and demanded the secrets of a Master, warning Hiram Abiff that he would die if he refused to comply with those evil and unworthy Masons' request. Hiram Abiff refused to divulge the secrets of a Master Mason without the consent and co-operation of Solomon King of Israel and Hiram King of Tyre, and he added that patience and industry would, in due time, entitle every worthy Mason to a participation of the secrets of a Master Mason. The evil Companion aimed a violent blow at Hiram Abiff, but he only glanced on Hiram Abiff's right temple. When Hiram Abiff recovered from the shock, he moved toward the North entrance of the Temple, where he was opposed by the second evil Companion, who was armed with a Level. After Hiram Abiff gave a similar answer to the second evil Companion, the latter struck him a violent blow on the left temple. Hiram Abiff, faint and bleeding, moved toward the East entrance of the Temple, where he was opposed by the third evil Companion, who was armed with a Maul. After Hiram Abiff gave a similar answer to the third evil Companion, the latter struck him a violent blow on the forehead, which was fatal.

Before the myth of Hiram Abiff, Freemasons were using other archetypes of the 'Architect,' precisely Noah and Bezalel. We can find several information about Noah in the book of Genesis, chapter 6. In Exodus 31:1–5, we read the following about Bezalel's Masonic profile: "Yahweh spoke to Moses, saying, 'Behold, I have called by name Bezalel the son of Uri, the son of Hur, of the tribe of Judah. I have filled him with the Spirit of God, in wisdom, and in understanding, and in knowledge, and in all kinds of workmanship, to devise skillful works, to work in gold, and in silver, and in bronze, and in cutting of stones for setting, and in carving of wood, to work in all kinds of workmanship.'" Moreover, according to Exodus 37:1–9, Bezalel was in charge of constructing the Ark of the Covenant.

The myth of Hiram Abiff constitutes an attempt by the Rev. Dr. John Theophilus Desaguliers and by the Rev. James Anderson, another prominent Freemason and Protestant clergyman, to merge the Biblical narratives about Hiram Abiff and the stories of old Masonic manuscripts referring to Noah and Bezalel, seeking thus to endow the Grand Lodge of London and Westminster with a distinctive Masonic identity, especially because, in those years, the Grand Lodge of London and Westminster was competing intensely with the Jacobites' Freemasonic forces. In February 1723, with the help of the Rev. Dr. John Theophilus Desaguliers, the Rev. James Anderson, a Scottish Presbyterian clergyman, compiled the *Book of Constitutions of the Free-Masons* (known also among Freemasons as Anderson's *Constitutions*), reflecting the ethos and the Masonic strategy of such prominent players in the politics of the Grand Lodge of London and Westminster as the two noble Grand Masters, the Duke of Montagu (1721) and the Duke of Wharton (1723), and the scientist and Deputy Grand Master at the time of the publication of the *Constitutions*, the Rev. Dr. John Theophilus Desaguliers.

The eighteenth century is a period of political and religious ferment in England, and, therefore, the Grand Lodge of London and Westminster cannot develop peacefully. In the years around 1740, there was a large number of Irish Freemasons in London, many of whom had been initiated into the Craft in Ireland. Many of those Irish Freemasons encountered difficulties in gaining entrance into London Lodges operating under the auspices of the Grand Lodge of London and Westminster. Therefore, in 1751, a group of those Irish Freemasons together with other Jacobite Freemasons founded a new Grand Lodge in London. According to their arguments, the Premier Grand Lodge had made innovations and had departed from "the landmarks," whereas they were practicing Freemasonry "according to the old institutions granted by Prince Edwin at York in AD 926." For this reason, they became known as the Ancients' Grand Lodge, and they were referring to their older rival, namely, the Grand Lodge of 1717, as "Moderns." In their Masonic certificates, issued to new members, the Ancients called themselves the "Grand Lodge of Free and Accepted Masons of England according to the Old Constitutions."[1]

As it has been pointedly observed by the historian Frank E. Halliday, "up to 1750, the century is that of [Alexander] Pope, [Jonathan] Swift, [Daniel] Defoe, and [Henry] Fielding, . . . in politics of [Robert] Walpole and the Whigs, who placed and kept the Hanoverians on the throne. It was the period of rationalism and materialism, when any form of 'enthusiasm' was suspect."[2] Desaguliers's and Anderson's Grand Lodge, that is, the Moderns' Grand Lodge—whose practice of Freemasonry consisted mainly in a system of simple moral, rational, and practical lessons combined with basic epistemological values—was outwardly part of the ethos of those early eighteenth century British rationalist scholars and Whig politicians. On the other hand, the Ancients' Grand Lodge was oriented toward a more esoteric approach to Freemasonry, and it was associated with the Jacobites' secret attempts to restore King James VII (of Scotland) and II (of England) and his heirs to the British throne. Although the Jacobite Rising of 1715 ended in defeat, many Freemasons continued to support the Stuart dynasty. The Hanoverian King George I and, generally, the supporters of the Hanoverian dynasty were concerned about the Jacobites' influence on London Freemasonry, which was a secret organization meeting in small

1 Riley, J. R., "Masonic Certificates," *Quatuor Coronati Antigrapha*, Vol. VIII, 1891.
2 Halliday, Frank E., *An Illustrated Cultural History of England*, London: Thames & Hudson, 1967, p. 193.

cabals, called Lodges, in the upper floors over inns, pubs, and coffee-houses around London. Thus, the supporters of the Hanoverian dynasty and the Whigs decided to reorganize, reform, and control Freemasonry. For this reason, the Grand Lodge of London and Westminster, which was founded in 1717, forbade all political and religious discussions within its Lodges, and it supported the House of Hanover. In addition, in its formative years, the Grand Lodge of London and Westminster, that is, the Moderns' Grand Lodge, methodically cultivated and promoted the opinion that the Craft's history officially began in 1717, and it suppressed information pertaining to the history and the ethos of other Freemasonic entities. The dominance of King George I and of the Whigs in the Grand Lodge of London and Westminster trapped Freemasonry in the conflict between the Vatican and Protestantism, and it played an important role in the Vatican's decision to launch a propaganda campaign against Freemasonry. In 1738, Pope Clement XII issued the first Papal prohibition on Freemasonry.

At the philosophical and cultural level, the Ancients' Grand Lodge of England is oriented toward the principles of traditionalism, Rosicrucianism, and, generally, mysticism (without, of course, negating the significance of natural sciences), whereas the Moderns' Grand Lodge of England is oriented toward the European Enlightenment and, generally, rationalism.[1] At the sociological level, the Ancients' Grand Lodge of England is closer to the conservatives (Tories) and the House of Stuart, whereas the Moderns' Grand Lodge of England is closer to the liberals (Whigs) and the House of Hanover. The social forces that are associated with the Ancients' Grand Lodge emphasize traditional values and the spiritual unity of society; hence, the traditional Tories' emphasis on the monarch, the traditional Church, and an organic view of society. On the other hand, the social forces that are associated with the Moderns' Grand Lodge endorse a pluralist view of society, and they emphasize rational speculation and debate as well as individualism; hence, the Whigs' emphasis on constitutionalism, toleration for nonconformist Protestants (e.g., the Presbyterians), and support for the great aristocratic families and the Protestant Hanoverian succession. Under the Hanoverian dynasty, the wealthy Whigs built their palaces and neoclassical mansions from monastic and other medieval ruins, and they established a social system that cannot really be determined as anything other than a liberal oligarchy, where the economic power oligopolies, or the 'oligarchs,' control the essence of the political process and yield only its formal trappings to the people's representatives.

---

1 For a thorough philosophical study of 'ratio,' see: Laos, Nicolas, *Methexiology: Philosophical Theology and Theological Philosophy for the Deification of Humanity*, Eugene, Oregon: Wipf and Stock Publishers, 2016.

In 1809, the Moderns' Grand Lodge instituted a "Lodge of Promulgation" to return their own ritual to regularity with Scotland, Ireland, and especially the Ancients' Grand Lodge. In 1811, both the Moderns and the Ancients appointed Commissioners, and, over the next two years, articles of Union were negotiated and agreed. In January 1813, the Duke of Sussex became Grand Master of the Moderns' Grand Lodge on the resignation of his brother, the Prince Regent, and, in December of that year, another brother, the Duke of Kent became Grand Master of the Ancients' Grand Lodge. On December 27, 1813 (day of St. John the Evangelist), the Moderns' Grand Lodge of England and the Ancients' Grand Lodge of England were amalgamated into the United Grand Lodge of England (UGLE), with the Duke of Sussex (who was the younger son of King George III) as Grand Master. Following the union in 1813, a "Lodge of Reconciliation" (1813–6) was formed to reconcile the rituals worked under the two former Grand Lodges. In 1823, an "Emulation Lodge of Improvement" was established (under the sanction of the Lodge of Hope No. 7), teaching the ritual settled by the Lodge of Reconciliation, known as the Emulation Ritual.

The Preliminary Declaration to the *Book of Constitutions* of the United Grand Lodge of England (UGLE) states the following: "By the solemn Act of Union between the two Grand Lodges of Freemasons of England in December 1813, it was 'declared and pronounced that pure Antient [*sic*] Masonry consists of three degrees and no more, viz., those of the Entered Apprentice, the Fellow Craft, and the Master Mason, including the Supreme Order of the Holy Royal Arch.'" According to the Emulation Ritual, Desaguliers's Hiramic legend is the main theme of the Third Degree, and, because of the untimely death of Hiram Abiff, the genuine secrets of a Master Mason are lost and cannot be communicated to any Freemason, since, "without the consent and co-operation" of the three Grand Masters (Solomon King of Israel, Hiram King of Tyre, and Hiram Abiff), they could never be divulged. However, according to the United Grand Lodge of England (UGLE), the genuine secrets of a Master Mason are restored in the Holy Order of the Royal Arch of Jerusalem, which is regarded by the UGLE as the completion and perfection of the Third Degree.

The Royal Arch Degree originally appeared in 1743, precisely, in *Faulkner's Dublin Journal*, dated January, 10–14, 1743, where an article reported that Youghall Lodge No. 21 celebrated St. John's Day with a parade in which there was "the Royal Arch carried by two excellent Masons." In 1744, in Dublin, Ireland, Fifield D'Assigny published a book entitled *A Serious and Impartial Enquiry into the Cause of the Present Decay of Freemasonry in the Kingdom of Ireland*, in which he argued that the Royal Arch Degree was conferred in Dublin "some few years ago," and that it had been brought there from the city of York. In

1746, the Irish-born Freemason Laurence Dermott, who would later become Grand Secretary (1752–71) of the Ancients' Grand Lodge of England, was exalted to the Degree of the Royal Arch in Dublin. According to Dermott, the Royal Arch was the fourth degree of Craft Masonry. Under Dermott's influence, the Ancients' Grand Lodge of England championed the Royal Arch Degree in England, while it was met with hostility in the Moderns' Grand Lodge of England. The earliest Masonic records referring to the Royal Arch Degree are to be found in the minutes of March 4, 1752 of the Grand Committee for the organization of the Ancients' Grand Lodge of England, and in the minutes of December 22, 1753 of the Fredericksburg Lodge in Virginia, U.S.A.

At this point, it is important to mention that Laurence Dermott wrote in the Ancients' book of constitution, entitled *Ahiman Rezon*,[1] that he believed the Royal Arch to be "the Root, Heart, and Marrow of Free-Masonry." The Moderns' Grand Lodge, which had never officially recognized or given sanction to the Royal Arch, responded to the popularity of the Royal Arch by simply tolerating those of its members who were enthusiastic about the Royal Arch. The Royal Arch is organized in a similar way as the Craft; each unit is called a Chapter instead of a Lodge, the ruling body of the Royal Arch is known as the Supreme Grand Chapter. An indication of the unofficial embrace of the Royal Arch on the part of officials of the Moderns' Grand Lodge is the fact that the Moderns' Grand Master Lord Blayney was exalted in the Royal Arch, and he became the Grand Master of the first Grand Chapter of the Royal Arch in the world; this was the body created when such distinguished officials of the Moderns' Grand Lodge as Lord Blayney, James Heseltine, and Thomas Dunckerley, as well as other members of an independent (that is, unrecognized by the Moderns' Grand Lodge) Royal Arch Chapter met at the Turk's Head tavern in Gerrard Street, Soho, on July 22, 1767, and, during that meeting, they drew up and signed what is now known as the Charter of Compact, converting their own independent Royal Arch Chapter into the Excellent Grand and Royal Arch Chapter, with Lord Blayney at its head.

The Third Degree of Symbolic Masonry is focused on the notions of 'death' and 'loss'; but that which was 'lost' in the Third Degree is 'found' in the Royal Arch. Harry Mendoza, Past Grand Officer of the Grand Chapter of the UGLE and Past Master of the Quatuor Coronati Lodge, No. 2076

---

1 The book of constitution of the Ancients' Grand Lodge of England was written by Laurence Dermott, and its title was *Ahiman Rezon*. The first edition of the *Ahiman Rezon* was published in 1756; a second one was published in 1764. It has often been said that the title *Ahiman Rezon* is derived from the Hebrew language and variously means 'to help a brother,' 'will of selected brethren,' 'the secrets of prepared brethren,' 'royal builders,' and 'Brother Secretary'; the reason why Laurence Dermott used it and its meaning to him remain unclear.

(UGLE), has argued that, when Symbolic Masonry refers to the Lost Word (i.e., the loss of the genuine secrets of a Master Mason), the term 'loss' does not mean that something was misplaced, but it should be interpreted as a failure "to keep something in mind," and, similarly, the term 'found' (i.e., the restoration of the genuine secrets of a Master Mason) should be interpreted as a discovery of "something for the first time," that is as a new awareness.[1]

The ceremony of the Royal Arch is based on the legend of the rebuilding of King Solomon's Temple after the Babylonian Captivity (sixth century BC). In fact, the main body of the Royal Arch Ceremony is based on the following two separate stories: (i) The true Biblical story describing the return from Babylon and the building of the Temple of Jerusalem (thus, the emblem of Royal Arch Masonry is the letter T, standing for the Latin word Templum, over the letter H, standing for the Latin word Hierosolymae, as shown in Figure 3).[2] (ii) The ancient Royal Arch legend describing the discovery of the Vault, the Altar, and the Sacred Word. According to the English Royal Arch's allegorical narrative, Jewish captives returning to Jerusalem, after the Babylonian Captivity, participate in the reconstruction of the Jerusalem Temple, and, while constructing the Second Temple of Jerusalem, they discover a large underground vault consisting of nine arches. Within this vault, they discover the true name of God, namely, YEHOVAH, engraved on the keystone of the ninth arch. The symbolic meaning of this discovery has been explained by Harry Mendoza as follows: what was lost by King Solomon and most of his successors for the next four centuries was the genuine metaphysical secrets of Judaism and, more particularly, the belief that Yehovah was the one and only true God of Israel. What was found by the time the captives returned to Jerusalem was an even broader awareness than the one which was lost: the exiles re-discovered the truth that Yehovah was the one and only true God of Israel, and that Yehovah was not merely the God of a specific nation, that is, Yehovah was not only the God of Israel among different 'national' deities, but He was the one and only universal

---

1 Mendoza, Harry, *Fifty Royal Arch Questions Answered*, England, private publication, 1994, p. 12. Harry Mendoza is a Past Master of the Quatuor Coronati Lodge No. 2076 of the United Grand Lodge of England and a Past Assistant Grand Sojourner of the Supreme Grand Chapter of Royal Arch Masons of England.

2 Babylonian Exile, also called Babylonian Captivity, is the forced detention of Jews in Babylon, following the destruction of Jerusalem by Nebuchadnezzar in 586 BC. The exile formally ended in 538 BC, when the Persian conqueror of Babylon, Cyrus the Great, gave the Jews permission to return to Palestine. The Biblical book of Ezra narrates the history of the Jewish exiles' return to Jerusalem and of the construction of the second Jerusalem Temple. In 536 BC, Zerubbabel, who was the grandson of Jechonias, penultimate king of Judah, led the people in rebuilding the altar and laying the second Jerusalem Temple's foundation. See also Pritchard, James B., *Archaeology of the Old Testament*, edited by K. C. Hanson, Eugene, Oregon: Wipf and Stock, 2008.

God. Thus, after the Babylonian exile, the Israelites developed a new, much deeper and more universal, awareness of monotheism.[1]

In the fifth century AD, Philostorgius, in his *Church History*, writing of the rebuilding of the Jerusalem Temple, refers to the discovery of the Vault, and this is the earliest framework of the Royal Arch legend. Additionally, in the fourteenth century, Nikephoros Kallistos Xanthopoulos (Latinized as Nicephorus Callistus Xanthopulus), in his *Ecclesiastica Historia*, refers to a similar legend. Moreover, there is Biblical evidence for the Holy royal Arch legend's reference to finding "part of the long-lost Sacred Law." In particular, in 2 Kings, chapter 22, and in 2 Chronicles, chapter 34, we find references to the priest Hilkiah discovering a law-book during the execution of repair work in the temple of Jerusalem. Biblical commentators commonly identify the previous book that was found by Hilkiah with the kernel of the Deuteronomy, and, in fact, this is the source of the Irish Royal Arch legend.

Figure 3: The characteristic symbol of the Royal Arch

Even though, in 1813, the United Grand Lodge of England proclaimed that the spiritually deep Holy Order of the Royal Arch of Jerusalem is an integral part of "pure Antient Masonry," in accordance with the Ancients' principles and ceremonies, the first Grand Master of the United Grand Lodge of England, namely, the Duke of Sussex, was an advocate of empirical positivism, in contradistinction to the Ancients' mystical perception of Freemasonry, an advocate of deism, in contradistinction to the traditional Biblical character of Freemasonry, and a devoted Whig, opposing the Stuarts' Freemasonic and, generally, cultural legacy and promoting a liberal bourgeois cultural and political monologue. Thus, the Duke of Sussex, Grand Master of the UGLE from 1813 until 1843, allowed and encouraged the initiation of non-Christians into Freemasonry, he discarded the traditional Christian color of Freemasonry, and he was negatively disposed toward the development of Freemasonic degrees and orders beyond the three Craft degrees (i.e., those of the Entered Apprentice, the Fellow Craft, and the Master Mason) and the Order of the Holy Royal Arch of Jerusalem.

---

1 Mendoza, *Fifty Royal Arch Questions Answered*, pp. 12–13.

C. The spread of Freemasonry

In France, Freemasonry developed mainly during the second decade of the eighteenth century, having come primarily from England. Moreover, exiled Scottish Freemasons, who had settled in France after the Jacobites' failure to restore James II Stuart to the British throne, exerted significant influence on the formation and organization of French Freemasonry. The first French Lodge whose existence is historically certain was founded by some Englishmen in Paris "around the year 1725," and it met at the house of the traiteur Huré on rue des Boucheries, "in the manner of English societies," mainly bringing together Irishmen and Jacobite exiles.[1]

In 1728, the French Freemasons proclaimed the Duke of Wharton (Philip Wharton, First Duke of Wharton) "Grand Master of the Freemasons in France." Wharton was a powerful Jacobite politician in England, even though his father, Thomas Wharton, First Marquess of Wharton, was a Whig partisan. In fact, Philip Wharton did not get control of his father's extensive estate, because it was put in the care of his parents' Whig party friends. In 1716, James Francis Edward Stuart, "The Old Pretender" and son of James II, created Philip Wharton Jacobite Duke of Northumberland. In 1718, King George I created Philip Wharton Duke of Wharton in order acquire his political support and appease the Jacobites. Moreover, in 1723, the Duke of Wharton became Grand Master of the Grand Lodge of London and Westminster (i.e., the Moderns' Grand Lodge). He was succeeded as Grand Master of the French Freemasons by two prominent Jacobite noblemen: first, by Sir James Hector MacLean, Fifth Baronet of Morvern, and then by Charles Radclyffe, Fifth Earl of Derwentwater.

On June 24, 1738, an assembly of representatives from all the "English" and the "Scottish" Lodges operating in France formed the first French Grand Lodge, called Grande Loge de France, and they proclaimed the Duke of Antin (Louis de Pardaillan de Gondrin, Second Duke of Antin) "general and perpetual Grand Master in the Kingdom of France."

In the 1740s, an original and mixed-sex form of Freemasonry, known as "Masonry of Adoption," arose among the French nobility, and the Duchess of Bourbon-Condé, sister of the Duke of Chartres, became the first Grand Mistress of Mixed Freemasonry. In 1743, after the death of the Duke of Antin, Louis de Bourbon-Condé, Count of Clermont, prince of the blood and future member of the Académie Française, succeeded him as "Grand Master of all regular Lodges in France." In 1771, Louis Philippe d'Orléans succeeded the Comte de Clermont as Grand Master, and, with the support of provincial Lodges, which were dissatisfied with the hegemonic attitude of Paris

---

1 *Mémoire historique sur la maçonnerie*, supplément de l'*Encyclopédie*, 1773.

Lodges, he reorganized French Freemasonry, and he changed the name of the Grand Lodge of France to the Grand Orient of France (in French, Grand Orient de France). However, some "Vénérables" (i.e., Presidents) of mainly Paris Lodges refused to comply with this reform, and, thus, they created a "Grand Lodge of Clermont," which lasted until May 1799, whereas the Grand Orient of France became the dominant force in French Freemasonry. The Grand Orient of France expressed a new Masonic current according to which new, higher Masonic degrees, primarily formed by Frenchmen and Scottish Jacobites, control the three degrees of the Craft. The earliest surviving record of a degree beyond the Craft, that is, beyond the Master Mason Degree, appears in the year 1733, when the term "Scots Master" was used in connection with regular meetings of Lodge No. 115 at the Devil's Tavern at London's Temple Bar (it is included in Rawlinson's List of Lodges). Moreover, on October 28, 1735, the Lodge at the Bear Inn in Bath records an "extraordinary" meeting of Lodge of Masters at which the Master, both Wardens, and nine brethren were made "Scots Master Masons."

After the French Revolution, the notorious Jesuit propagandist Augustin Barruel wrote that Freemasons had actively prepared the 1789 revolution, but the truth is that there were Freemasons in both the Republican and monarchical camps. In 1789, the Grand Orient of France proclaimed its attachment to the democratic political regime, but, due to the Reign of Terror, it was forced to cease its activities between 1793 and 1796, and, of the nearly one thousand Lodges active on the eve of the French Revolution, only seventy-five managed to resume their activities in 1800. The plebiscite of November 6, 1804 legitimized the First French Empire of Napoleon I, and, very soon thereafter, the French Masons learned that his brother, namely, Joseph Bonaparte, had been named Grand Master of the Grand Orient of France, with its administration effectively assigned to Jean-Jacques-Régis de Cambacérès, First Duke of Parma, lawyer, and author of the Napoleonic Code. During the First Empire, the Grand Lodge of France was placed under the direct control of the French political establishment, and, gradually, it put all French Freemasonry under its authority.

In 1804, Count Alexandre de Grasse-Tilly came to France from his birthplace in the Antilles, having been authorized by the "Supreme Council of Sovereign Grand Inspector General of the 33rd and Last Degree of the Ancient and Accepted Scottish Rite for the United States of America" to disseminate this new Masonic Rite in France and establish the Supreme Council of the Ancient and Accepted Scottish Rite (AASR) for France (for further details, see chapter 7). Indeed, Count Alexandre de Grasse-Tilly established a Supreme Council of France and contributed to the creation of a "General Scottish Grand Lodge of France," under the protection of

François Christophe Kellermann, who, under Napoleon Bonaparte, was named successively Senator (1800), President of the Senate (1801), Marshal of France (1804), and Duke of Valmy. However, due to Napoleon's policy of state centralism, the Supreme Council of the AASR for France and the General Scottish Grand Lodge of France were merged into one Masonic institution within few years after their formation.

In 1814, at the start of the Bourbon Restoration, Count Alexandre de Grasse-Tilly reignited the conflict between the Grand Orient of France, which wanted to be the central authority of all French Freemasonry, and the Supreme Council of the AASR for France, which pursued the independence of the AASR. In 1870, the Grand Orient of France numbered around 18,000 Freemasons, and the Supreme Council of the AASR for France around 6,000.[1]

In the nineteenth century, radical trends expanded throughout French Freemasonry, a large portion of which endorsed anticlerical attitudes, thus setting the stage for the outbreak of a cultural clash between the Grand Orient of France and the Vatican. Additionally, in the nineteenth century, many French Freemasons endorsed radical political beliefs. Several French Freemasons participated in the July Revolution (1830), and, with the exceptions of Lamartine and Ledru-Rollin, all the members of the provisional government of 1848 were Freemasons.[2] Moreover, in 1871, many Parisian Freemasons were involved in the Paris Commune. During the Paris Commune, Professor Eugène Thirifocq, a militant socialist and member of the "Le Libre Examen" Lodge of the Supreme Council of the AASR for France, argued that Masonic banners should be set up on Paris's ramparts, and that they should be "avenged" in case they were torn by the bullets of the anti-Commune forces. However, unlike the Parisian Lodges, the provincial ones did not support the Commune, and, ultimately, the Grand Orient of France officially disavowed the action of the Parisian Lodges, and it rallied to Adolphe Thiers (who attempted to win monarchists over to his vision of a conservative, bourgeois republic) and the French Third Republic, in which the Grand Orient of France played a leading role.

In 1875, Jules Ferry (a promoter of laicism and colonial expansion, who became minister of public education of the Third Republic between 1880 and 1881 as well as between 1883 and 1885) and Émile Littré (a prominent lexicographer best known for his *Dictionnaire de la langue Française*) were initiated into Freemasonry in the "La Clémente Amitié" Lodge. In 1877, in the context of and in accordance with the Third Republic's policy of "laïcité" and bourgeois political economy, the Grand Orient of France decided to abolish its requirement that its members believe in the existence of God and the

---

1 Ligou, Daniel, *Histoire des francs-maçons en France*, France, private publisher, 2000, Tome 1, p. 76.
2 Ibid., p. 41.

immortality of the soul and for its Lodges to work "for the Glory of the Great Architect of the Universe." In 1894, the Grand Orient of France's decision to admit atheists triggered a Masonic schism, since a group of French Lodges wishing to require a belief in the Great Architect of the Universe and the immortality of the soul broke off from the Grand Orient of France, and they formed the Grand Lodge of France (in French, Grande Loge de France; the second organization of that name).

In 1876, acting in line with the ethos of the Third Republic, the Grand Orient of France, and the French-Jewish national liberal lobby, Crémieux, the then Grand Commander of the Supreme Council of the AASR for France, who was also the founder of a Zionist organization called "Alliance Israélite Universelle," decreed that his jurisdiction should not impose any doctrine with regard to the Great Architect of the Universe, thus promoting a secular and agnostic attitude. In reaction to the French Supreme Council's previous policy, a group of its high-degree Lodges decided to secede from its jurisdiction, and, ultimately, the French Supreme Council granted them their independence, merging them into the more traditional Grand Lodge of France.

In 1913, two lodges ("Le Centre des Amis" and the "Loge Anglaise") seceded from the Grand Orient of France, and they founded the "National Independent and Regular Grand Lodge," which fully endorsed and complied with the policy and the rules of the United Grand Lodge of England, which, in turn, immediately recognized it. In 1948, it changed its name to the National Grand Lodge of France (in French, Grande Loge Nationale Française).

In Germany, Freemasonry arrived in the first half of the eighteenth century, coming primarily from England and France. The first German Royal Prince who was initiated into Freemasonry was Francis Stephen, Duke of Lorraine, afterwards the husband of Maria Theresa (1736), co-ruler of Austria, (1740), and eventually Emperor of Germany (1745). In particular, he was initiated by the Rev. Dr. John Theophilus Desaguliers, the well-known leading Freemason of the Grand Lodge of London and Westminster, in a Special Lodge held at the Hague in 1731. According to William Preston's *Illustrations of Masonry* (originally published in 1772), in 1733, the Earl of Strathmore, Grand Master of the Grand Lodge of London and Westminster, granted to eleven German Masons a deputation to found a Lodge at Hamburg. This is usually supposed to have developed into Lodge Absalom, but the two numbers are distinct on the engraved lists, since the Warrant of the latter was dated October 23, 1740. In general, the first German Lodges were founded by German Freemasons mostly initiated in England and acting on the basis of Warrants issued by the Grand Master of the Grand Lodge of London and Westminster. Moreover, during the formative years of German

Freemasonry, the Grand Lodge of London and Westminster used to organize most of the German Masonic Lodges into districts and provinces, yet some of the German Masonic Lodges, especially those in major German cities, declared themselves as Mother and Grand Lodges for their own jurisdiction. On August 14, 1738, the Crown Prince of Prussia— afterwards Frederick the Great—was initiated into Freemasonry at Brunswick by a deputation from the Lodge at Hamburg. When he succeeded to the throne, Frederick the Great founded a Lodge in Berlin; that Lodge was called "Three Globes," and its first meeting was held on September 13, 1740. During the next ensuing years, the "Three Globes" Lodge granted several warrants of Constitution to subordinate Lodges, and, on June 24, 1744, it assumed the title of the "Grand Mother Lodge of the Three Globes."

By the 1930s, the following eleven Grand Lodges had been operating in Germany:

1. Grand Mother Lodge of the Three Globes at Berlin, originally founded in 1740,

2. Grand Lodge of Prussia (called the Royal York of Friendship), founded in 1760,

3. National Grand Lodge of German Freemasons at Berlin, founded in 1770,

4. Grand Lodge of Hamburg, founded in 1743,

5. Grand Lodge of the Sun in Bayreuth, founded in 1741,

6. Mother Grand Lodge of Eclectic Union at Frankfurt, founded in 1742,

7. National Grand Lodge of Saxony at Dresden, founded in 1811,

8. Grand Lodge "Concord" at Darmstadt, founded in 1846,

9. Grand Lodge "Chain of German Brotherhood" at Leipzig, founded in 1924,

10. Grand Lodge "Freimaurerbund" at Nuremberg, later at Hamburg, founded in 1907,

11. Symbolic Grand Lodge at Hamburg, later at Berlin, founded in 1930.

The first three of the aforementioned eleven Grand Lodges, all based at Berlin, have been known as the "Old Prussian Lodges," they generally enjoyed the protection of the Prussian Kings, and they only admitted men professing the Christian Faith. The Grand Lodges number 4–9 in the aforementioned list, admitted men of any monotheistic faith, and they have been known as the "Humanitarian Lodges." The last two Grand Lodges (numbers 10 and 11) in the aforementioned list were not recognized by the other nine, because they did not conform to several of the traditional landmarks of mainstream German Freemasonry.

In the middle of the eighteenth century, the Rite of Strict Observance arose in Germany, cultivating the concept of higher degrees in German Freemasonry. The founder of the Rite of Strict Observance was Karl Gotthelf, Baron von Hund und Altengrotkau, who claimed to have been initiated into the higher degrees of freemasonry by Scottish Jacobites who guarded the secret knowledge of the Knights Templar. Under the leadership of Baron von Hund, the Rite of Strict Observance, which is strongly Templar in tone and cultivates principles of esoteric Christianity and benevolence, became the predominant form of Freemasonry in Germany. According to the authoritative Masonic historian Robert Freke Gould, the whole system of the Rite of Strict Observance was based on a fictional narrative according to which, at the time of the destruction of the Templar Order, a certain number of Knights Templar took refuge in Scotland, and there preserved the existence of the Order.[1]

On August 24, 1764, Johann W. von Zinzendorf, one of the most prominent German Freemasons, signed the Act of Strict Observance at Halle, and he was made a Strict Observance Knight Templar by Baron von Hund, the head of the Order of Strict Observance, on October 3, 1764. In June 1765, Zinzendorf was elected Grand Master of the Grand Mother Lodge of the Three Globes, which, in 1766, was constituted a Scottish Lodge authorized to warrant Strict Observance Lodges. The subordinate Lodges under the Grand Mother Lodge of the Three Globes adopted the new system, with the exception of the Royal York Lodge, which temporarily placed itself under the protection of the Grand Lodge of London and Westminster, but afterwards it reasserted its independence.

In 1766, Zinzendorf renounced the Rite of Strict Observance, and, in the same year, he resigned the office of the Grand Master of the Grand Mother Lodge of the Three Globes. In 1767, he retired altogether from the Grand Mother Lodge of the Three Globes, and, in 1768, by virtue of his inherent authority as a "Scottish Master," and having previously procured the Swedish Rite, he founded his first Lodge on the Swedish Rite at Potsdam; a second was formed at Berlin in 1769, and, by 1770, at least twelve had been operating in Germany. In 1770, the previous Swedish Rite Lodges assumed the title of the National Grand Lodge of German Freemasons at Berlin. In 1773, a compact between the National Grand Lodge of German Freemasons and the Grand Lodge of London and Westminster was concluded.

Albert G. Mackey, in his seminal *Encyclopedia of Freemasonry*, aptly describes the Swedish Rite of Freemasonry as a synthesis of the pure Rite of York, the French high degrees, the Templarism of the Rite of Strict Observance, and Rosicrucianism. In Sweden, Freemasonry was developed in

---

1 Gould, Robert F., *The History of Freemasonry*, Vol. V, London: Caxton, 1931.

the first half of the eighteenth century under strong French influences. The chief architect of the Swedish Rite was Carl Friedrich Eckleff, who created a system of nine degrees. However, Duke Karl of Södermanland—the later King Karl XIII of Sweden—who was a keen Freemason, redesigned Eckleff's constitution of the Swedish Rite to contain ten degrees. The Swedish Rite system is grouped into three divisions as follows:

St. John's Degrees:
    I. Apprentice
    II. Fellow Craft
    III. Master Mason

St. Andrew's Degrees
    IV&V. Apprentice and Companion of St. Andrew (a double degree)
    VI. Master of St. Andrew

Chapter degrees:
    VII. Very Illustrious Brother, Knight of the East
    VIII. Most Illustrious Brother, Knight of the West
    IX. Enlightened Brother of St. John's Lodge
    X. Very Enlightened Brother of St. Andrew's Lodge.

On the top of the Swedish Rite system is the XIth Degree, called Most Enlightened Brother, Knight Commander of the Red Cross, and few, carefully selected members of the Swedish Rite attain this degree. The rank of Grand Master is sometimes referred to as the XIIth Degree.

In the 1770s, several controversies emerged among the members of the Rite of Strict Observance, and they were discussed at the different conventions held by the order: at Kohl in 1772, Braunschweig in 1775, Wiesbaden in 1776, Wolfenbüttel in in 1778, and Wilhelmsbad in 1782. Under the influence of French brothers, the Wilhelmsbad convention renounced the claim that the Rite of Strict Observance had a historical link with the medieval Knights Templar. In the late 1780s, the Rite of Strict Observance fell into decay. However, the French brothers of the Rite of Strict Observance had introduced a fundamental change at their Lyon convention in 1778: they transformed the Order of the Strict Observance into a Christian Masonic Order of Chivalry under the names of "Rectified Scottish Rite" (RSR) and "Order of the Knights Beneficent of the Holy City" (KBHC); in French, Chevaliers Bienfaisants de la Cité Sainte. In the nineteenth century, the Rite of Strict Observance had become defunct, but the RSR/KBHC continued to exist in Switzerland, and it was from Geneva that the RSR/KBHC became reestablished in France, the U.S.A., England, Germany, and Belgium in the twentieth century.

The Nazis' rise to power, in 1933, had a devastating impact on German Freemasonry. By 1935, all Lodges in Germany had been dissolved, and their property had been confiscated by the Nazi regime. Thereupon, German Freemasonry remained completely suppressed until 1945.

In 1949, representatives of 151 German Lodges met at Frankfurt and founded the United Grand Lodge of German Freemasons (in St. Paul's Church in Frankfurt). However, complete unity was still not achieved, because former members of the old National Grand Lodge at Berlin stood out, pursuing to protect their traditional Swedish Rite system, and the Swedish Rite Lodges formed the Grand Lodge of the Freemasons' Order (GLFD). In 1958, the former United Grand Lodge of Germany (now the Grand Lodge of Ancient Free and Accepted Masons of Germany) and the Grand Land Lodge of the Freemasons of Germany joined together in a new Masonic institution that was called United Grand Lodges of Germany (the plural form is of particular significance). The basis of the unity was a *Magna Carta of German Freemasons* that transferred sovereignty to the United Grand Lodges of Germany, but it maintained the two forming bodies—namely, the Grand Lodge of Ancient Free and Accepted Masons of Germany and the Grand Lodge of the Freemasons' Order (now the Grand Land Lodge of Freemasons in Germany)—as Provincial (Land) Grand Lodges. Additionally, a Senate was formed for the United Grand Lodges of Germany, with each party having five Senate members. In 1970, the Grand National Mother Lodge "The Three Globes," the German District Grand Lodge of the United Grand Lodge of England (now the Grand Lodge of British Freemasons in Germany), and the American-Canadian Provincial Grand Lodge (now the American-Canadian Grand Lodge of Ancient Free and Accepted Masons) also joined the United Grand Lodges of Germany on the basis of the previous *Magna Carta of German Freemasons*. Thus, the status of the three latterly joining Grand Lodges was raised under an amended *Magna Carta of German Freemasons*, according to which Grand Lodge of Ancient Free and Accepted Masons of Germany has five Senate members, the Grand Land Lodge of Freemasons in Germany has three Senate members, the Grand National Mother Lodge "The Three Globes" has one Senate member, the Grand Lodge of British Freemasons in Germany has one Senate member, and the American-Canadian Grand Lodge of Ancient Free and Accepted Masons has one Senate member.

In Italy, Freemasonry arrived in the first half of the eighteenth century, coming primarily from England and France. The first Lodge in Italy was set up in Florence, sometime before August 1732, by the British nobleman, politician, opera impresario, and cricketer Lord Charles Sackville, then Earl of Middlesex, later the second Duke of Dorset. The previous Lodge attracted Italian noblemen and intellectuals, but it also attracted the interest of the Papal Inquisition, and its Secretary, Tommaso Baldasarre Crudeli (1702–1745), a Florentine poet, lawyer, and champion of free thought, was imprisoned and tortured, later dying as a result. Moreover, two Lodges were formed in Livorno in 1763 and 1765 under auspices of the Ancients' Grand Lodge of England, and the Moderns' Grand Lodge of England warranted two more Lodges in the same city in 1771.

In 1733, an English-speaking Jacobite Lodge was formed in Rome, and it admitted the exiled Scottish nobleman George Seton, Fifth Earl of Winton, who had taken part in the Jacobite rising of 1715, supporting "The Old Pretender" James Stuart. In 1737, the previous Jacobite Lodge was closed down, and its officers were arrested by the Papal Inquisition. In 1738, the Roman Catholic Church published *In Eminenti*, the first papal bull against Freemasonry. However, foreign Masons continued to meet in secret, and a permanent Lodge was founded in Rome in 1787, but it was closed down by the Papal Inquisition in 1789, the same day that Count Alessandro di Cagliostro (pseudonym of the Italian occultist and adventurer Giuseppe Balsamo) was arrested and imprisoned in the Castel Sant'Angelo (soon afterward he was sentenced to death on the charge of being a Freemason, but the Pope changed his sentence to life imprisonment in the Castel Sant'Angelo). In 1789, Cagliostro was invited by the painters and sculptors of the French Academy in Rome to attend the reunions of their Lodge, and he tried to set up his own Lodge, which, in his opinion, would have been working in accordance with the Egyptian ritual (nowadays Memphis and Misraim). But, according to Pope Pius VI, Freemasonry and revolution were almost synonymous. Indeed, the French Academy in Rome was rallying in support of Republicanism, and Cagliostro's presence in the "Amis Sincères" Lodge instigated the Pope to give a hard lesson to those French artists and their new Masonic leader. Freemasonry flourished in Rome after the French invasion of 1809, but a new wave of suppression was launched by the Papacy in 1814.

In Milan, two Swiss citizens, Pierre George Madiott and a certain Moussard, founded the first Lodge around 1756. The abbot Pavesi, the monk Celestino Scalzi, Marquess Ottaviano Casnedi, Count Conte Belgioioso, doctor Vincenzo d'Adda, general Joseph Esterhazi, and some officials of the Army were member of the Lodge. In 1776, another Lodge was established in Cremona; its Worshipful Master was Count Pasquale Biffi, a close friend of Cesare Beccaria and of the Verri brothers.

In Naples, Freemasonry started developing in the 1760s. In 1759, King Charles VII of Naples, who was also King Charles V of Sicily, a proponent of enlightened despotism, succeeded to the Spanish throne, and he reigned as Charles III, King of Spain and the Spanish Indies, from 1759 until 1788. Upon succeeding to the Spanish throne, Charles abdicated the Neapolitan and Sicilian thrones in favor of Ferdinand, his third surviving son, who became

Ferdinand I of the Two Sicilies. In the 1760s, the Grand Lodge of London and Westminster was quarrelling with the Grand Lodge of Holland over the control of the Masonic jurisdiction of Naples, and they both warranted Provincial Grand Lodges of Naples. However, in 1775, Francesco d'Aquino, Prince of Caramanico, who was ambassador to London and Paris for the Kingdom of Naples and later viceroy of Sicily, founded "Zelo" Lodge, claiming independence from any foreign Obedience. Moreover, in 1775, King Ferdinand I of the Two Sicilies forbade any Masonic activity, but Freemasonry was not eliminated in Naples. In 1776, Diego Naselli was elected Grand Master of the Grand Lodge of Naples, and the English Provincial Grand Lodge of Naples continued its operation; the first's Masonic ethos was characterized by esotericism, whereas the latter was oriented toward the principles of the European Enlightenment and civil Democracy. As a result of the French Revolution and the following reaction, both the Grand Lodge of Naples and the English Provincial Grand Lodge of Naples were dissolved.

In 1805, the Grand Orient of Italy (in Italian, Grande Oriente d'Italia) was founded in Milan under the regency of Eugène Rose de Beauharnais (the stepson and adopted child of Napoleon I). It was the epoch of Napoleonic Freemasonry. The previous Grand Orient of Italy was dissolved in 1814 upon the fall of Napoleon. During the same period, the Ancient and Accepted Scottish Rite (AASR) was introduced in Italy, and a Supreme Council of the AASR for Italy was formed at Milan in 1805, and it is from this body that the current Grand Orient of Italy claims its direct descent. Additionally, by 1861, three Grand Orients were in operation in Italy: at Naples, Turin, and Palermo. In 1867, Giuseppe Garibaldi, one of Italy's "fathers of the fatherland" and most prominent Freemasons, united the previous three Italian Grand Orients at a meeting of all Italian Lodges, out of which it came a Grand Orient to govern the Craft degrees and a Scottish Rite Supreme Council to govern the Degrees 4°–33° of the AASR. These two bodies endured until 1925, when Benito Mussolini's fascist regime ruthlessly suppressed Freemasonry.

The Grand Orient of Italy was revived in 1945, and it was recognized by the United Grand Lodge of England in 1972. Moreover, in the 1970s, many Grand Lodges around the world, following the policy of the United Grand Lodge of England, recognized the Grand Orient of Italy.

In 1980, the "Propaganda Due," or "P2," Lodge scandal broke out in Italy. In particular, in the 1970s, the "P2" Lodge, which was an elitist and clandestine Lodge under the auspices of the Grand Orient of Italy, was involved in political intrigues and terrorist operations organized by NATO and by U.S. and Italian intelligence agencies with the aim of manipulating the Italian political system. In fact, the "P2" Lodge was part of Operation Gladio ('Gladio' is the Italian form of 'gladius,' a type of Roman sword). Operation Gladio was the codename for a clandestine NATO 'stay-behind' operation in Europe during the Cold War. The purpose of Gladio was to maintain paramilitary networks that would continue anti-communist actions in the event of a Soviet invasion and conquest. Gladio operated under different codenames in Italy, Germany, France, Belgium, the Netherlands, Greece, Luxemburg, Great Britain, Norway, Portugal, Spain, Austria, Turkey, Denmark, Switzerland, and Sweden.[1] It was part of a series of national operations first coordinated by the Clandestine Committee of the Western Union (CCWU), founded in 1948, but, after the creation of NATO in 1949, CCWU was integrated into NATO's Clandestine Planning Committee founded in 1951 and overseen by SHAPE (Supreme Headquarters Allied Powers, Europe). CIA Director Allen Dulles played a key role in the creation of Gladio networks, and many of Gladio's operations were financed and supported by the CIA and by CIA-controlled networks of organized crime and terrorism.[2]

Neofascist extremists, such as the far-right "Ordine Nuovo" subversive organization and the "P2" clandestine Masonic Lodge headed by Licio Gelli, executed Gladio's "strategy of tension" in Italy in the 1960s and the 1970s. In Italy, Gladio's "strategy of tension" included the following operations: the 1964 silent *coup d*'état through which General Giovanni de Lorenzo, who was the head of the Italian SIFAR intelligence agency, forced the Italian socialist ministers to leave the government; the 1969 Piazza Fontana bombing; the 1970 failed coup attempt "Golpe Borghese"; the 1972 Peteano massacre; the 1973 bombing of the airplane Argo 16; the 1974 Piazza della Loggia bombing; the 1978 murder of the then Italian Prime minister Aldo Moro, who was pursuing the so-called "historic compromise" between the Christian Democrats and Italian Communist Party (PCI); the 1980 Bologna massacre, etc.[3] Through the previous "strategy of tension," the Euroatlantic ruling elite aimed at terrorizing Italian citizens in order to stop the rise of left-wing political forces in Italy and to implement Henry Kissinger's anti-communist policy, since Kissinger had warned the then Christian Democrat Prime Minister of Italy, Aldo Moro, not to bring all Italian political forces into direct collaboration. In 1978, Aldo Moro was kidnapped and assassinated by the Italian leftist terrorist organization called "Red Brigades," which worked closely with the Hyperion Language School in Paris. An Italian police report referred to the Hyperion Language School as "the most important CIA office in Europe."[4]

On October 24, 1990, the then Italian Christian Democrat Prime Minister Giulio Andreotti publicly recognized the existence of Gladio. On

1 Ganser, Daniele, *NATO's Secret Armies*, Oxford: Frank Cass, 2005.
2 Ibid.
3 Ibid.
4 Ibid.

March 26, 2001, the British newspaper *The Guardian* wrote that General Giandelio Maletti, commander of the counter-intelligence section of Italy's military intelligence service from 1971 to 1975, told the Milan court the following: "The CIA [Central Intelligence Agency], following the directives of its government, wanted to create an Italian nationalism capable of halting what it saw as a slide to the left, and, for this purpose, it may have made use of rightwing terrorism."[1] On November 22, 1990, the European Parliament passed a resolution (Nr. C 324/201) condemning Gladio.

In 1992, Licio Gelli, the Venerable Master of the "P2" Lodge, was sentenced to eighteen years and six months of prison after being found guilty of fraud concerning the collapse of the banking company Banco Ambrosiano, whose main share-holder was the Vatican Bank, that is, the Istituto per le Opere di Religione. However, Gelli's sentence was reduced by the Court of Appeal to twelve years. Gelli disappeared on the eve of being imprisoned, in May 1998, while under house arrest in his mansion near Arezzo, but finally he was arrested in the French Riviera, in Cannes. On July 19, 2005, Gelli and the former Mafia boss Giuseppe Calò were formally indicted by Roman magistrates for the murder of Roberto Calvi, Chairman of Banco Ambrosiano, which collapsed in 1982. Calvi, known also as "God's banker," was the link between the "P2" Lodge and the Vatican. Before the court, Gelli stated that people connected with Calvi's banking activities were involved in financing the Polish "Solidarity" movement on behalf of the Vatican. Gelli was accused of having provoked Calvi's death in order to punish him for having embezzled money owed to the "P2" Lodge and the Mafia, and the Mafia, in particular, wanted to prevent Calvi from revealing how Banco Ambrosiano had been used for money laundering. Finally, in May 2009, the case against Gelli was dropped, because, according to the magistrate, there was insufficient evidence to argue that Gelli had been involved in the planning and execution of the crime. Moreover, Gelli has been implicated in Aldo Moro's murder, since the then Italian chief of intelligence, accused of negligence, was a member of the "P2" Lodge.

In 1993, the then Grand Master of the Grand Orient of Italy, Giuliano Di Bernardo, arguing that there were irregularities in the operations of the Grand Orient, seceded and formed the Regular Grand Lodge of Italy (in Italian, Gran Loggia Regolare d'Italia), endorsing the United Grand Lodge of England's model of Freemasonry. The Grand Lodges of England, Ireland, Scotland, and a few others, withdrew recognition from the Grand Orient of Italy, and they recognized the new Regular Grand Lodge of Italy. But the

---

1 Willan, Philip, "Terrorists 'Helped by CIA' to Stop Rise of Left in Italy," *The Guardian*, March 26, 2001; see: http://www.theguardian.com/world/2001/mar/26/terrorism

majority of the American and the Australian Grand Lodges continued to recognize the Grand Orient of Italy.

In December 1997, fifteen Lodges under the Regular Grand Lodge of Italy seceded and formed the Grand Lodge of the Union (in Italian, Gran Loggia dell'Unione). Moreover, in 1998, a further group of Lodges seceded from the Regular Grand Lodge of Italy to create the United Grand Lodge of Italy (in Italian, Gran Loggia Unita d'Italia). In June 1999, the Grand Lodge of the Union founded a body known as the Federation of Grand Lodges of Italy, whose purpose is to unite all regular Grand Lodges operating in Italy. Of the many other Grand Lodges in Italy, the most important are the Grand Lodge of Italy of the Ancient Free Accepted Masons, the Unione Massonica di Stretta Osservanza Iniziatica (U.M.S.O.I.), the Italian Masonic Grand Lodge, the Grand Orient of Naples and the two Sicilies, and the Feminine Grand Lodge of Italy (a women-only Masonic organization).

The history of U.S. Freemasonry is inextricably linked to that of European Freemasonry. In fact, the differences among the various European Masonic Obediences (e.g., English Freemasonry, Scottish Freemasonry, French Freemasonry, etc.) have manifested themselves in the United States of America. In 1680, the first known Freemason settled in what is known today as the United States of America: he was called John Skene, and he was a member of the Lodge of Aberdeen in Scotland. In that time, the one fifth of the members of the Lodge of Aberdeen were operative Masons (i.e., stonemasons), while the rest were speculative (symbolic) Masons, that is, 'Freemasons.' In general, when we talk about Scottish Masonic Lodges before the 1720s, we talk about Lodges that were primarily made up of stonemasons. However, in the 1670s, only approximately twenty percent of the members of the Lodge of Aberdeen were stonemasons, the rest being 'accepted,' that is, symbolic Masons. For instance, John Skene was not a stonemason, but he was a merchant, and he fled to New Jersey in order to escape religious persecution. In particular, Skene settled on the north side of the Raritan River in New Jersey, where he founded what is known today as Perth Amboy, after the name of Perth, the ancient capital of Scotland. A few years later, Skene was joined by another Scottish Mason called John Cockburn, who emigrated to New Jersey in 1684. John Cockburn was a member of a Masonic Lodge in Melrose, which is in the Scottish borders, and he was a working stonemason. The Lodge of Melrose, to which John Cockburn belonged, was entirely made up of stonemasons devoted to the building of castles and abbeys near the Scottish borders. In New Jersey, John Cockburn founded the town of Melrose, after his hometown. Moreover, John Cockburn wrote back to his mother Lodge in Scotland, proposing to his Masonic brothers to emigrate to America and mentioning that, in America, there were all sorts of business opportunities, especially for stonemasons. John Skene, a symbolic Mason from Aberdeen, and John Cockburn, an operative Mason from Melrose, cooperated with each other on several building projects in New Jersey.

In 1702, Colonel Daniel Coxe arrived in New York with Lord Cornbury. Coxe had strong ties with the Hanoverian dynasty of Great Britain, and he was appointed Commander of military forces in West New Jersey. In 1730, the Duke of Norfolk, who was then the Grand Master of the Moderns' Grand Lodge of England, appointed Coxe Provincial Grand Master for the Masonic Provinces of New York, New Jersey, and Pennsylvania. Other Lodges in the colony received Charters from the Ancients' Grand Lodge of England, the Grand Lodge of Scotland, and the Grand Lodge of Ireland.

In 1752, an American called George Washington—the later first President of the U.S.A.—became a Freemason in a Scottish Lodge at Fredericksburg in Virginia. In 1752, that Scottish Lodge at Fredericksburg, in which George Washington was initiated into the Craft, was a clandestine, or 'irregular,' Masonic Lodge, in the sense that it had not received a Charter from the Grand Lodge of Scotland. However, in 1758, George Washington's Lodge was granted a Charter from the Grand Lodge of Scotland.

Starting in 1765, members of American colonial society rejected the authority of the British Parliament to tax them without any representatives in the government. During the following decade, protests by colonists, known also as Patriots, continued to escalate. In December 1773, in the context of the Boston Tea Party, which was a political protest by the Sons of Liberty[1] in Boston, Patriots destroyed an entire shipment of tea sent by the East India Company. The British Empire responded by imposing punitive laws, known as the Coercive Acts, on Massachusetts in 1774 until the tea had been paid for. On the other hand, colonists, known as Loyalists, preferred to remain subjects of the British Crown. Claiming that King George III's rule was tyrannical and infringing the colonists' rights, the Continental Congress declared the colonies free and independent states in July 1776. The Patriots' leaders professed the political philosophies of Liberalism and Republicanism to reject monarchy and aristocracy, and they proclaimed that all men are created equal.

The founders of the U.S.A. had good intentions, but they were insufficiently educated to understand the intrigues of conceptual thinking

---

1 The Sons of Liberty was a semiclandestine organization of American colonists that was founded in 1765 in response to the Stamp Act, which instituted a tax intended to fund the British Armed Forces stationed in the American colonies as a result of the French and Indian War. One of the most prominent leaders of the Sons of Liberty was Paul Revere, who became the Worshipful Master of the St. Andrew's Lodge in Boston, Massachusetts, in 1770. Moreover, Paul Revere was the Grand Master of the Grand Lodge of Massachusetts from 1794 until 1797.

(which are often more complex and more important than political intrigues), and they were too opportunistic to resist the temptation of giving primacy to the 'urgent' and 'immediate' over the 'significant.' Thus, Charles Thomson—who was one of America's most important founders and the Congressional Secretary from 1774 to 1779—wrote a detailed history of the events that took place during the American Revolution and of the men who had been celebrated as heroes across the newly-founded U.S.A., but, ultimately, he decided to destroy his manuscript by arguing as follows: "Let the world admire the supposed wisdom and valor of our great men," and he added the following: "I shall not undeceive future generations."[1] It is worth pointing out that even the self-esteem of the social establishment of the newly-founded republic of the U.S.A. was largely dependent on the opinion that particular members of European elites, such as Alexis de Tocqueville and Marquis de Lafayette, had about the American Revolution.

In addition, to a large extent, the ideology of the American Revolution itself can be ascribed to an English Whig political theorist and activist called Thomas Paine, whose pamphlet entitled *Common Sense* (1775–6), actually, became the most important philosophical/ideological underpinning of the U.S. Declaration of Independence. Not only was Thomas Paine a Whig political activist, but also he was a Whig 'theologian.' In his book *The Age of Reason*, Paine endorsed a radically positivist attitude on the basis of which he discarded the Bible and openly stated that he was contending against the Gospel of Jesus Christ. Through rationalism, Paine attempted to elevate his intellect, precisely, his "common sense," to an ontologically sufficient criterion of truth. Hence, ultimately, the U.S.A. was politically and intellectually dominated by the principles and mentalities of the English Whigs and of Puritanism, which is a positivist distortion of Christianity. In the late twentieth century, the U.S.A. became the vanguard of a liberal globalist ideology that not only aims at substituting the great cultural traditions of humanity with a particular liberal monologue, but also it undermines people's ability to appreciate high culture, thus, actually, dehumanizing humanity in the name of and through liberal humanism.

After the American Revolution, gradually, U.S. Freemasonry was dominated by the concept and the principles of "regular Freemasonry" that were developed by the Moderns' Grand Lodge of England and, after 1813, by the United Grand Lodge of England (UGLE). The U.S.A. does not have a national Masonic leader, because each State has its own Grand Lodge whose presiding officer is the Grand Master of that State. The U.S. Grand Lodges that operate in conformity with the landmarks of the UGLE are deemed to

---

1 Charles Thomson as recorded by Dr. Benjamin Rush, quoted in Saussy, F. Tupper, *Rulers of Evil: Useful Knowledge about Governing Bodies*, HarperCollins, 2001, p. 125.

be "regular," and they recognize each other, while maintaining independence and sovereignty over their subordinate Lodges.

D. Mystical imperialism

In the nineteenth century, under the House of Hanover and the House of Saxe-Coburg and Gotha, the British monarchy and its government—having placed the United Grand Lodge of England (UGLE) under their direct control, since the latter's foundation in 1813—fabricated an imperialist British-Israel mythology, which they promoted through English Masonic Lodges, Pentecostal Churches (e.g., the Bible-Pattern Church Fellowship), and fanciful nationalist "pyramidologists" (e.g., Herbert Aldersmith).[1]

According to the British-Israel mythology, the tribes of Israel wandered into northern Europe, Queen Victoria was descended from the Biblical King David and, thus, a descendant of the Davidic family tree that produced Jesus Christ, the British are the real "Chosen People," and the British Empire had a God-given mission to accomplish. Furthermore, according to British Israelism, the modern Jews are not the historical Hebrews of Biblical Israel, but rather the British are. However, according to the eschatology of the British-Israel mythology, the modern Jews should be put into Palestine in order to fulfill prophecy, fight a great war against the Muslims, and bring about the End Times. Thus, British Israelism is strongly linked to Zionism, which is a distortion of traditional, Torah Judaism and irrelevant to the esoteric teachings of the Kabbalah.

From the perspective of Torah Judaism, the Sinaitic Law is the essence of Judaism, but Reformed Judaism has subordinated the Sinaitic Law to historicity, it has compromised the Sinaitic Law with the spirit of Western modernity, and it allows and encourages rabbis to pick and choose which of the Torah commandments to obey. Whereas Torah Judaism means subservience to God and that man should emulate God, Zionism is a sect of Reformed Judaism, and it is founded on nationalism and the desacralization of reality. Zionism understands and defines 'Judaism' according to secular and nationalist criteria, and, in essence, it is the ideological underpinning of the Zionist State of Israel. The term 'Zionism' was coined in 1893 by Nathan Birnbaum, but Theodor Herzl (1860–1904), an Austrian Jew born to a bourgeois Budapest family, is the acknowledged founder of Zionism, and, in 1896, he published his seminal book *The Jewish State*, where he argued that the cure for anti-Semitism was the establishment of a Jewish state on the model of modern Western European nation-states. However, Herzl himself did not hesitate to indirectly promote anti-Semitism in order to convince

---

1 See, for instance: Garnier, John, *Israel in Britain*, London: Robert Banks & Son, 1890; Poole, Rev. W. H., *Anglo-Israel*, Toronto: Bengough Bros., 1879.

as many Jews to embrace his Zionist ideology as possible. In his diary, on page 16, Herzl argued that "anti-Semitism helps to build this kind of Jew, education that will bring to assimilation,"[1] and, on page 68 of his diary, Herzl wrote the following: "an idea rose on my heart to bring on anti-Semitism and to obliterate Jewish wealth."[2]

Whereas Torah Judaism is founded on the revelation at Sinai (Exodus 19), Zionism is an attempt to build a Jew without Torah and a modern Western European type of Jewish state, as Amnon Raz-Krakotzkin, historian at the University of Ben-Gurion, has pointed out.[3] In particular, the so-called Revisionist Zionism is the founding ideology of the non-religious right in Israel, which has led to the development of the Likud Party. The ideology of Revisionist Zionism was originally developed by Ze'ev Jabotinsky, who was a Russian Jewish activist and author, and, with the Russian Jewish activist Joseph Trumpeldor, he co-founded the Jewish Legion of the British Army in World War I.

To provide fuel for the aforementioned British-Israel mythology, Albert Edward, Prince of Wales (King of Great Britain and Ireland as Edward VII from 1901), who was the Grand Master of the UGLE from 1874 until 1901, visited Jerusalem in 1862, and, in 1865, the Palestine Exploration Fund was founded under the royal patronage of Queen Victoria. In the 1870s, several British soldier-archeologists were dispatched to the Holy Land in order to dig up supposed religious relics that might help the promotion of British Israelism. However, in 2003, Tudor Parfitt, Professor of Jewish Studies at the School of Oriental and African Studies (SOAS), in London, published a book entitled *The Lost Tribes of Israel*, in which he declared that "the Lost Tribes are indeed nothing but a myth," and that "this myth is a vital feature of colonial discourse throughout the long period of European overseas empires, from the beginning of the fifteenth century, until the later half of the twentieth."[4]

One can fully realize the cynical character of the British-Israel mythology by studying the changes in its narrative. In particular, according to the original version of the British-Israel mythology, the Nordic Aryans, that is, both the British and the Germans, were the wandering "Chosen People," but, after the 1870s, Germany broke from allegiance to Great Britain's free trade policy, and, therefore, members of the British social establishment articulated a new version of the British-Israel mythology, according to which only the British were the wandering "Chosen People," whereas modern Germans

---

1 See: http://www.nkusa.org/Historical_Documents/Herzl_quotes.cfm
2 Ibid.
3 See: https://bgu.academia.edu/AmnonRazKrakotzkin
4 Parfitt, Tudor, *The Lost Tribes of Israel: The History of a Myth*, London: Phoenix, 2003, pp. 1, 225

were descendants of ancient Assyrians. Thus, an 'occult war' broke out in Europe.

In the late nineteenth and the early twentieth centuries, the British ruling elite articulated a strategy of 'mystical imperialism' grounded in the ethos of the era's British Freemasonry, the British orientalist Edward Granville Browne's radical pantheism, and the modernist Arab Masonic society. The goals of that British strategy of mystical imperialism were to infuse a sense of the divine into the British Empire's politics and grand strategy and to solidify the British Empire by creating a syncretistic, unified field theory of religion, thus establishing a cultural monologue through modernism and spiritual syncretism, instead of merely pursuing the more traditional divide-and-conquer technique. As a counterattack against the aforementioned British-Israel mythology, nationalist and racist German occultists articulated an Aryan mythology by synthesizing Hindu-Vedic, Nordic-Germanic, and neo-Gnostic religious traditions. Thus, in 1939, Heinrich Himmler, head of the Gestapo and the Waffen-SS, sent an expedition led by the Nazi scholar Ernst Schäfer to Tibet in the hopes of uncovering proof of Aryan links to modern Germany in Central Asia.

The Nazis' and some Eurasianists' Aryan/Indo-Aryan theories—according to which, a tribe of all-conquering Central Asian chariot-riders and horse lords supposedly swept through India and Iran ("land of the Aryans") approximately 3,500 years ago before depositing their linguistic legacy in what is now Europe—are mainly ideologues' attempts to fabricate a distinct prestigious identity in order to justify their existential and imperialist claims and visions. However, in 2011, scientific evidence published in the *American Journal of Human Genetics* by a team spearheaded by the Centre for Cellular and Molecular Biology in the southern Indian city of Hyderabad showed that no such clear distinct Aryan/Indo-Aryan racial identity ever existed and that the Aryans of Nazi repute were never as pure or as real as the Nazis' racialist ideologues would hope.[1]

Characteristic representatives of occult German nationalism and racism are the Thule Society (Thule-Gesellschaft),[2] Karl Maria Wiligut (1866–1946), Savitri Devi Mukherji (1905–82), and Miguel Serrano (1917–2009).[3] The Thule Society, a German occultist and *völkisch* group founded in Munich by Rudolf

---

1 Tharoor, Ishaan, "The Aryan Race: Time to Forget It?" *Time*, December 15, 2011; see: http://world.time.com/2011/12/15/the-aryan-race-time-to-forget-about-it/

2 The Thule Society was founded in 1918 by Rudolf Freiherr von Sebottendorff (or von Sebottendorf), whose real name was Adam Alfred Rudolf Glauer. Sebottendorff was a Freemason, a Sufi of the Bektashi Order, and a practitioner of meditation, astrology, numerology, and alchemy.

3 Goodrick-Clarke, Nicholas, *The Occult Roots of Nazism: Secret Aryan Cults and Their Influence on Nazi Ideology*, London: I. B. Tauris & Co., 2004; Flowers, S. E., and Moynihan, M., *The Secret King: The Myth and Reality of Nazi Occultism*, revised and expanded edition, Port Townsend, WA: Feral House, 2007.

von Sebottendorf, is notable chiefly as the organization that sponsored the Deutsche Arbeiterpartei (DAP), which was later reorganized by Adolf Hitler into the National Socialist German Workers' Party (NSDAP or Nazi Party). Karl Maria Wiligut was an Austrian occultist and SS-Brigadeführer who argued that "Irminenschaft" (known also as Irminism)—a current of Ariosophy based on a Germanic deity Irmin—was the true German ancestral religion, thus merging Neopaganism, Wicca (pagan witchcraft), and the Nazi political ideology into a unified totalitarian system. Miguel Serrano was a Chilean diplomat, journalist, and poet, who wrote books on occultism and "Esoteric Hitlerism," and he reformulated Jung's theory of collective archetypes in a racist way. Savitri Devi was a Nazi spy and scholar, and she articulated a synthesis between Nazism and Hinduism in the context of which she proclaimed Adolf Hitler to have been sent by Providence, much like an avatar of the Hindu god Vishnu. In other words, the Thule Society, Savitri Devi, Karl Maria Wiligut, and Miguel Serrano have used mythology and esotericism as a fig leaf for stunningly brutal and simplistic political movements.

In general, in the late nineteenth and the early twentieth centuries, mythology and, generally, spirituality were systematically distorted, abused, desecrated, and manipulated by British and German imperialists. Moreover, in that milieu of mystical imperialist strategies, Russian occultists, primarily Madame Helena Petrovna Blavatsky, the founder of a mystical 'school' called Theosophy, articulated a Eurasian theory of mystical imperialism. Blavatsky was a friend of Russian Tsar Nicolas II and the Oriental enthusiast Prince Esper Ukhtomsky, a close confidant of Tsar Nicolas II. Moreover, Blavatsky was connected with Ukhtomsky's Tibetan friend Shamzaran Badmaev, who lobbied for the unification of Russia, Mongolia, and Tibet into a peculiar mystical Eurasian entity, and with the imperialist Russian publicist Mikhail Katkoff. In fact, Blavatsky fascinated Tsar Nicolas II and his wife, the notoriously superstitious Tsarina Alexandra Feodorovna, with her book *The Secret Doctrine*. Blavatsky's book *The Secret Doctrine* is a synthesis of several mystical traditions, but it is primarily focused on Indo/Tibetan spirituality. Many of Blavatsky's adherents formed the impression and cultivated the belief that Tsar Nicolas II was the prophesied northern "White Tsar," uniquely gifted and divinely destined to balance the British Empire, to fight against materialism and rationalism, and to become a Eurasian emperor.

Far from being a cultural representative and guardian of Byzantine Christianity and of the legacy of the Eastern Roman Empire, the Romanov Dynasty of Russia was descended from the same Germanic-Bohemian group as the royal families of Germany and Hanoverian Britain. The early Romanovs were so strongly committed to the Germanic ethos that they looked down upon Russians as being too Asiatic, and, in particular, Tsar Peter the Great even tried to forcibly implant German culture in Russia. Moreover, the Romanovs were susceptible to occult brainwashing and to German romanticism. Arthur Dee (1579–1651), the son the English magus, spy master, alchemist and Rosicrucian John Dee, was appointed one of the physicians to the Tsar Michael I of Russia. Blavatsky was among the elite of Russian nobility, and she was a cousin of Tsarist Prime Minister Count Witte.

In 1886, Jamal ad-Din al-Afghani, who had named himself "Philosopher of the East," visited Russia "invited by the order of the Russian government,"[1] and he joined up with Blavatsky's publisher, Mikhail Katkoff, who wanted to implement an imperialist Russian-Orientalist ideological and geostrategic policy in Central Asia and India. Al-Afghani was descended from a Shiite Azerbaijani family from the Asadabad village of Iran, but he used the name al-Afghani to hide his Iranian and Shiite origin because he was generally active within predominantly Sunni areas. Al-Afghani established his own Masonic organization under the auspices of the Grand Orient of France. Al-Afghani's ideology was a peculiar combination of radical, anti-Western Pan-Islamism and an attempt of utilizing Western rationality and technology in order to invigorate Islam.

The nineteenth century Russian establishment cooperated with Blavatsky, Jamal ad-Din al-Afghani, and several spiritualists in order to conduct its own 'occult war,' thus betraying its Byzantine Christian roots and departing from the legacy of the Eastern Roman Empire. As a result, when Russian Tsar Nicolas II and Tsarina Alexandra Feodorovna visited France in 1896, the French occultist Papus (whose real name was Gérard Anaclet Vincent Encausse), the founder of the Martinist Order, sent them a greeting on behalf of the "French Spiritualists."[2] Furthermore, by establishing the Kabbalistic Order of the Rose-Croix as the 'inner circle' of the Martinist Order, Papus, Oswald Wirth, and Stanislas De Guaita attempted to unite occultists into a revived Rosicrucian brotherhood, as an international occult absolutist order, in which they hoped Tsarist Russia would play a leading role as a Eurasian entity bridging East and West within the context of the Martinists' occult syncretistic and absolutist system. In general, the Slavic cultural revival of the nineteenth century imitated the era's techniques of mystical imperialism combined with local Slavic mystical traditions and superstitions. In particular, the Slavic cultural revival of the nineteenth century was an ideological mixture of Asian mentalities (Orientalism), German romanticism, and Slavic chauvinism, and, therefore, it rendered

1 Livingstone, David, *Black Terror White Soldiers: Islam, Fascism, and the New Age,* U.S.A.: Sabilillah Publications, 2013, p. 194.
2 Ibid.

Russia spiritually incapable of successfully performing its historical role as an heir to the Eastern Roman Empire and as the 'Third Rome.'

With regard to Blavatsky's work, it is worth mentioning Max Müller's criticism. Friedrich Max Müller was a German Indologist who was contemporary to Blavatsky and spent most of his working life as professor of comparative philology at Oxford. Irrespectively of the value of Max Müller's substantial arguments about the Indian mythology, his epistemological criticism of Blavatsky's work is apt. Van den Bosch has summarized Müller's epistemological criticism of Blavatsky's work as follows:

> Müller was of the opinion that Blavatsky had not understood Indian religions . . . She was, according to him, deceived by others and had been carried away by her own imagination . . . He argued that her secret doctrines were contrary to Indian religious tradition. There was no esoteric interpretation of the *Shastras* and other ancient Indian scriptures that could possibly support Blavatsky's theosophy.[1]

With regard to Freemasonry itself, Blavatsky's movement, namely, the Theosophical Society, and her epigones have given rise to a neo-Orientalist and totally dechristianized Freemasonic movement. In the nineteenth century, in France, the International Order of Mixed Freemasonry "Le Droit Humain" was founded by Maria Deraismes, a well-known humanitarian, feminist author, and lecturer, and Georges Martin, a French doctor, politician, and Freemason. Several prominent members of the Theosophical Society, including Annie Besant (a prominent British socialist, theosophist, women's rights activist, writer, orator, and supporter of Irish and Indian self-rule), Charles W. Leadbeater (occultist and co-initiator with J. I. Wedgwood of the Liberal Catholic Church), Curuppumullage Jinarajadasa (a U.S. occultist), and Henry Steel Olcott (a U.S. military officer, journalist, lawyer, and an advocate of a peculiar modernist Buddhist movement) joined Co-Freemasonry and started promoting their views and mentalities through Freemasonry. Moreover, given that the Theosophists' main contact in India was with the Arya Somaj movement, whose creed was national regeneration based on a return to the ancient Veda religion, the Theosophists' infiltration into Co-Freemasonry gave rise to new Freemasonic organizations that mixed Freemasonry with Oriental occult belief systems, and with Hindu and other Central Asian nationalist movements.

In particular, on September 26, 1902, Annie Besant and officers of the Supreme Council of the French "Maçonnerie Mixte" (known today as "The International Order of Freemasonry for Men and Women, Le Droit

1 Quoted in Van Olst, Bas Rijken, "Max Müller and H. P. Blavatsky," *Sunrise: Theosophical Perspectives*, June/July 2006 (Theosophical University Press); see: http://www.theosophy-nw.org/theosnw/world/general/ge-bas2.htm

Humain") founded the "Order of Universal Co-Freemasonry in Great Britain and the British Dependencies"; Leadbeater served as the presiding officer of the Sydney Lodge No. 404 and of various other Freemasonic organizations. Besant's and Leadbeater's movement of Co-Freemasonry has sometimes been called "Occult Freemasonry," because it is founded on an occult syncretic attitude toward great Oriental spiritual traditions. However, the spiritual identity of this Order of Co-Freemasonry is neither European nor Asian, in the sense that it is not based on the study of the authentic great mythologies of Europe or Asia, but it consists in an occult cultural melting pot fabricated by Annie Besant and Charles W. Leadbeater. However, in the 1920s, Besant was discredited, because she claimed that her protégé and adopted son Jiddu Krishnamurti, an Indian occult writer, was the new Messiah and incarnation of Buddha, but, in 1929, Krishnamurti officially and publicly rejected these claims.

E. The old Masonic manuscripts and the true Noachites

Noah is an emblematic figure in several systems of Western esotericism. Freemasonry is a characteristic case in point. One of the earliest surviving documents of Freemasonry, the *Graham Manuscript*, apparently dated October 24, 1726, explicitly refers to the sons of Noah seeking the secret that their dead father had possessed. Hence, the previous manuscript gives a Noah story as the legend of the Third Degree of Symbolic Masonry. Additionally, if one looks at Anderson's 1738 *Constitutions of Freemasonry*, he realizes the key importance of Noah for early Freemasons: Freemasons see themselves as true Noachites, that is, as children of Noah.

According to the book of Genesis, Noah distributed different spiritual characteristics among different people. His sons were equal to each other, in the sense that they all sprang from the same source, but each one of them was different from his brothers, in the sense that each of Noah's sons had his own distinctive spiritual identity.

We read in the book of Genesis 9:20–27: "Noah, a man of the soil, was the first to plant a vineyard. He drank some of the wine and became drunk, and he lay uncovered in his tent. And Ham, the father of Canaan, saw the nakedness of his father, and told his two brothers outside. Then Shem and Japheth took a garment, laid it on both their shoulders, and walked backward and covered the nakedness of their father; their faces were turned away, and they did not see their father's nakedness. When Noah awoke from his wine and knew what his youngest son had done to him, he said, 'Cursed be Canaan; lowest of slaves shall he be to his brothers.' He also said, 'Blessed by the LORD my God be Shem; and let Canaan be his slave. May God make space for Japheth, and let him live in the tents of Shem; and let Canaan be his slave.' After the flood Noah lived three hundred fifty years. All the days of Noah were nine hundred fifty years; and he died."

The three children of Noah are three very well-known persons. Shem is the father of the Hebrews and a forebear of Abraham (1 Chronicles 1:17–27). Ham is the father of Canaan and Misraim (Genesis 10:6 and 1 Chronicles 1:8), and, according to Clement of Alexandria (*Homily IX*, 3–7), the races of the Egyptians, the Babylonians and the Persians are descended from Misraim. Japheth is the father of Javan, and the sons of Javan are Elishah, Tarshish, the Kittim and the Rodanim (Genesis 10:2–4). Thus, the Bible tells us that Japheth was the father of Ion (Javan) and, therefore, the father of the Greeks. According to the Greek mythology, Ion was the son of Apollo and Creusa, daughter of Erechtheus and wife of Xuthus, and, when his mother abandoned him, he was saved and raised by a priestess of the Delphic Oracle. His story is told in the tragedy Ion by Euripides. According to mythological accounts, Ion is the father of one of the primary tribes of Greece, specifically, the Ionians.

Many philologists identify Iapetos (or Japetus), who, according to the ancient Greek mythology, was the Titan of mortal life, the son of Uranus and Gaia, with Japheth, who, according to the Bible, was one of Noah's sons, for the following reasons: (i) there is a linguistic connection between the names Iapetos and Japheth; (ii) according to the Greek mythology, Cronus, a brother of Iapetos, castrated their father, which echoes the sinful act of Ham, the brother of Japheth; (iii) both Japheth and Iapetos are related to a deluge: the first through his father Noah, and the latter through his grandson Deucalion; (iv) Iapetos was the husband of Asia.

The Biblical story of Noah has great ontological significance. First of all, it is interesting that Noah cursed his son Ham, because the latter saw him naked. The previous attitude of Noah should not be interpreted as a manifestation of anger by a prudish old man. It is has a much deeper meaning.

The name Noah means 'relief.' The father of Noah was Lamech, the sixth generation descendant of Cain (Genesis 4:18). Lamech named his son Noah, prophesizing the following: "Out of the ground that the LORD has cursed this one shall bring us relief from our work and from the toil of our hands" (Genesis 5:29). Noah relieved the humankind and, in general, every animate being from the curse of the Deluge. Thus, according to Matthew 24:36–39, Noah can be considered as a type of Christ: "Heaven and earth will pass away, but my words will not pass away. But of that day and hour no one knows, neither the angels of heaven, nor the Son, but the Father alone. For as it was in the days of Noah, so it will be at the coming of the Son of Man. In (those) days before the flood, they were eating and drinking, marrying and giving in marriage, up to the day that Noah entered the ark. They did not know until the flood came and carried them all away. So will it be (also) at the coming of the Son of Man."

Furthermore, according to the book of Genesis 9:20, Noah is the first farmer. He transformed, or one could even say 'transmuted,' the 'cursed' land into a nourisher of the human being, and also he transformed labor into a source of reward. One day, as he had passed from labor to refreshment, Noah drank wine from his vineyard, he became inebriated, and he put off his clothes.

Nakedness is a kind of revelation, precisely, it reveals one's body. In the context of Biblical anthropology, the human body is not merely a system of flesh and bones, but it is something much more than that. The human body discloses the whole human being. In other words, the human body is inextricably linked to the human mind, and it is the mediator between the reality of consciousness and the reality of the external, physical and historical world. The Apostle Paul wrote that the body is meant "for the Lord, and the Lord for the body" (1 Corinthians 6:13). Since the body substantiates the human person, the disclosure of the naked body should not take place without certain presuppositions. The disclosure of a person's body means the revelation of what that person really is, and, therefore, this act presupposes deep awareness of the holiness of that moment, that is, it presupposes a kind of initiation. 'Initiation' means the ability to see when your eyes are shut, that is, it means the ability to see beyond sensible phenomena. The presence of any being of the sensible world in human consciousness is determined by the significance that human consciousness assigns to the given sensible being. Thus, the ability to see beyond sensible phenomena means that one is able to see the spiritual reality in which the objects of his consciousness are embedded. In the context of the previous analysis, showing one's body without initiation is an ontological degradation of the human being, since, in this way, man behaves like animals.

If we are not 'initiated', the human body is clothed, which means that one's being is concealed. Thus, according to the book of Genesis, God covers the fallen man with clothes: "For the man and his wife the LORD God made leather garments, with which he clothed them" (Genesis 3:21). Furthermore, on several occasions, the Bible stresses the social and cultural functions performed by clothing: "Life's prime needs are water, bread, and clothing, a house, too, for decent privacy" (Sirach 29:21). According to Deuteronomy, food and clothing are some of God's blessings (Deuteronomy 10:18), whereas, if man is abandoned by God's grace, he lives "in hunger and thirst, in nakedness and utter poverty" (Deuteronomy 28:48). Clothes protect us from adverse environmental conditions, and, therefore, according to Exodus 22:25, "if you take your neighbour's cloak as a pledge, you shall return it to him before sunset." Clothing helps us to distinguish between male and female, and it can function as a symbol of their relations (Deuteronomy 22:5). Furthermore, clothing indicates social life, since giving one's clothes to someone else is a sign of brotherhood (1 Samuel 18:3–4), and, according to Ezekiel 18:7, justice requires that we should "clothe the naked." In the same spirit, Isaiah teaches that the act of "clothing the naked when you see them" is an act of spiritual rebirth (Isaiah 58:7). Moreover, Jesus Christ said: "If anyone wants to go to law with you over your tunic, hand him your cloak as well" (Matthew 5:40), meaning that we must be personally available to the fellow human who seeks communion with us. Clothing, by being an objectification of the intentionality of human consciousness, implies that, through clothes, our body can exist in many different ways that reflect our personhood and not only in accordance with the impersonal and coercive logic of nature.

After the aforementioned analysis, we are able to understand the meaning of Ham's act. Ham disgraced initiation, that is, he disgraced the human personhood by treating the human being as if it were merely an object of the natural world. Shem and Japheth did the opposite: "Shem and Japheth, however, took a robe, and holding it on their backs, they walked backward and covered their father's nakedness" (Genesis 9:23). In other words, Shem and Japheth safeguarded the personal mode of existence of the human being, and they respected the existential otherness of Noah, in particular, and of every human being, in general, instead of treating them like same units of the natural world. Thus, Noah cursed Ham and prophesied the following: "Blessed be the LORD the God of Shem; and let Canaan be his slave. May God extend the territory of Japheth, and let him live in the tents of Shem; and let Canaan be his slave" (Genesis 9:26–27). Japheth, the founder of the Greek civilization, will worship the God of Shem, but Japheth will not reign only in the land of Shem. Japheth's dominion will expand worldwide.

In terms of the mythological language of the book of Genesis, a Noachite is a person or a society whose existence has the following four dimensions: the first dimension is symbolically represented by the Hebrews, who are descended from Shem, and it corresponds to the principle of prophetic and charismatic religion; the second dimension is symbolically represented by the Egyptians, who are descended from Ham, and it corresponds to the principle of tradition;[1] the third dimension is symbolically represented by the

---

1 The archetypal relationship between ancient Egypt and the principle of tradition was emphasized by Plato in his dialogue *Timaeus*, 21e–25b, where Plato narrates a conversation between Egyptian priests and the great Athenian sage Solon. According to the Egyptian priest, the Egyptians' relationship with tradition is, first of all, due to the climate of Egypt: in Egypt, "neither then nor at any other time does the water pour down over our fields from above, on the contrary it all tends naturally to well up from below," and, therefore, "it is, for

Greeks, who are descended from Japheth, and it corresponds to philosophy (including philosophical theology); the fourth dimension is symbolically represented by the Egyptians, who are descended from Ham, and it corresponds to the principle of technology and, generally, the utilization of knowledge for the achievement of economic goals.[1] In the consciousness

these reasons, that what is here preserved is reckoned to be most ancient"; on the other hand, according to the Egyptian priest, in Greece, and generally "in every place where there is no excessive heat or cold to prevent it there always exists some human stock, now more, now less in number" (Ibid., 22e). Hence, the natural climate of Greece makes the Greeks feel secure about the preservation of their nation and of their stock of knowledge, and, therefore, they do not need to depend on rigid traditional structures for their survival; in the Egyptian priest's own words: "the Goddess [Athina, the founder of Athens] . . . established your State, choosing the spot wherein you were born since she perceived therein a climate duly blended, and how that it would bring forth men of supreme wisdom" (Ibid., 24c). Furthermore, the Egyptian priest said to Solon that the Greeks' dynamic relation to tradition is related to the use of written language: "if any event has occurred that is noble or great or in any way conspicuous," it is "recorded from of old and preserved" in Egyptian temples, whereas, according to the Egyptian priest, the Greeks and the others "are but newly equipped . . . with letters" and, therefore, they lack certain memories.

1 The archetypal relationship between the Arab mentality and the utilization of knowledge for the achievement of economic goals has been emphasized and analyzed by the Arab historian and economist Ibn Khaldun, who wrote the seminal book *Muqaddimah*, also known as Ibn Khaldun's *Prolegomena*, in 1377. In particular, in the "Second Prefaratory Discussion," in the first book of his *Prolegomena*, Ibn Khaldun divides the cultivated part of the earth into seven zones, and he observes that the level of civilization in each of them depends on the corresponding climatological conditions. However, Ibn Khaldun assigns great importance to the economic and sociological characteristics of civilization, too. In his chapter on "Bedouin Civilization, Savage Nations and Tribes and their Conditions [of Life] Including Several Basic and Explanatory Statements," Ibn Khaldun argues that the differences of condition among people are the result of economic factors, and he observes that "sedentary people" (that is, the inhabitants of cities and countries, some of whom are craftsmen and others are merchants) earn more and live more comfortably than Bedouins, because they live above subsistence level. In addition, in his chapter "On the various aspects of making a living, such as profit and the crafts," Ibn Khaldun writes that the ancient and the early medieval Arabs, of all people, were least familiar with crafts, because the center of the Arabs' life was in the desert, and the Arabs were more remote from sedentary civilization than anybody else, whereas, in the same periods, the non-Arabs in the East and the Christian Mediterranean nations were very well versed in the crafts because they had developed sedentary civilizations. In his chapter on "The various kinds of sciences," Ibn Khaldun points out that his contemporaries' sciences were developed and cultivated by the two greatest pre-Islamic civilizations, namely, by the Persian civilization and the Greek civilization. According to Ibn Khaldun, when the Muslims conquered Persia, Sa'd ibn Abi Waqqas wrote to 'Umar ibn al-Khattab, asking him for permission to take the Persians' scientific books and distribute them as booty among the Muslims, but 'Umar ordered him to destroy them on the grounds that Islam was a self-sufficient system of knowledge. Thus, due to the Muslims, the sciences of the Persians were lost. Furthermore, Ibn Khaldun points out that the Greek scientific books continued to exist during the Eastern Roman Empire, known also as the Byzantine Empire, and, when the Arabs started depriving the Byzantines [Rum], as well as other nations, of their realms, they came in touch

of a true Noachite, the previous four principles, or existential dimensions, always co-exist and interact with each other, and they are interwoven with each other; none of the previous four principles exists completely separated from the other three principles. The synthesis of the previous four principles is the defining characteristic of the true Noachites and, generally, of genuine, traditional Freemasonry.

F. Gematria

Gematria is congruent to the Kabbalah, and it consists in a system of correspondences between letters and numbers, which allows one to investigate the relation between words or phrases that have identical numerical values. This is not a vulgar system of numerology, but it is a complex and creative way of reading and thinking that helps one to understand and appreciate the literary and conceptual beauty, complexity, and brilliance of sacred texts. The Hebrew Gematria applies to the Old Testament, which was written in Hebrew, and the Greek Gematria, which is based on Pythagorean numerology, applies to the New Testament, which was written in Greek.

For instance, the numerical value of the Tetragrammaton (the ineffable name of God in Judaism) is 26. In particular, the Tetragrammaton (Yehovah) consists of the following four Hebrew letters, which are characterized by the following correspondences:

Yod = 10 (Fire)
He = 5 (Water)
Vav = 6 (Air)
He = 5 (Earth).

Furthermore, the number 26 corresponds to the Middle Pillar of the Kabbalistic Tree of Life:

First sefira: Kether: 1
Sixth sefira: Tifereth: 6
Ninth sefira: Yesod: 9
Tenth sefira: Malkuth: 10
Sum: 1+6+9+10 = 26.

According to the terminology of Plotinus's *Enneads*, Malkuth is "Nature," and Kether is "Nous" (mind); everything between them signifies stages of becoming. However, many philosophies, especially, Oriental ones, have been confused by the intense desire of the human nous (mind) to unite with

---

with Greek scientific works. Ibn Khaldun writes that, at the beginning, the Arabs disregarded the crafts, but, eventually, they developed a sedentary civilization, they became versed in many different crafts and sciences, and, ultimately, they desired to study philosophy.

the Source. This bewilderment has given rise to various dualistic doctrines, whose advocates, having failed to understand the dynamic unity between the Physical and the Spiritual, completely disregard the human body. For instance, in the context of particular Gnostic dualistic 'schools,' the material nature, in general, and the human body, in particular, are viewed as a prison to the omnipotent Spirit, leaving the following basic questions unanswered: How omnipotent is a spirit that can be confined by something as frail as the human body? How omnipotent is a spirit that is not free, but it is pervaded by deterministic laws of spiritual progression and regression? Moreover, in the context of Dionysius the Areopagite's hierarchical ordering of beings, matter is not merely described as non-being, since, according to Dionysius the Areopagite, there is an epistemological, yet non-ontological, continuity between the Source and the created material world.

When and to the extent that, during our life in the physical plane, we are united with the Absolute, precisely, with the source of the significance and *telos* of the beings and things in world, we should live in such a way as to gain as much experience as humanly possible. From this perspective—that is, when and to the extent that a human being, as a psychosomatic whole, lives in the physical plane united with the Absolute, that is, with the ultimate, transcendent meaning of life—experience is knowledge, existence is pure joy, and sorrow is knowledge without understanding. Man can only understand his historical adventure if he is united with the Absolute, and, thus, if he is capable of viewing beings and things from the perspective of their significance. The capability of viewing beings and things from the perspective of their significance, that is, divinely, precludes sorrow and depression. Thus, the first word that Jesus Christ said to his disciples after his Resurrection was "Rejoice!"[1] In the same spirit, the Apostle Paul, having understood that the end of the human being is to experience Jesus Christ's Resurrection, and, thus, to be deified, writes to the Philippians: "Rejoice in the Lord always! Again I will say, 'Rejoice!'"[2]

G. The Bavarian Illuminati: Their rise and fall

The term 'Illuminati' (plural of the Latin term *Illuminatus*, enlightened) usually refers to the Bavarian Illuminati, an esoteric society founded on May 1, 1776, by Adam Weishaupt (1748-1830), who was the first lay professor of Canon Law at the University of Ingolstadt.[3] The Order of the Illuminati

---

1 Matthew 28:8.
2 Philippians 4:4.
3 The suppression of the Jesuit Order in 1773 by Pope Clement XIV made it possible for Adam Weishaupt, who was not a Jesuit, to assume the post of Professor of Canon Law at the University of Ingolstadt.

was modelled on Freemasonry, and it was made up of freethinkers.[1] Given that, by the middle of the eighteenth century, many Freemasonic Orders had been placed under the control of despotic social elites and Royal Houses and many Freemasons had developed a petty-bourgeois mentality, Adam Weishaupt attempted to politicize the humanist ethos of Freemasonry by creating a new esoteric society whose members would be capable of contemplating the political ramifications of Freemasonic and Rosicrucian moral legends and teachings and of undertaking humanist and essentially liberating political initiatives. According to the instructions that Weishaupt wrote for the Illuminati's Regent Degree, if the Order of the Illuminati cannot establish itself in any particular place with all the forms and regular progress of its degree system, it must operate under a cloak of secrecy, and "the inferior Lodges of Freemasonry are the most convenient cloaks" for the Illuminati's grand object. Weishaupt himself was initiated in the Masonic Lodge "Theodor zum guten Rath" at Munich in 1777. The degree system of the Order of the Illuminati is as follows: Novice, Minerval, Illuminatus Minor, Illuminatus Major, Illuminatus Dirigens, Epopt (or Priest of Illuminism), Regent (or Prince of Illuminism), Magus-Philosopher, and Rex (or Man-King).

Very soon after the foundation of the Order of the Bavarian Illuminati, a fierce disagreement broke out between Adam Weishaupt, who was the Chairman of the Illuminati's Areopagus (peak administrative apparatus), and Adolph Freiherr von Knigge, who was a very influential member of the Illuminati's Areopagus and senior official of the Freemasonic Order of Strict Observance. Whereas Weishaupt was oriented toward the classical Greek civilization and the golden age of the ancient city-state of Athens, and he wanted to promote a radical political program for the liberation of humanity from corrupt despotic regimes and superstition, von Knigge was oriented toward his contemporary romantic neo-mythologies about the Knights Templar and Oriental schools of mystical belief. Inspired by classical Greece, Weishaupt combined metaphysics with the affirmation of history, and, indeed, he endorsed the metaphysics of the early Christian Church in order to endow his program for the liberation of humanity with ontological underpinnings. On the other hand, von Knigge's Oriental mysticism was 'infected' by the peculiar historical nihilism that characterizes many Oriental spiritual schools, which deny the value of history, and, thus, they yearn for the end of this world and pursue man's individuation only in another world.

---

1 Originally called the Order of the Perfectibilists, Weishaupt's Order of the Illuminati should not be confused with other esoteric societies that have used the terms 'Illuminatus,' or 'Illuminati,' such as, for instance, the Société des Illuminés d'Avignon (founded in 1786 by Dom Antoine-Joseph de Pernéty) and the VIIIth Degree of Aleister Crowley's Ordo Templi Orientis.

In 1777, Karl Theodor, a proponent of Enlightened Despotism, became ruler of Bavaria, and, in 1785, he banned all secret societies, including the Illuminati. Thus, the Order of the Illuminati was shattered in Bavaria. However, Adam Weishaupt had already resigned from his official position of power in the Order at an Illuminati congress convened in Weimar in 1784. The authoritarian Bavarian political regime that was established by Karl Theodor and the Jesuits conducted a vicious propaganda campaign against Adam Weishaupt and the Illuminati in Bavaria and throughout Europe. Moreover, many Freemasons, mainly out of fear of being persecuted by political and religious authorities, denounced the Illuminati.

In his own defense of the Order of the Illuminati, Weishaupt[1] explained that the proper candidate for the Order of the Illuminati is a person who has the following qualities: (i) he "does not close his ear to the lamentations of the miserable"; (ii) he does not close his heart to "gentle pity"; (iii) he is "the friend and brother of the unfortunate"; (iv) he has "a heart capable of love and friendship"; (v) he is "steadfast in adversity, unwearied in the carrying out of whatever has been once engaged in, undaunted in the overcoming of difficulties"; (vi) he "does not mock and despise the weak"; (vii) he is "susceptible of conceiving great designs, desirous of rising superior to all base motives, and of distinguishing himself by deeds of benevolence"; (viii) he "shuns idleness"; (ix) he "considers no knowledge as unessential which he may have the opportunity of acquiring, regarding the knowledge of mankind as his chief study"; (x) "when truth and virtue are in question", he is "sufficiently courageous to follow the dictates of his own heart," "despising the approbation of the multitude." Furthermore, in the Epopt Degree of the Order of the Illuminati, Adam Weishaupt exposed his revolutionary vision about the autonomy and happiness of mankind, and he clarified that "Morality shall alone produce this great Revolution."

According to the rituals of the Order of the Illuminati, the members of the Illuminatus Major Degree should obtain a deep awareness of the following issues: the extent to which men have failed to actualize their ontological potential; the extent to which and the manners in which civil institutions have degenerated into new kinds of despotism; the errors that lie in the means that have been hitherto employed by the sages; the abandonment of the world to "the yoke of the wicked"; the persecution and misfortune of the honest man in the present, corrupt polities; and the sacrifice of the better part of humanity to selfish interest. In addition, according to their ritual, the members of the Illuminatus Major Degree should promise to co-operate with the other members of the Order of the Illuminati in order to promote

---

1 Adam Weishaupt has elucidated the ethos and the structure of the Order of the Illuminati in his book entitled *Apologie der Illuminaten* (1786).

the spiritual and political emancipation of humanity. Weishaupt's political thought was founded on his conceptions of natural law, natural freedom, and natural way of life.

The Epopt Degree of the Order of the Illuminati places the candidate under much more solemn and weighty obligations, and it urges him to work for the establishment of the "empire of reason," in the context of which political and spiritual prejudices and contradictions will be eliminated and all the people will be capable of undertaking their existential responsibilities and of governing themselves. Furthermore, according to the Illuminati's rituals and Weishaupt's directions, promotion to the Regent Degree presupposed that the candidate was "as much as possible free man and independent of all Princes" and also that the candidate had shown how ardently he wished for a change in the political system. In particular, according to Weishaupt's "Code of the Illuminati," the Epopts who were worthy to be promoted to the Regent Degree are persons that unite prudence with the liberty of thinking and acting, that know how to combine transcendence of wit with gravity and dignity of manners, and that their heart is entirely devoted to the Order's mission for the welfare of humanity. Thus, according to the Regent Degree Ritual, the initiator tells the candidate: "You are now strong enough to conduct yourself, be then in future your own guide . . . Be free; that is to say, be a man, and a man who knows how to govern himself, a man who knows his duty, and his inalienable rights . . . Here, take back the engagements you have hitherto contracted with us. To you we return them all."

On January 31, 1800, Thomas Jefferson,[1] the principal author of the United States Declaration of Independence (1776) and third President of the United States of America, wrote to Bishop James Madison about Adam Weishaupt and about the Illuminati and Freemasonry. In his correspondence with Madison, Jefferson argued as follows: Weishaupt was a humanist, he believed in the infinite moral improvement of mankind, and he wanted to develop people's capacity for self-government; Weishaupt's political views were touching closest to William Godwin's anarchist political philosophy, and, therefore, absolutist religious and political authorities, using propaganda mechanisms and techniques, attempted to present Weishaupt's political principles as "a conspiracy against all government"; Weishaupt believed in the purity of the early Christian Church's ethos and wanted to restore it through the moral system of the Order of the Illuminati, since, according to Weishaupt, Freemasons had failed to do so and most Freemasonic Orders had lost touch with the genuine meaning of their rituals and were infiltrated by representatives of political and spiritual despotism; Weishaupt created a

---

1 See: *The Thomas Jefferson Papers*, Washington, D.C.: The Library of Congress, Federal Edition.

secret society in order to protect himself and other freethinkers against the tyrannical regime of Bavaria.

The history and the ethos of Weishaupt's Bavarian Illuminati remind every true Freemason of the diachronic need for a global humanist 'conspiracy' against tyrannical political and spiritual regimes, against material decadence and poverty, against depression, as well as against superstition. On the other hand, Weishaupt's attempt to create a new humanist movement was fragmentary, and, therefore, it ultimately degraded into a source of inspiration for conspiracy theorists, fanciful mimics, and various pseudo-Illuminati organizations. Moreover, even though Weishaupt intended to philosophically and politically found his Bavarian Illuminati on the ethos of classical Athens (i.e., of the Athenian society of the fifth century BC), he mainly embraced Rousseau's primitivism and social contract theory, ignoring the anthropological and, broadly, spiritual difference between classical Athens and Rousseau's political philosophy.

Jean-Jacques Rousseau (1712–78) proposes the merits of the primitive natural way of life and the idea of virtue as it was cultivated in ancient Greek city-states. According to Rousseau, the established type of modern state cannot cultivate virtue, because it is an artificial and mechanistic association in which the logic of money and power prevails. Rousseau and Weishaupt seek to restore humanity to what they consider to be its natural state of freedom. As George H. Sabine and Thomas L. Thorson have pointedly argued, the true hero of Rousseau's primitivism was "the irritated and bewildered bourgeois."[1] Both Rousseau and Weishaupt maintain that their ideal of a society formed by social contract is based on the ethos of the ancient Greek city-state. But, even though Rousseau and Weishaupt were influenced by the political system of classical Athens, and they were looking back with admiration to the city-states of ancient Greece, Rousseau's and Weishaupt's political thought is conditioned by modern Western conceptions of 'society' and 'individuality.' In the context of modern Western political thought, the concept of justice is focused on the modern subject's rights, precisely, on the protection of individual rights, whereas, in the context of classical Greek civilization, the concept of justice is inextricably linked to the sociality of the ancient Greek man, precisely, it refers to the idea that each citizen contributes to the prosperity of his city-state in proportion to his respective abilities.

There is a sharp anthropological and ontological difference between ancient Greece's sociocentric political thought and modern Europe's collectivist theories. Based on rather ambiguous ideological conceptions of

---

1 Sabine, G. H., and Thorson, T. L., *A History of Political Theory*, 4th edition, Fort Worth: Holt, Rinehart and Winston, 1973, p. 531.

social equality and on organic and, hence, totalitarian conceptions of social unity, modern collectivist political theorists, such as Rousseau (who ushered the age of totalitarian democracy by equating the will of the collectivity, or 'the people,' with the will of God), Weishaupt, and Karl Marx, interpret man as a being determined by historical and natural necessities, and, ultimately, they degrade man into a bio-economic unit. Such a degradation of the human being was impossible in the context of classical Greek civilization, because, from the perspective of classical Greek political thought, social unity does not consist in a form of cooperation among individual owners of economic wealth, simply because the modern cultural-anthropological category of the individual is irrelevant and, indeed, alien to classical Greek civilization. From the perspective of the modern Western subject, 'nobility' primarily refers to and depends on what one possesses in terms of private property and individual power, whereas, from the perspective of the ancient Greek person, 'nobility' primarily refers to and depends on what one can contribute to the well-being of his community in order to be worthy of it.

4. Ancient And Accepted Scottish Rite

By the term Ancient and Accepted Scottish Rite, or simply Scottish Rite, we mean a Masonic Order that consists of thirty-three degrees, precisely of the three Craft degrees (i.e., the Entered Apprentice, the Fellow Craft, and the Master Mason Degrees) plus thirty more degrees. However, in several Masonic Obediences around the world, Craft Lodges operate under the authority of Grand Lodges, not the Scottish Rite, that is, in such Obediences, the Scottish Rite does not exercise authority over its first three degrees, recognizing the independence of the Craft from the Scottish Rite. There are usually five coordinate bodies within a Scottish Rite Jurisdiction, namely:

1. Lodge of Perfection: it controls the degrees 4th through 14th, known also as the Ineffable Degrees, since their principal purpose is the investigation and contemplation of the ineffable name of the deity. The presiding officer of a Lodge of Perfection is called the Venerable Master.

2. Chapter of Rose-Croix: it controls the degrees 15th through 18th, whose purpose is to invest the candidate with a deeper understanding of religion, philosophy, ethics, and history. The presiding officer of a Rose-Croix Chapter is called the Wise Master.

3. Council of Kadosh: it controls the degrees 19th through 30th, which have a chivalric, philosophical, and mystical character. The presiding officer of a Lodge of Perfection is called the Commander.

4. Consistory: it controls the degrees 31st and 32nd, which are concerned with the relationship between the spiritual and the temporal. The presiding officer of a Consistory is called the Master of Kadosh.

5. Supreme Council: it consists of the holders of the 33rd Degree, and it is the supreme authority of the Scottish Rite within its corresponding Jurisdiction. The presiding officer of a Supreme Council is called the Grand Commander.

The Scottish Rite Degrees are the following:

Symbolic Lodge: Degrees 1°–3° are identical with the three Craft degrees:
The three great, symbolic lights in Freemasonry are the Volume of Sacred Law (i.e., the Holy Bible), the Square, and the Set of Compasses. The Volume of Sacred Law is a manifestation of the Divine Logos. The Square is a symbol of morality, and the Set of Compasses is a symbol of self-mastery. The three lesser lights of Freemasonry are situated East, South, and West, respectively representing the Sun, that is, the ruler of the day, the Moon, that is, the ruler of the night, and the Master of the Lodge, that is, the facilitator of the Lodge.

The symbolic meaning of the First Degree Tracing Board was expounded by the distinguished Scottish author and Freemason William Preston in his book entitled *Illustrations of Masonry*, published in 1772, as follows:

The form of a Symbolic Lodge is a regular parallelepipedon, whose length extends from East to West; its breadth extends from North to South; and it is as deep as the earth and as high as the heavens; these dimensions of a Symbolic Lodge symbolize the universality of Symbolic Masonry and the infinity of a True Freemason's charity.

A Symbolic Lodge is situated due East and West, because the material Sun, which is a *sine qua non* source of material life and a natural symbol of the uncreated Glory of God, namely, of the divine Sun, rises in the East and sets in the West. Moreover, the noblest form of culture originated in the East, and, thence, it expanded westward.

Masonic Lodges are supported by three great pillars, which are called Wisdom, Strength, and Beauty, and they respectively represent Solomon King of Israel, because of his Wisdom in building, completing, and dedicating the Temple at Jerusalem to God's service, Hiram King of Tyre, because of his Strength in supporting King Solomon with men and materials, and Hiram

Abiff, because of his profound workmanship in beautifying and adorning King Solomon's Temple. Moreover, the three great pillars of a Masonic Lodge, namely, Wisdom, Strength, and Beauty, correspond to the following three noble Architectural Orders: the Ionic, the Doric, and the Corinthian, respectively.

The ceiling of a Masonic Lodge symbolically corresponds to the Heavens, to which Freemasons hope to ascend by the assistance of a mysterious ladder, in Scripture called Jacob's ladder. It is composed of many staves or rounds, which point out as many virtues. However, the three principal virtues are Faith (F), Hope (H), and Charity (C): Faith in God, Hope in salvation, and to be in Charity with all men. The previous mysterious ladder reaches to the Heavens, and it rests on the Volume of the Sacred Law.

The floor of a Masonic Lodge is a Mosaic pavement, which, by reason of its being variegated and chequered, points out that the sensible world is characterized by duality, contradictions, and diversity.

The Blazing Star, or Glory in the center of a Masonic Lodge refers us to the uncreated light of God's grace, which enlightens the human mind.

The Indented or Tessellated Border refers us to the Planets, the eternal physical beings, or the celestial spheres, which imitate the perfection of the divine mode of life through their harmonious motions. As Aristotle writes in his *Physics*, V, 265a, God is the direct object of the universal eros that characterizes the celestial spheres.

The Furniture of the Lodge consists of the Volume of the Sacred Law, the Square, and the Set of Compasses.

The Jewels of the Lodge are three movable and three immovable. The Movable Jewels are the following: the Square, which teaches morality; the Level, which teaches unity in diversity and equality in difference; and the Plumb Rule, which is a symbol of rectitude of conduct, integrity of life, and that uprightness of moral character which makes a good and just man. The Master is distinguished by the Square, the Senior Warden by the Level, and the Junior Warden by the Plumb Rule. The Immovable Jewels are the Tracing Board, the Rough Ashlar, and the Perfect Ashlar. The Tracing Board is for the Master to lay lines and draw designs on; the Rough Ashlar for the Apprentice to work, mark, and indent on; and the Perfect Ashlar for the experienced Craftsman to try, and adjust, his jewels on.

The working tools of an Apprentice are the 24-inch Gauge, the common Gavel, and Chisel. The 24-inch Gauge is a measurement tool that refers us to the twenty-four hours of the day, which we should use wisely. The common Gavel symbolizes the force of conscience: we resort to our inner judge, precisely, to our conscience, because conscience has correctly been characterized as "the natural Bible," and those who study it have an experience of divine perception; additionally, our conscience knows our intentions, and, therefore, it can inform us about what is really good and judge dishonesty. The Chisel is an emblem of the advantages of education, which underpin true nobility.

William Preston, in his book entitled *Illustrations of Masonry*, published in 1772, expounded the Second Degree Tracing Board as follows:

At the porchway or entrance of the Temple at Jerusalem, which was completed by King Solomon, there were two magnificent, great Pillars. That on the left was called Boaz, which denotes in strength; that one the right Jachin, which denotes to establish; and when conjoined stability; for God said: "In strength I will establish this Mine house to stand firm forever." Those Pillars were made of molten brass, and the superintendent of the casting was Hiram Abiff.

Those Pillars were adorned with two chapiters, which were enriched with network, which denotes unity, lily-work, which denotes peace, and pomegranates, which denote plenty. Additionally, those Pillars were adorned with two spherical balls on which ware delineated maps of the celestial and terrestrial globes, pointing out the universality of the Craft.

At the building of King Solomon's Temple, many Masons were employed, and they had their own place, which was called the Middle Chamber. They got there by the porchway or entrance on the south side. After those Masons had entered the porch, they arrived at the foot of the winding staircase which led to the Middle Chamber. The qualifications requisite to gain admittance to that Middle Chamber were Fidelity, Hospitality, and Taciturnity. When Masons were in the Middle Chamber of the Temple, their attention was peculiarly drawn to the Mosaic Pavement, the Blazing Star, the Tasselled Border, and the letter G. The Mosaic Pavement represents the Law delivered by God to Moses on Mount Sinai. The Blazing Star represents the Glory of God appearing on Mount Sinai at the deliverance of that Law. The Tasseled Border represents ornaments of a virtuous life, living in conformity to that Law. The letter G stands for Geometry and Gnosis. In this case, Gnosis means that kind of knowledge which is derived from the uncreated grace of God, that is, from the divine illumination of the human mind.

In the entire history of humanity, only one Temple has ever been more important than King Solomon's Temple: the mystical Temple of Christ's body. The qualifications requisite to gain admittance into this Temple's Middle Chamber are Faith, Hope, and Charity.

The working tools of a Companion are the Square, which teaches morality, the Level, which teaches equality, and the Plumb Rule, which teaches justness and uprightness of life and actions.

According to William Preston's *Illustrations of Masonry*, the Third Degree Tracing Board represents the tomb of Hiram Abiff in accordance with the Hiramic legend, which I expounded in Chapter 3. The working tools of a

Master Mason are the following: the Skirret, which points out that straight and undeviating line of conduct laid down for our pursuit in the Volume of Sacred Law; the Pencil, which symbolizes moral responsibility; and the Set of Compasses, which reminds us of God's perfect justice.

First Degree Tracing Board, engraved by F. Curtis, printed by John Cole in his *Illustrations of Freemasonry* published in 1801:

Figure 4: The Tracing Boards of the three Degrees of Symbolic Masonry[1]

---

1 See Dwor, Mark S., "The Tracing Boards," presented at the Vancouver Grand Masonic Day, October 16, 1999, Centennial-King George Lodge No. 171; see: http://freemasonry.bcy.ca/texts/gmd1999/tb_history03.html

From left to right: Second Degree and Third Degree Tracing Boards, engraved by F. Curtis, printed by John Cole in his *Illustrations of Freemasonry* published in 1801:

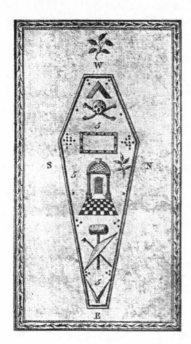 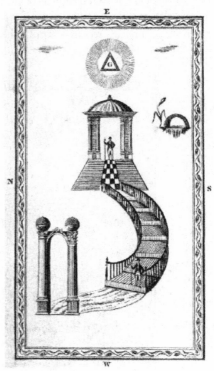

Lodge of Perfection:

4° Secret Master: in this degree, the aspirant undertakes to use the secrets of the Master Mason Degree in order to improve oneself.

5° Perfect Master: symbolically speaking, the Perfect Masters are those Freemasons who have buried Hiram Abiff. The Freemasons who are initiated into this degree are aware that they must first bury the 'old man' before they become capable of acting for the good of humanity, that is, they must achieve self-mastery and dispel the clouds of superstition and of prejudice.

6° Intimate Secretary: this degree teaches that we must first achieve inner balance before we become capable of offering spiritual or psychological help to others.

7° Provost and Judge: this degree teaches that we must embrace the following maxim: "with whatever measure you measure, it will be measured to you."[1]

8° Intendant of the Building: this degree teaches that the cooperation among all Freemasons is a necessary prerequisite for the accomplishment of the Freemasonic Work, and that international cooperation can avert several evils, including unjust wars.

9° Elu (or Elected Master/Knight) of the Nine: according to the didactic legend of this degree, one of the Elus of the Nine, acting in self-defense, killed one of Hiram Abiff's assassins, and, because of his action, he almost voluntarily appeared before the Court in order to give an account of his doings.

10° Elu (or Illustrious Elect) of the Fifteen: according to the didactic legend of this degree, the rest of Hiram Abiff's assassins were arrested, they were taken to King Solomon's Court to stand trial, and they were ultimately found guilty and executed. The ninth and tenth degrees teach that no one should take the law into one's own hands, and that no one should resist to the true and regular administration of justice.

11° Elu (or Sublime Knight Elect) of the Twelve: this degree teaches that a Freemason should be a defender of human rights.

12° Master Architect

13° Royal Arch of Solomon: The twelfth and the thirteenth degrees teach that only through the complete and correct fulfillment of one's duty and through the complete and correct actualization of the noble potentialities of the human being can humanity accomplish great achievements. The legend of the Royal Arch is based on the rediscovery of God's name by the Israelites during the rebuilding of the Jerusalem Temple, in accordance with what I mentioned in Chapter 3 with regard to the Holy Order of the Royal Arch.

14° Perfect Elu (or Grand Elect, Perfect and Sublime Mason): this degree refers to those sages who preserved the deepest knowledge, the memory, and the name of the Great Architect of the Universe, even after the Grand Masters of the Temple, that is, the true Gnostics (namely, the true masters of the sacred Gnosis/Knowledge), were dispersed and taken captive by King Nebuchadnezzar II of Babylon after the destruction of the Jerusalem Temple (sixth century BC). The jewel of the fourteenth degree is a set of compasses, opened upon a quarter of a circle, and surmounted by a pointed crown; between the legs of the set of compasses is a medal representing, on one side, the sun and, on the other, a five-pointed star, in the center of which is a delta and on that the Holy Tetragrammaton (that is, the name of God in Hebrew characters: Yod-He-Vav-He).

---

1 Matthew 7:2.

Chapter of Rose-Croix:

15° Knight of the East, of the Sword, or of the Eagle: this degree is dedicated to Zerubbabel. In 538 BC, the Persian King Cyrus II, who had already captured Babylon, issued a decree allowing the Jews to return home to "rebuild the house of the Lord, the God of Israel,"[1] and he restored the Temple's treasures that the Babylonians had stolen. Zerubbabel was placed in charge of the returning Jews and given the title "governor of Judah." Zerubbabel kept his promise to rebuild the Temple of Jerusalem. Zerubbabel's leadership was by right and recognition: he was a descendant of David, and he had personal leadership qualities. When the Jews returned to Jerusalem, they established living quarters, and they were called to begin to work. They began neither by building city walls nor by constructing public buildings, but by rebuilding the altar, worshiping God together. Under Zerubbabel's leadership, the Jews founded their building efforts on spirituality. A key Biblical excerpt about the ethos of Zerubbabel and his regime is the following: "This is the word of the LORD to Zerubbabel, saying, 'Not by might, nor by power, but by my Spirit,' says the LORD Almighty. Who are you, great mountain? Before Zerubbabel you are a plain; and he will bring out the capstone with shouts of 'Grace, grace, to it!'"[2]

16° Prince of Jerusalem: this degree, in continuation of the fifteenth degree, narrates that, under the protection of King Darius, who was the successor of King Cyrus II, the Jews subdued the Samaritans, who had been heckling the Jews' efforts to rebuild the Jerusalem Temple, and, thus, ultimately, the Jews managed to indulge undisturbed in their building efforts. The subjugation of the Samaritans by the Jews teaches that Freemasons must willfully and wisely subdue their passions and remain faithful to their duty in order to work together harmoniously for the building of a civilization that will glorify God.

17° Knight of the East and West: this degree is the completion of the previous two ones, and it refers to the conquest of the Holy Land by the Crusaders in the eleventh century AD. Even though the Ancient and Accepted Scottish Rite (AASR) rejects the methods and, generally, the militaristic mentality of the medieval Papacy's religious warriors, the seventeenth degree of the AASR refers to the Crusading Order of Malta as a type of synthesis between Eastern spirituality and Western historical activism and as a model of international cooperation for achieving a noble goal.

18° Knight Rose-Croix: this degree is dedicated to Rosicrucianism, to which I referred in Chapter 1, and to Jesus Christ as the channel of God's love in our world. According to the 18th Degree Ritual, the candidate is

---

1 Ezra 1:3.
2 Zechariah 4:6–7

symbolically admitted in a Chapter of Knights Rose-Croix "at the ninth hour of the day," when the earth quakes, the rocks are rent, the veil of the Temple is rent in twain and darkness overspreads the earth, highlighting the Passion Narrative in Matthew 27:50–51. In a series of highly mystical experiences, the 18th Degree Ceremony expresses the figurative passage of man through the darkest veil, accompanied and sustained by the three theological virtues (namely, Faith, Hope, and Charity), and it teaches that, assisted by these virtues, the candidate will succeed in attaining the Rosicrucians' ultimate goal, which is that Word on which the eternal salvation of humanity depends, namely, "Emmanuel."

The manner in which the Rose-Croix Degree is worked by the United Traditionalist Grand Sanctuaries of the Ancient and Primitive Rite Memphis–Misraim seeks to inculcate a thorough understanding of the Christ Mystery. In his *Two Hundred Texts on Theology and the Incarnate Dispensation of the Son of God (written for Thalassius)*, Maximus the Confessor elucidates the mystery that is hidden in the age at which Jesus Christ started his earthly ministry.[1] According to the New Testament, Jesus Christ started his earthly ministry when he became thirty years old. When adequately understood, Maximus the Confessor maintains, the number thirty (30) presents Lord Jesus Christ as the Creator and Preserver of time and nature as well as of the world of ideas, because of the following reason: the number seven alludes to the Creator of time, because time is divided into weeks and each week has seven days, and because, according to Moses's cosmogony, "on the seventh day God ended his work which he had done";[2] the number five alludes to the Creator of nature, because there are five senses; the number eight alludes to the Creator of the intelligible world, or the world of ideas, because the intelligible world transcends the sensible (temporal) world, and the latter is represented by the number seven; the number ten alludes to the Preserver of the world, because, according to the Bible, God gave ten Commandments for the moral perfection of mankind,[3] and because the first letter of the name of the Incarnate Logos in Greek—namely, ΙΗΣΟΥΣ (JESUS)—is the tenth letter of the Greek alphabet. Thus, if we add the numbers five, seven, eight, and ten, we get the important symbolic number thirty. If we add the number three—that is, the number of the Holy Trinity—to the number thirty, we get the number thirty-three, which symbolizes the Exaltation of Jesus Christ.

To explain the meaning of the Christian Trinitarian formula, one can use the following metaphor about a poet, e.g., T.S. Eliot: the poetry of T.S. Eliot is his 'logos', or word; Eliot's word proceeds from Eliot's 'nous' (mind); and

---

1 See *The Philokalia*, Vol. 2, edited and translated in English by Bishop Kallistos Ware, G. E. H. Palmer, and Philip Sherrard, London: Faber and Faber, 1982.
2 Genesis 2:2.
3 Exodus 20:1–17; Deuteronomy 5:4–21.

Eliot's word gives to its readers the 'spirit' of Eliot, i.e., a special feeling of participation in the personal world of Eliot. The spirit of Eliot remains with the readers of Eliot's word even when they do not have his poems in front of them. By analogy, 'God the Father' is the Nous, or Mind, of God, 'God the Son' is the Logos, or Word, of God, and the 'Holy Spirit' is the Spirit of God. However, in the case of the Holy Trinity, the Nous of God (Father), the Logos of God (Son), and the Spirit of God (Holy Spirit) are not attributes or functions of a being, but they are three Hypostases (modes of being) of the same Divine Nature.

Pontius Pilate—who served as the fifth prefect of the Roman province of Judaea under Emperor Tiberius and is best known from the biblical account of the trial and crucifixion of Jesus[1]—represents natural law. The Jews who shouted against Jesus, "Crucify! Crucify!"[2] and that "he must die, because he claimed to be the Son of God,"[3] represent written law. He who has not been raised above both natural law and written law through the mystery of faith cannot accept the truth that transcends nature and reason, and he crucifies the divine Logos, assuming that the Gospel is a "stumbling block" or a "foolishness."[4]

Figure 5: The Knight Rose-Croix emblem: a set of compasses surmounted by a rose and celestial crown, a rose-cross is between the legs of the set of compasses, and under it is a pelican pecking its breast to feed its seven young (an ancient symbol of the Savior); the inscription I.N.R.I. means 'Iesus Nazarenus Rex Iudaeorum' (i.e., Jesus, the Nazarene, the King of the Jews) and the alchemical aphorism 'Igne Natura Renovatur Integra' (i.e., All Nature will be Renewed by Fire).

Council of Kadosh:

19° Grand Pontiff: Pontiff literally means bridge-builder, and, thus, the nineteenth degree teaches that we should build bridges among humans, serving the principles of Justice, Truth, and Toleration.

---

1 Matthew 27:2, 19; John 18:31–37, 19:12–13; Mark 15:5, 15.
2 John 19:6.
3 Ibid., 19:7.
4 1 Corinthians 1:23.

20° Master of the Symbolic Lodge, or Grand Master of All Symbolic Lodges: this degree teaches the aspirant that, actually, a Freemason is a philosopher who experiences philosophy as a way of life whose end is one's union with the deity. Additionally, this degree informs the aspirant that, on certain occasions, during the course of history, ignorance and humble aspirations engaged in the fabrication of particular Masonic degrees, and that whoever has received the twentieth degree of the AASR has to be a vigilant instructor of pure, ancient Masonry and a true master of oneself. The virtues that help to give us that mastery are represented by the angles of five squares and three triangles on the Twentieth Degree Tracing Board:

The Squares:
The first square represents Prudence, Temperance, Chastity, and Sobriety.
The second square represents Heroism, Firmness, Equanimity, and Patience.
The third square represents Purity, Honor, Fidelity, and Punctuality.
The fourth square represents Charity, Kindness, Generosity, and Liberality.
The fifth square represents Disinterestedness, Mercy, Forgiveness, and Forbearance.

The Triangles:
The first triangle represents Veneration, Devotedness, and Patriotism.
The second triangle represents Gratitude to God, Love of Mankind, and Confidence in human nature.
The third triangle represents Truth, Justice, and Toleration.

21° Noachite, or Prussian Knight: this degree teaches justice, and that it is our duty to shield and protect the innocent and to assist the distressed.

22° Knight of the Royal Axe, Prince of Libanus: the name of this degree commemorates a contract that was made between Solomon King of Israel and Hiram King of Tyre, wherein cedar logs from the mountains of Lebanon and pine were gathered and sent downstream for the specific purpose of building the Temple of Jerusalem. In particular, in 2 Chronicles 2:3, we read the following: "Solomon sent to Hiram King of Tyre, saying, 'As you dealt with David my father, and sent him cedars to build him a house in which to dwell, so deal with me.'" The twenty-second degree teaches that labor is honorable, and that we should strive to improve the condition of humanity by remaining focused on the principle of the 'sacred.'

23° Chief of the Tabernacle: this degree is focused on the Tabernacle, which, according to the Bible, was the portable dwelling place for the divine presence from the time of the Exodus from Egypt through the conquering of the land of Canaan, and its form is distinctly defined.[1] In the book of Exodus, chapters 25 through 31 record God's directions for building the Tabernacle: the high quality of the precious metals that were used for the construction of the Tabernacle show God's greatness and transcendence; the curtain surrounding the Most Holy Place shows God's moral perfection as symbolized by his separation from the profane and unclean; the portable nature of the Tabernacle shows that God wanted to be with his people as they traveled. The twenty-third degree of the AASR teaches that only those who are psychically cleansed of all impurity are commended in the performance of the holy rites.

24° Prince of the Tabernacle: this degree is a continuation of the previous one, and it teaches the aspirant that he must labor incessantly for the glory of God, the honor of his nation, and the happiness of his brothers and sisters, as well as to offer thanks and prayers to God in lieu of old-type, material sacrifices.

25° Knight of the Brazen Serpent: this degree relates to the time when, after the death of Aaron, the Israelite community "traveled from Mount Hor by the way to the Red Sea, to go around the land of Edom," and "the soul of the people was very discouraged because of the journey," and they "spoke against God and against Moses."[2] God used venomous snakes to make the people realize the consequences of their unbelief and grievance. Finally, the people realized their error, and they said to Moses: "We have sinned, because we have spoken against Yahweh and against you. Pray to Yahweh, that he take away the serpents from us."[3] Moses, following God's instructions, "made a serpent of bronze, and set it on the pole. If a serpent had bitten any man, when he looked at the serpent of bronze, he lived."[4] It was not the brazen snake that healed the people, but their belief that God would heal them and their focus on the ultimate purpose of their journey. Jesus Christ explained that, just as the Israelites were healed of their sickness by looking at the brazen snake on the pole, all believers today can be saved from the sickness of sin by looking at Jesus's Crucifixion.[5] The duties of the Knight of the Brazen Serpent is to purify the soul in order to become spiritually free and participate in the ultimate source of being.

26° Prince of Mercy: this degree honors the memory of the Christians who were secretly gathering in Catacombs under Rome, during the reign of the Emperor Diocletian (284-305 AD), which marked the final widespread

---

1 Exodus 25:1ff.
2 Numbers 21:4–5.
3 Ibid., 21:7.
4 Ibid., 21:9.
5 John 3:14–15.

persecution of Christians in the Roman Empire. In addition, in this degree, the aspirant is encouraged to study the spiritual traditions that are hidden in the Buddhist pagoda on the Isle of Salsette, in the roofless fanes of Persia, in the forest temples of the Druids, in the pyramids of Memphis, in the vaults of Crete and Samothrace, in the great temple of Eleusis, and in the inner sanctuary of the Jerusalem Temple. The emblem of the 26th Degree is as follows: an equilateral triangle of gold; in the center of the triangle, also of gold, is a flaming heart; engraved on the heart are the letters I∴H∴S∴, which stand for 'Iesus Hominum Salvator' (Jesus the Savior of Humanity) and 'Imperium, Harmonia, Sapientia' (Empire, Harmony, Wisdom).

27° Knight Commander of the Temple: Even though the Ancient and Accepted Scottish Rite rejects the use of weapons as a means for propagating any religion, this degree refers to the Knights Templar and, generally, to the medieval Crusaders in order to inculcate the chivalric values of Humility, Temperance, Chastity, Generosity, and Honor, as well as in order use the medieval Crusaders as symbols of heroic commitment to a noble goal.

28° Knight of the Sun, or Prince Adept: this degree is focused on the sun in order to symbolize pure monotheism, the presence of God's light in Nature, and the divine illumination of the human mind.

A 28th-Degree Chapter is structured as follows: in the East is the seal of the Macrocosm (i.e., the hexagram of Solomon) with the up-pointing triangle in black and the down-pointing triangle in white, and under the words "Lux e Tenebris"; in the West is the seal of the Microcosm (i.e., the Pentagram) in white and vermillion; in the South is a representation of the Temple of Solomon with a man holding a lamb between the columns of Jachin and Boaz; in the North is a symbol from the *Zohar*, with two man's heads and arms forming a hexagram.

In this degree, the following correspondences are taught:

Angelic Name (Malakim)	Planet	Color	Hebrew Letter	Egyptian Names	Metal
Michael/ Shemesh	Sun	Purple and Gold	Resh	Ra	Gold
Gabriel/ Levannah	Moon	Black, Blue, and Silver	Gimel	Hathor	Silver
Samael	Mars	Green and Red	Peh	Set and Horus	Bronze, Iron, and Brash

Raphael/ Beit	Mercury	Sky Blue & Yellow	Beth	Thoth	Quicksilver, Aluminum
Sachiel/ Tzadkiel	Jupiter	Orange, Purple, and Blue	Kaph	Isis and Horus	Tin, Brass, and Bronze
Anael/ Haniel	Venus (The Morning and Evening Star, Star of Love)	Red, Dark Green, and Royal Blue	Daleth	Osiris and Isis	Copper and Brass
Cassiel/ Kafziel	Saturn	White, Black, Dark Green Indigo or Maroon	Tau	Nephthys and Horus	Lead

29° Scottish Knight of St. Andrew: the emblem of this degree is the Cross of St. Andrew (i.e., the X-shaped Cross), which, in heraldry, is termed the Cross Saltire, and it is an emblem of suffering and humility. St. Andrew, the Patron Saint of Scotland, is regarded as the symbol of Scottish Freemasonry. In 1320, the Declaration of Arbroath cited Scotland's conversion to Christianity by Andrew, "the first to be an Apostle." A disciple of John the Baptist, the Apostle Andrew only left that Master to follow Jesus Christ, and he sealed the faith that he held and the love that he bore to humanity with his blood. St. Andrew symbolizes the transition from the Old Law, proclaimed by Moses, to the Universal Law of Love and Brotherhood, proclaimed by Christ. By analogy, Hiram Abiff, the great Masonic exemplar, symbolizes humanity's transition from moral philosophy to higher spheres of spirituality.

30° Knight Kadosh, or Knight of the White and Black Eagle: In Hebrew, 'Kadosh' means designated, differentiated or set aside for a purpose. Moreover, according to Numbers 16:7, Kadosh is God's chosen, and, according to Isaiah 5:16, Kadosh is fervent and righteous. A primary meaning of the double-headed eagle is balance or equilibrium and universality. The plot of this degree has deep meanings.

A Knight of St. Andrew wishes to become a Knight Kadosh. Thus, according to the thirtieth-degree ritual, initially, the aspirant listens to the history of the Knights Templar and the values of chivalry, to which I referred in Chapter 2. The thirtieth degree of the Ancient and Accepted Scottish Rite of Freemasonry denounces political and spiritual despotism and corrupt authorities by referring to the betrayal and persecution of the medieval Knights Templar by their own political and religious superiors, namely by King Philip IV of France and Pope Clement V. The truth is that the Knights Templar had committed religious crimes, since they were Papal Crusaders, and they had practiced usury; however, King Philip IV of France and Pope

Clement V persecuted and suppressed the Order of the Knights Templar not because of its real crimes, but in order to confiscate its assets, and because both the French King and the Pope were afraid of the Templars' great military and economic power. Hence, according to an old maxim of the thirtieth degree of the AASR, "Nec proditor, nec proditus, innocens feret" (i.e., neither the one who has betrayed nor the one who has been betrayed is innocent).[1] In other words, the thirtieth degree of the AASR refers to the history of the Knights Templar not in order to praise medieval warrior-monks, but in order to teach important lessons about the spiritual and political freedom of man and in order to remind Freemasons that corrupt and authoritarian regimes, such as those of King Philip IV of France and Pope Clement V, do not hesitate to persecute and kill even their own soldiers and servants in order to advance their own interests.

In the context of the 30th Degree ceremony, after having become a sworn adversary of political and spiritual tyrants, the aspirant is instructed to ascend and descend the mysterious ladder of the Knight Kadosh. This ladder has two supports and seven steps. The first support on the right is called "Oheb Eloah," meaning love of God, and the second support on the left is called "Oheb Kerobo," meaning love of one's neighbor. The seven ascending steps on the left part are the seven Liberal Arts, which allow us to know the universe and ascend to high levels of conceptual thinking, whereas the seven descending steps remind us of the most important virtues through which we should serve our fellow humans and work for the happiness of humanity 'down here,' in this world. In particular, the seven ascending steps of the Knight Kadosh's mysterious ladder are the following (from bottom to top):

1. Grammar,
2. Rhetoric,
3. Logic,
4. Arithmetic,
5. Geometry,
6. Music,
7. Astronomy.

The seven descending steps of the Knight Kadosh's mysterious ladder are the following (from top to bottom):

---

1 Farina, Salvatore, *Il Libro Completo dei Riti Massonici*, Milan: Gherardo Casini Editore, 2009; *Typikon tou Triakostou Vathmou* (Ritual of the Thirtieth Degree), Athens: Supreme Council of the 33rd Degree of the Ancient and Accepted Scottish Rite for Greece, 1998 (in Greek), published by command of the then Supreme Council of the AASR for Greece, whose Sovereign Grand Commander was Georgios Chalkiotis, and whose Lieutenant Grand Commander was Christos Maneas.

1. Tsedakah, meaning justice and charity,
2. Schor Laban (literally white ox), meaning goodness and innocence,
3. Mathok, meaning blandness,
4. Emounah, meaning truthfulness,
5. Hamal Saghia, meaning tolerance and open-mindedness,
6. Sabbal, meaning moral duty,
7. Ghemoul Binah Thebounah, meaning that prudence leads to wisdom.

Consistory of Sublime Princes:

31° Inspector Inquisitor Commander: this degree is concerned with Masonic justice, and it urges the aspirant to study moral philosophy and philosophy of law, to pay particular attention to the moral theories and the normative thought of such great lawgivers as Moses (the main author of the Pentateuch), Zoroaster (the founder of the religion of ancient Persia), Confucius (the great Chinese philosopher and author of his seminal *Analects*), Hermes Trismegistus, Socrates, Mohammed (the Prophet of Islam), and Alfred the Great (King of Wessex from AD 871 to 899), and to remain committed to the following teachings of Jesus Christ: "if you forgive men their trespasses, your heavenly Father will also forgive you. But if you don't forgive men their trespasses, neither will your Father forgive your trespasses."[1] "Don't judge, so that you won't be judged. For with whatever judgment you judge, you will be judged; and with whatever measure you measure, it will be measured to you."[2] "Don't judge according to appearance, but judge righteous judgment."[3] "Blessed are the merciful, for they shall obtain mercy."[4]

32° Master (or Sublime Prince) of the Royal Secret: this degree urges the aspirant to review the previous thirty-one degrees and to study metaphysics and philosophy of religion in order thus to be able to fully appreciate and understand the "royal secret" of Freemasonry, which consists in a peculiar, symbolic Masonic Crusade whose purpose is to take possession of a mystical 'Jerusalem' that consists in the achievement of the following Masonic ends: to heal all inner dissensions and produce peace and harmony in the external world; to make charitable judgment universal; to spiritually elevate the masses of mankind in order to become aware of their true interests; to substitute the fraternal spirit for tyranny and usurped privilege; and to establish a social order in the image of the divine order.

---

1 Matthew 6:14–15.
2 Ibid., 7:1–2.
3 John 7:24.
4 Matthew 5:7.

Supreme Council:

33° Inspector General: this degree is mainly executive, and it is conferred as an honorarium on those who for great merit and long and arduous services have deserved well of the AASR. The earliest thirty-third degree ritual "is in the handwriting of the Reverend Frederick Delcho . . . The document, likely written about 1801, was the basis for subsequent versions and is now in the collection of the Supreme Council, 33o, N.M.J. [Northern Masonic Jurisdiction of the U.S.A.]."[1] The Supreme Council of the AASR for the Northern Jurisdiction continued to use a post-1804 revision of the Frederick Delcho ritual until the "Union of 1867" (when the N.M.J. merged with the competing Cerneau Supreme Council in New York), at which time the N.M.J. adopted Henry C. Atwood's version of the James Foulhouze ritual, which was based on the ritual used by the Grand Orient of France in 1845.[2]

The thirty-third degree teaches the aspirant that our goal, as the Order's Inspectors General, is not to cause fruitless battles and bloodshed in order to recapture the land that was sacralized by the life and the death of our Puissant Lord, Jesus Crist, but to recapture our God-given rights, to substitute truth for error, and to substitute freedom and justice for despotism and anomy; for, then and only then, will we have recaptured the "the only true Holy Land," which is "the patrimony of love, intelligence, and charity, which our Father has given us."[3] The Banner of the Order is white, bordered with a fringe of gold, and having in the center a double-headed black eagle, its wings displayed, beak and legs gold, holding with one claw the hilt, gold, and with the other the blade, steel, of a sword placed horizontally, hilt to the right and point to the left; from the sword hangs, lettered, gold, the motto, in Latin, DEUS MEUMQUE JUS (God and My Right). The eagle is crowned with a rayed equilateral triangle of gold bearing the inscription 33.

---

1 Hoyos, Arturo de, "On the Origins of the Prince Hall Scottish Rite Rituals," in *Freemasonry in Context: History, Ritual, Controversy,* edited by A. de Hoyos and S. B. Morris, Lanham, Maryland: Lexington Books, 2004, p. 51.
2 Ibid.
3 *Typikon tou Triakostou Tritou Vathmou* (Ritual of the Thirty-Third Degree), Athens: Supreme Council of the 33rd Degree of the Ancient and Accepted Scottish Rite for Greece, (in Greek), based on the original Greek edition of the Thirty-Third Degree Ritual, which was compiled by the first Scottish Rite Supreme Council that was founded in Greece on July 24, 1872 by Demetrios Rhodocanakis, as a thirty-third-degree member of the Supreme Council of the AASR for Scotland.

Figure 6: The emblem of the 33rd Degree of the AASR with its mottos: 'Ordo ab Chao' (Order from Chaos) and 'Deus Meumque Jus' (God and my Right).

In France, there is a long tradition of 'Scottish Masonry,' mainly associated with the exiled Jacobites. In 1744, a pamphlet entitled *Le Parfait Maçon* claimed to offer "the true secrets of the four degrees of Apprentice, Companion, Master Ordinary, and Scottish." According to the previous pamphlet, "there are still other degrees above the Master's . . . Some say six, other seven. Those who are called Scottish Masons claim to constitute the Fourth Degree." Additionally, in 1742, the Mother Lodge of the "Three Globes" at Berlin founded the Scottish Lodge "Union" to work the Fourth or "Scottish" Degree.

The Scottish adherents of the exiled British King James II who followed him into exile (after the landing of the Prince of Orange in 1688) brought to the English Court at St. Germain (which had been placed at the disposal of James II by the French King Louis XIV) Scottish Masonic traditions intermingled with Templarism. The development of Scottish Masonry and of Masonic Templar degrees and legends in France was significantly boosted by the seminal *Ramsay's Oration*, written in 1737. The Chevalier Andrew Michael Ramsay was a native of Scotland, a Knight of the French Order of St. Lazarus, and, in 1724 and 1725, tutor to the two sons of the exiled James III ("The Old Pretender"), the son of Great Britain's exiled King James II. In fact, Ramsay was born in Ayr, Scotland, the son of a baker, he was educated at the University of Edinburgh, and, when King James II threw the mace into the Thames and fled to Paris, he went to the Netherlands, where he served with the English auxiliaries and studied mystical theology. Ramsay was attracted to the mysticism of quietism as practised in the circle of George Garden, a Scottish Church minister and leading figure of the early Scottish Episcopal Church, at Rosehearty, in the historical county of Aberdeenshire in Scotland. In 1710, Ramsay travelled to Rijnsburg to meet Antoinette Bourignon de la Porte, a French-Flemish mystic and adventurer, and, afterword, he also met Jeanne-Marie Bouvier de la Motte-Guyon, known simply as Mme Guyon, who was a prominent French mystic and advocate of quietism. Mme Guyon was emphasizing and teaching meditation on love. In August 1710, Ramsay went on to stay with François Fénelon, a French Roman Catholic archbishop, mystical theologian, poet, writer, and preceptor of the grandsons of Louis XIV. Under Fénelon's influence, Ramsay was converted to Roman Catholicism. In January 1724, Ramsay was sent to Rome as tutor to James III's two sons, Charles Edward and Henry, but in November 1724 Ramsay was back in Paris.

In 1737, in Paris, Ramsay delivered a thought-provoking and controversial Oration before the English Provincial Grand Lodge of France, of which he was Grand Chancellor and Orator.[1] In his Oration, Ramsay argued that the founders of Freemasonry "were not simple workers in stone," but crusader knights "who vowed to restore the Temple" in the Holy Land, in imitation of the ancient Israelites, who, "while they handled the trowel and mortar with one hand, in the other, they held the sword and buckler." Thus, Ramsay attempted to integrate the institution and the ethos of medieval chivalry into Freemasonry and to cultivate mystical theology through legends about the cultural interaction between crusading knights, especially the Templars, and Eastern mystics during the Crusaders' expeditions in the Eastern Roman Empire and the Middle East.

In particular, according to the Chevalier Ramsay's aforementioned oration, at the time of the Crusades, many princes, lords, and knights associated themselves and vowed to restore the Christians' Temple in Jerusalem and to employ themselves in restoring the traditional form and glory of their architecture. Thus, they agreed upon several secret ancient signs and symbolic words drawn from the Christian religion in order to recognize themselves among the heathens and Saracens. Furthermore, according to the same oration, those secret signs and words were only communicated to those who promised solemnly never to divulge them. As a result, the chevalier Ramsay maintains, the previous sacred promise, often associated with the Templars' inner circle, was not heretical, but instead it was a holy bond to unite Christians of all nationalities into one confraternity. Moreover, according to Ramsay, sometime afterward, Masonry was somehow united with the Knights of St. John, and, from that time, the Masons' Lodges took the name of Lodges of St. John. The previous speculations have inspired the fabrication of several 'Templar' Masonic side-degrees, such as the Royal Order of Scotland (which is organized into two degrees, namely, that of the

---

1 Ramsay's oration was intended to be delivered on March 21, 1737. It was first printed in 1741 in the periodical *Almanach des Cocus* (see also *Ars Quatuor Coronatorum* 32 (1919), Part 1).

Royal Order of Heredom and that of the Knights of the Rosy Cross) and the Chevaliers Bienfaisants de la Cité Sainte.

According to the legends (which must not be mistaken for actual history) taught by the Royal Order of Scotland, by Baron von Hund's Rite of Strict Observance, and by the Chevaliers Bienfaisants de la Cité Sainte, their lineages can be traced to Templars who escaped from the pogrom that was unleashed against the Templar Order in 1311 and fled to different lands: Pierre de Beaujeu took refuge in Sweden, while Pierre d'Aumont, Provincial Grand Master of Auvergne, fled with two Commanders and five Knights to the British Isles, and, ultimately, they settled in the island of Mull, in Scotland, where they met George Harris, Grand Commander of Hampton Court. The legend of Pierre d'Aumont is the mythological foundation of many continental Masonic groups, including the French Chapter of Clermont. Additionally, according to the traditional (precisely, legendary) history of the Royal Order of Scotland, in particular, the Degree of Knight of the Rosy Cross was instituted by Robert the Bruce (who was King of Scots from 1306 until his death in 1329) on the battlefield of Bannockburn, on June 24, 1314, to commemorate the valor of a band of Knights Templar who had rendered him significant aid in that victory against the English King, Edward II.

The lineage of the Ancient and Accepted Scottish Rite (AASR) can be traced to an older Freemasonic Order called the Rite of Perfection, which had twenty-five degrees and was strongly Templar in tone. The most important forerunner of the AASR was the Chapter of Clermont, which was founded in 1754 outside Paris by the Chevalier de Bonneville, and it was working Scottish degrees beyond the three Craft degrees. The Chapter of Clermont, which was honoring the Duke of Clermont, then Grand Master of the English Provincial Grand Lodge of France, and was strongly associated with the Jacobites, lasted for about four years. The Chapter's demise gave rise to two mutually competing Masonic groups: the former was known as the Knights of the East, representing mainly the bourgeoisie and the middle class as well as the Whig ideology, whereas the latter was known as the Emperors of the East and West, representing mainly the nobility and the old conservative ideology. In 1761, the Emperors of the East and West managed to defeat the Knights of the East.

The full name of the Emperors of the East and West, who emerged in the 1750s on the basis of mystical Templar legends and in continuity with the Chapter of Claremont, was "Emperors of the East and West, Sovereign Prince Masons, Substitutes General of the Royal Art, Grand Surveillants and Officers of the Grand Sovereign Lodge of St. John of Jerusalem." The Emperors of the East and West were also known as the Heredom of Perfection or Kilwinning. After the formation of the Emperors of the East and West, the

Rite of Perfection was established, comprising twenty-five degrees, twenty-two of which were what the French called the "high degrees," and they were added to the three Craft degrees. The highest of these degrees was that of Sublime Prince of the Royal Secret, a precursor of the AASR's 32nd Degree. Moreover, in 1761, a document pertaining to the Rite of Perfection, which is known as the *Secret Constitutions of 1761*, designated the Rite's supreme officers as Inspectors General.

In particular, the twenty-five degrees of the Rite of Perfection were the following:

1° Apprentice
2° Companion
3° Master
4° Secret Master
5° Perfect Master
6° Intimate Secretary
7° Intendant of the Buildings
8° Provost and Judge
9° Master Elect of the Nine
10° Master Elect of the Fifteen
11° Illustrious Elect Chief of the Twelve Tribes
12° Grand Master Architect
13° Knight Royal Arch
14° Grand, Elect, Ancient, Perfect Master
15° Knight of the Sword or of the East
16° Prince of Jerusalem
17° Knight of the East and West
18° Knight Rose-Croix
19° Grand Pontiff or Master *ad Vitam*
20° Grand Patriarch Noachite
21° Grand Master of the Key of Masonry
22° Prince of Libanus, Knight Royal Axe
23° Knight of the Sun, Prince Adept, Chief of the Grand Consistory
24° Illustrious Chief Grand Commander of the White and Black Eagle, Grand Elect Kadosh
25° Most Illustrious Sovereign Prince of Masonry, Grand Knight, Sublime Knight Commander of the Royal Secret.

In order to understand the historical development of the Scottish Rite, it is also important to bear in mind that, by the 1740s, at Avignon, the capital of the department of Vaucluse, there already existed several centers of Hermetic studies, often working in the context of Freemasonry and practicing the three Craft degrees and other higher Scottish degrees. One of the most influential members of the Hermetic community of Avignon was Dom Antoine-Joseph de Pernéty, who was librarian to Frederick the Great, and he wrote the *Dictionnaire Mytho-Hermé*tique (1758). There is an important intellectual link between the Scottish Rite of Freemasonry and the Société des Illuminés d'Avignon, which was founded in 1786 by Dom Antoine-Joseph de Pernéty and a Polish Count called Thaddeus Leszczy Grabianka. The Société des Illuminés d'Avignon was derived from an esoteric society that existed in Berlin prior to 1779, when Pernéty joined it, and it was organized in two classes superior to Symbolic Masonry: the Novices or Minors, and the Illuminés; their head was called Magus and Pontiff. Moreover, the "Illuminés d'Avignon" were influenced by German Templar and Scottish Masonic degrees and legends related to Baron von Hund's Rite of Strict Observance and the Chevaliers Bienfaisants de la Cité Sainte at Lyons. In 1783, Pernéty left Berlin, and he took up residence at a house he called Tabor near Avignon provided by one of his disciples, Marquis Vernety de Vaucroze. There, Pernéty set up a lodge room for those who came to be known as the Illuminés d'Avignon. Among the Illuminés d'Avignon were Baron de Staël-Holstein, the Swedish ambassador, and the Duchess Württemberg.

In the second half of the eighteenth century, several new Masonic and quasi-Masonic Orders and Rites were formed in France, such as the Ellus Coens, the Illuminés du Zodiaque, the Frères noirs, etc. By 1766, a French Freemasonic fraternity called the "Mother Lodge of Comtat-Venaissin" (in French, known as the "Mère Loge du Comtat-Venaissin") was already working the following degrees beyond the three Craft degrees: 4° True Mason, 5° True Mason on the Right Road, 6° Knight of the Golden Key, 7° Knight of Iris, 8° Knight Argonaut, 9° Knight of the Golden Fleece. However, in 1775, the "Mother Lodge of Comtat-Venaissin" was suppressed by the Roman Catholic Inquisition.

In 1766, the chief seat of Scottish Masonry in Paris was the "Social Contract" Lodge (in French, "Le Contrat Social"), originally called the "Saint Lazarus" Lode, which was working according to a "Philosophical Scottish Rite" (in French, "Rite Ecossais Philosophique") founded by the French physician and Hermeticist M. Boileau, who was a student of de Pernéty, under the auspices of the Grand Lodge of France. The degrees of the Philosophical Scottish Rite were the following:

1°–3°: Knight of the Black Eagle or Rose-Croix of Heredom (divided into three parts)
4° Knight of the Phoenix
5° Knight of the Sun
6° Knight of Iris
7° True Mason

8° Knight Argonaut
9° Knight of the Golden Fleece
10° Grand Inspector Perfect Initiate
11° Grand Inspector Perfect Initiate
12° Sublime Master of the Luminous Ring.

In August 1766, the "Mother Lodge of Comtat-Venaissin" amalgamated with the "Social Contract" Lodge. Thus, after its suppression at Avignon by the Roman Catholic Inquisition, the "Mother Lodge of Comtat-Venaissin" was revived in the bosom of the "Social Contract" Lodge in Paris under the auspices of the Grand Lodge of France and, from 1772 onward, under the auspices of the Grand Orient of France, which, however, for years, refused to recognize the "Social Contract" Lodge as a "Mother Lodge," that is, as a Lodge with power to warrant other Lodges, and, ultimately, it erased the "Social Contract" Lodge from the roll. In 1781, on the basis of a new Concordat, the "Social Contract" Lodge was reinstated as a daughter of the Grand Orient of France as regards the three Craft degrees, but the "Social Contract" Lodge was given sole control over the higher Scottish degrees, and it was permitted to affiliate itself to other French Lodges and endow them with Chapters and Tribunals of the higher degrees. Moreover, in 1780, an Academy of the Sublime Masters of the Luminous Ring was established in France. That Academy was teaching that Freemasonry was originally founded by Pythagoras of Samos, and it was primarily concerned with the study and the elucidation of Pythagoras's teachings.

The Council of the Emperors of the East and West, to which I referred above, was working the Rite of Perfection. In 1761, just three years after its foundation, the Council of the Emperors of the East and West granted a patent to a merchant called Stephen Morin[1] to propagate the Rite of Perfection and installed him as a Grand Inspector of the Rite of Perfection. The original of this document has not been found, but Freemasons know about it only from the copy preserved in the *Golden Book* of the Comte de Grasse-Tilly, founder of the Supreme Council of the Ancient and Accepted Scottish Rite for France. In 1761, Morin arrived in San Domingo, where he started propagating the Rite of Perfection, and, by virtue of his patent, he appointed many Inspectors for both the West Indies and the United States of America.

Morin was by no means the proper person to act as the Grand Inspector and chief propagator of the Rite of Perfection in America. His philosophical and Masonic education was poor, he had not managed to subdue his sexual

---

1 According to Albert G. Mackey's *Encyclopedia of Freemasonry*, most probably, Stephen Morin was a member of a French-American Huguenot family.

passion (contrary to the teachings of the Entered Apprentice ritual[1]), and the reports on his misdoings had once obliged the Council of the Emperors of the East and West to reconsider the appointment of Morin as the chief propagator and the head of the Rite of Perfection in America. Furthermore, Morin made wrong decisions with regard to the choice of his lieutenants. In particular, he appointed several Jewish merchants of dubious morality and rather bad reputation as his lieutenants, and, thus, unworthy persons played an instrumental role in the history of the Rite of Perfection in America for approximately the next forty years.

Morin appointed Henry Andrew Francken as Deputy Inspector General, who played an important role in the formation and development of the Rite of Perfection in the American colonies. In 1766, Francken went to New York, where he appointed Moses Michael Hays, a Jewish banker and merchant, as a Deputy Inspector General, he issued a patent for a Lodge of Perfection at Albany, and he conferred the degrees on a number of Masons there. In 1781, Hays installed eight Deputy Inspectors General, four of whom were later important in the establishment of the first Supreme Council of the Ancient and Accepted Scottish Rite in South Carolina, namely: Isaac da Costa, Deputy Inspector General for South Carolina, Abraham Forst, Deputy Inspector General for Virginia, Joseph M. Myers, Deputy Inspector General for Maryland, and Barend M. Spitzer, Deputy Inspector General for Georgia. In February 1783, Da Costa went to Charleston, South Carolina, where he established the "Sublime Grand Lodge of Perfection." After Da Costa's death in November 1783, Hays appointed Myers as Da Costa's successor. In 1801, at Charleston, Myers, Forst, and Spitzer fabricated additional high degree bodies, beyond the Rite of Perfection. Thus, in 1801, the ruling bodies of the Rite of Perfection in South Carolina, which were originally established by Da Costa in 1783, became the Supreme Council of the Ancient and Accepted Scottish Rite (AASR) for the Southern Jurisdiction, which has authority to confer thirty-three degrees, most of which existed in parts of previous degree systems. The formation of the "Mother" Supreme Council of the AASR took place at Charleston, in May 1801.

During this obscure, formative period of the American Lodges of the Rite of Perfection and of the AASR, there emerged a peculiar Masonic myth, according to which Frederick the Great, King of Prussia, was the Supreme

---

1 In 1827, William Morgan published a book entitled *Illustrations of Masonry*, which includes lectures on the three Craft Degrees. A lecture on a Masonic degree is a recapitulation and explanation of the corresponding degree's ceremonies and forms by way of question and answer. In Morgan's *Illustrations of Masonry*, precisely, in the First Section of the Lecture on the First Degree of Masonry, we read the following: "*Question*: What comest thou hither to do? *Answer*: To learn to subdue my passions, and improve myself in the secret arts and mysteries of ancient Freemasonry."

Head of the Rite of Perfection. Additionally, according to the same myth, Frederick the Great, on his death-bed, ratified the Grand Constitutions of 1786, which underpin the structure and the operation of the Ancient and Accepted Scottish Rite (AASR), and he personally instituted the 33rd Degree of the AASR, delegating his powers as a Sovereign of Masonry to local Supreme Councils, each one of which would govern the AASR in its jurisdiction. The original Grand Constitutions of Scottish Masonry had been written in French, but, in 1834, a Latin version of them alleged to have been signed by Frederick the Great was accepted as genuine by the Supreme Council of the AASR for France; however, this document is a forgery. The previous myth, according to which Frederick the Great was the Supreme Head of the Rite of Perfection, the author of the Grand Constitutions of 1786, and the creator of the 33rd Degree of the AASR, was, most probably, fabricated by unworthy Jewish and other founding Grand Inspectors of the Rite of Perfection in America in order to increase the commercial value of the Rite's degrees and as a marketing tool for the promotion of the 33rd Degree of the AASR.

The truth is that Frederick the Great was never actively involved in the Rite of Perfection, and that he neither ratified the Grand Constitutions of 1786, which have been, falsely, attributed to him, nor instituted the 33rd Degree of the AASR. Nevertheless, the Grand Constitutions of 1786 constitute the fundamental law of the AASR in every Supreme Council that has been regularly derived from the Charleston Supreme Council (i.e., the "Mother" Supreme Council of the world), and Albert Pike, who was the Sovereign Grand Commander of the Southern Jurisdiction of the AASR for the U.S.A. from 1859 until his death in 1891, believed that the Grand Constitutions of 1786 were authentic and had been ratified by Frederick the Great. On December 19, 1861, the Grand Lodge of the "Three Globes" at Berlin published a Protocol, in which it officially stated the following:

> Frederick the Great is said to have revised, reorganized, and increased from 25 to 33 degrees the system of High Degrees in a Supreme Council held at Berlin . . . With regard to this subject, Bro. Le Blanc de Marconnay sent a letter dated May 25, 1833 from New York to the Directory of the Grand National Mother Lodge of the Three Globes . . . Are these historical traditions founded on truth? . . . The answer that the Directory returned, on August 17, 1833, says: "The Grand National Mother Lodge of the Three Globes was founded on September, 13, 1740, under the authority of Frederick the Great, who was its first Grand Master. He never had anything to do with the organization and legislation of the Grand Lodge. Anything that concerns his having, in 1786, originated a high Masonic Senate, etc.,

has no historical basis" . . . [Georg Franz Burkhard] Kloss attends to this subject in a long examination in his *History of Freemasonry in France* and stamps the Constitutions and Statutes of the Ancient and Accepted Rite as "the grand lie of the Order." As harsh as this judgment may appear at a first glance, the Directory of the Grand Lodge of the Three Globes, after repeated researches in the archives and historical collections, cannot help sustaining it.[1]

After the formation of the "Mother" Supreme Council of the AASR at Charleston, in May 1801, other Supreme Councils of the AASR were formed in Saint-Domingue in 1802, in France in 1804, in Italy in 1805, in Spain in 1811, etc. On May 1, 1813, an officer from the Supreme Council at Charleston elevated several New York Masons to the thirty-third degree of the AASR and, thus, organized a Supreme Council of the AASR for the "Northern Masonic District and Jurisdiction."

In March 1853, Albert Pike, an attorney, journalist, soldier, and writer, who had fought in the Mexican–American War, and, who took the side of the Confederacy when the American civil War broke out, received the 4th through the 32nd Degrees of the AASR from Albert G. Mackey at Charleston, South Carolina, and he was appointed Deputy Inspector for Arkansas that same year. In 1855, the Supreme Council of the AASR for the Southern Jurisdiction appointed a committee in order to compile and formalize rituals for the 4th through the 32nd Degrees; the members of that committee were the following: Albert G. Mackey, John H. Honour, William S. Rockwell, Claude P. Samory, and Albert Pike. Of these five committee members, Pike was the only one who actually wrote rituals for the 4th through the 32nd Degrees, whose first complete version he published in 1857. However, this version of the 4°-32° ritual was never adopted by the Supreme Council, and, on several occasions, it was used only as a source of inspiration for future ritual revisions. Moreover, Pike wrote lectures for all the degrees of the AASR, which he published in 1871 under the title *Morals and Dogma of the Ancient and Accepted Scottish Rite of Freemasonry*.

Pike's *Morals and Dogma* reflects a fundamentally dualistic way of thinking, which has often been used by enemies of Freemasonry in order to accuse Pike of Satanism. Pike's dualistic way of thinking and approach to Freemasonry express a tragic way of experiencing life. Furthermore, sometimes, Pike's dualism becomes so radical that it, actually, deprives the human being of one's existential possibility to transcend the realm of duality and become a partaker of the pure, real good. If dualism is an ontological necessity, as Pike seems to contend, then spiritual freedom is essentially impossible.

1 See Findel, J. G., *The History of Freemasonry: From Its Origin Down to the Present Day*, 2nd revised edition, London: George Kenning, 1869, pp. 698–9.

With regard to Albert Pike's ideology and political role in the American system, it is important to mention that he acted as a secret 'asset' of the British Empire in America. During the American Civil War, Great Britain had several secret 'assets' in the United States, such as August Belmont, John Slidell, Albert Pike, etc. The principal authors of the Confederacy used the issue of slavery and abolition in order to carve up the United States into several contesting powers, thus facilitating and prolonging Victorian Britain's hegemony over America; that project was chiefly devised by Lord Palmerston (Henry John Temple, Third Viscount Palmerston), who served, under Queen Victoria, as Great Britain's Prime Minister twice (1855–8 and 1859–65) and as Great Britain's Foreign secretary three times (1830–4, 1835–41, 1846–51). Palmerston's sympathies in the American Civil War (1861–5) were with the secessionist Southern Confederacy, because, even though he professed opponent of the slave trade and slavery, he believed that the dissolution of Abraham Lincoln's Union would weaken the United States and, therefore, enhance British power.

In 2000, the Southern Jurisdiction of the AASR for the U.S.A. made significant revisions in its ritual. Moreover, the Supreme Councils of the AASR for other countries around the world have revised their rituals on several occasions in accordance with the corresponding Supreme Council's own ethos and mentality.

5. Ancient And Primitive Rite Memphis–Misraim

The Ancient and Primitive Rite Memphis–Misraim (or simply the Memphis–Misraim Rite) is a Masonic rite that was formed in 1881 as an amalgamation of the Scottish Rite, the Rite of Memphis, and the Rite of Misraim.

The name of the Rite of Misraim is taken from the Hebrew word for Egypt. The Rite of Misraim has played an important part in the development of what would later be called "Egyptian Masonry."[1] After the late 1780s and especially during the 1790s, modern Egyptology blossomed, because Napoleon the Great extended the French Empire into Egypt and brought Egyptian treasures and artifacts to Europe. Moreover, in 1799, the Rosetta Stone was discovered.[2] Thus,

1 Faulks and Cooper, *The Masonic Magician: The Life and Death of Count Cagliostro and His Egyptian Rite.*
2 The Rosetta Stone is a granodiorite stele inscribed with a decree issued at Memphis, in Hellenistic Egypt, in 196 BC on behalf of King Ptolemy V. The decree appears in three scripts, precisely, in ancient Egyptian hieroglyphs, in the demotic Egyptian

at the end of the eighteenth century and at the beginning of the nineteenth century, Europe experienced a phase of intense fascination with ancient Egypt. The origins of "Egyptian Masonry" can be traced to the Egyptian Rite of Masonry that was developed by Cagliostro at the end of the eighteenth century.

John Yarker, in his book entitled *The Arcane Schools* (originally published in Manchester, England, in 1909), writes that the Rite of Misraim with its ninety degrees was originally structured and established in a formal way in Italy in 1804–5. Its degrees were collected from several Masonic, Hermetic, Neoplatonic, Kabbalistic, Alchemical, and Rosicrucian sources. At this time, the head of the Misraim Rite was Le Changeur of Milan, who played a major role in the systematization of the Rite. In 1813, the Milan "Mother" Lodge of Misraim granted Patents of the 90th Degree to a few French Masons. From 1814 onward, under the leadership of bothers Joseph, Michel, and Marc Bèdarride, the Rite of Misraim developed quickly in France. Initially, the Grand Orient of France accepted the authority of the Misraim Rite, but, in December 1817, the Misraim Rite asserted its independence, and, thus, the Grand Orient of France started treating the Misraim Rite in a rather inimical way. It is worth pointing out that several attempts were made to place the Rite of Misraim under the auspices of the Grand Orient of France, but, ultimately, they were denied by the latter on the ground that the antiquity of the Misraim Rite had not been proved and that the sixty-eight out of the ninety degrees of the Rite were already included in the French Masonic system.

In 1845, in Paris, Marc Bèdarride's book entitled *De l'Ordre Maçonnique de Misraim* was published. In this book, Marc Bèdarride writes that the Misraim Rite has been originated from the ancient Egyptian rite of Isis. Moreover, in the same book, he maintains that the ritual represents the contests of Osiris and Seth as well as the death, the resurrection, and the triumph of the former and the destruction of the latter. Marc Bèdarride was initiated into Freemasonry at Cesina in 1801, he received the Rose-Croix Degree and the 31st Degree of the Ancient and Accepted Scottish Rite (AASR) at Paris, and, as he himself has stated, he was elevated to the 90th Degree of the Misraim Rite at Naples, in Italy.

During the nineteenth century, in France, the Rite of Misraim served as a meeting-place of opponents to the regime. Moreover, during the nineteenth century, the Carbonari recruited members in Misraim and Memphis Lodges. The Carbonari were an Italian revolutionary secret society, which, in 1814, attempted to obtain a constitution for the Kingdom of the Two Sicilies

---

language, and in ancient Greek. Thus, the Rosetta Stone provided the key to the modern understanding of Egyptian hieroglyphs.

---

by force, and, in 1820–1, it began resisting the French occupiers, notably Joachim Murat, the Bonapartist King of Naples. Thus, finally, the Carbonari became a liberal nationalist secret society expressing militant opposition to Austria's regime (precisely, Emperor Francis I of Austria and Austrian State Chancellor Prince Klemens von Metternich) and to the Holy Alliance, in general. They were instrumental in organizing revolutions in Italy in 1820–1 and in 1831.

The Rite of Misraim established a presence in England in 1870, but, after a few years of quarrels between its members and England's Supreme Council of the Ancient and Accepted Rite, the English Obedience of the Rite of Misraim started declining. In the 1870s, in England, the Rite of Misraim came under the control of John Yarker, an English Freemason, author, and mystic. In 1878, Yarker merged the Rite of Misraim with the rival Rite of Memphis to form the Rite of Memphis–Misraim. In his book entitled *Notes on the Scientific and Religious Mysteries of Antiquity; The Gnosis and Secret Schools of the Middle Ages; Modern Rosicrucianism; and the Various Rites and Degrees of Free and Accepted Masonry* (London: John Hogg, 1872, pp. 157–8), John Yarker argues that, "as the Masonic fraternity is now governed, the Craft is fast becoming the paradise of the *bon vivant*; of the 'charitable' hypocrite . . . the manufacturer of paltry Masonic tinsel; the rascally merchant . . . and the masonic 'Emperors' and other charlatans," and he proposes "the appointment of a higher (not pecuniary) standard of membership and morality, with exclusion from the 'purple' of all who inculcate frauds, sham, historical degrees, and other immoral abuses."

The Memphis Rite (also known as the Oriental Rite) is a modification of the Misraim Rite, and it was originally organized in Paris, in 1838–9, by Jacques-Etienne Marconis de Nègre, who had previously been a member of the Rite of Misraim. The Memphis Rite was composed of ninety working and six honorary and/or administrative degrees. References to an Egyptian system of Masonry were made in a pamphlet entitled *Master of Masters*, which appeared in Paris, in 1815. In fact, by that time, French Freemasonry had already been established in Egypt by the armies of Napoleon the Great, and, from thence, mingled with Hermetic and other local mystical traditions, it was transplanted to Montauban in France, in 1816, by the French Freemasons Gabriel-Mathieu Marconis de Nègre, Baron Dumas, Petite, Labrunie, Samuel Honis, etc. Thus, the Rite of Memphis was formed. After an interval of inactivity, this system of Egyptian Masonry was revived in Brussels and Paris, in 1838–9, by Jacques-Etienne Marconis de Nègre, son of Gabriel-Mathieu Marconis de Nègre.

In France, the newly-established Memphis Rite gained a certain success among military Lodges, and, within its Lodges, were grouped semi-retired members of Napoleon Bonaparte's armies, faithful Bonapartists, and a few radical ideologists, such Louis Blanc, a socialist scholar envisioning a corporatist system and the establishment of an association monopoly within each trade. Thus, the Rite of Memphis was suppressed by the French police as a subversive secret society, but, in 1848, with the overthrow of Louis-Philippe (King of the French from 1830 to 1848 as the leader of the Orléanist party), Jacques-Etienne Marconis de Nègre revived the Rite of Memphis.

In 1850, a Lodge called "Les Sectateurs de Ménès" was founded in London by non-English Masons belonging to various Masonic Orders, and it proved popular with refugees fleeing France for London at that time. Between 1851 and 1856, French refugees established several Lodges of the Rite of Memphis in London, the most important of which being "La Grand Loge des Philadelphes," formed out of the French refugee membership of "Les Sectateurs de Ménès" at the end of 1850. The constitution of the "Grand Loge des Philadelphes" was ratified by the Conseil Supreme de l'Ordre Maçonnique de Memphis on January 31, 1851; originally it was working the ninety-five degrees of the Rite of Memphis, but, after April 8, 1857, it was working only the three Craft degrees.

On December 2, 1851, a coup d'état was staged in France by Prince Louis-Napoléon Bonaparte, at the time President of the French Second Republic. A year later, the Prince-President reclaimed his uncle's throne as Emperor of the French under the regnal name Napoleon III. After Napoleon III's coup d'état, the Rite of Memphis was suppressed in France, and, in 1853, the "Grand Loge des Philadelphes" became the real Grand Lodge of the Memphis Rite. During the regime of Napoleon III, the Rite of Memphis was a major center of political opposition and conspiracy against his regime. However, ultimately, in 1862, Jacques-Etienne Marconis de Nègre placed the Rite of Memphis under the auspices of the Grand Orient of France, which assimilated the French members of the Memphis –Misraim Rite into its own Masonic system and took the Memphis degrees out of circulation. The "Grand Loge des Philadelphes" ceased to exist in the late 1870s.

The Rite of Memphis was introduced into America in 1856, and, by 1872, it was already present in Egypt, Romania, Great Britain, and Ireland. In 1871, John Yarker joined the Rite of Memphis during a visit to New York, and, in 1872, he received a charter for the Rite from its Grand Master in America, Harry Seymour. In 1872, John Yarker merged the Rite of Memphis and the Rite of Misraim, and he founded a Sovereign Grand Sanctuary of the Rite of Memphis and Misraim at his hometown of Manchester. In 1902, Yarker was proclaimed International Grand Master of the Rite of Memphis–Misraim.

However, before Yarker, in 1881, General Giuseppe Garibaldi,[1] had already initiated a process of merging the Rite of Memphis and the Rite of Misraim with the Scottish Rite; Garibaldi's previous initiative was accomplished in 1889, and Garibaldi was proclaimed International Grand Master of the Rite of Memphis–Misraim.

The Memphis–Misraim Degrees are the following:

Lodge:

    1º Apprentice
    2º Companion
    3º Master

College:

    4º Secret Master
    5º Perfect Master
    6º Intimate Secretary
    7º Provost and Judge
    8º Intendant of the Buildings
    9º Master Elect of Nine
    10º Illustrious Elect of Fifteen
    11º Sublime Prince Elect
    12º Grand Master Architect
    13º Royal Arch
    14º Grand Elect, Perfect and Sublime Master

Chapter:

    15º Knight of the East or Knight of the Sword
    16º Prince of Jerusalem
    17º Knight of the East and West
    18º Knight of the Rose Cross

Senate:

    19º Grand Pontiff
    20º Knight of the Temple
    21º Patriarch Noachite
    22º Knight of the Royal Axe
    23º Chief of the Tabernacle

---

1 Giuseppe Garibaldi (1807-82) was an Italian general and politician who is considered, with Camillo Cavour, Victor Emmanuel II, and Giuseppe Mazzini, as one of Italy's "fathers of the fatherland." He played a protagonist role in Risorgimento (i.e., the political and social movement for the unification of Italy), and he was appointed general by the provisional government of Milan in 1848, and General of the Roman Republic in 1849 by the Italian Minister of War.

24º Prince of the Tabernacle
25º Knight of the Brazen Serpent
26º Prince of Mercy
27º Commander of the Temple
28º Knight of the Sun or Prince Adept
29º Knight of St. Andrew

Areopagus and Tribunal:
    30º Grand Elected Knight Kadosh
    31º Grand Inspector Inquisitor Commander
    32º Sublime Prince of the Royal Secret
    33º Sovereign Grand Inspector General

The first thirty-three degrees of the Memphis–Misraim Rite are similar to those of the Scottish Rite. Most of these degrees are conferred on the candidate 'by name'; only the first three degrees (namely, the three Craft Degrees), the fourteenth degree, the eighteenth degree, the thirtieth degree, the thirty-first degree, the thirty-second degree, and the thirty-third degree are worked in full. The peculiar Sacred Words of these degrees are the following: (i) Apprentice: BOAZ; (ii) Companion: JACHIN; (iii) Master: MAH-HAH-BONE or MOABON (meaning 'of the Father'); (iv) Grand Elect, Perfect and Sublime Master: JEHOVAH; (v) Knight of the Rose Cross: I.N.R.I.; (vi) Grand Elected Knight Kadosh: NEKAM ADONAI (meaning 'revenge, O, LORD'), and the reply is PHARASCH CHOL (meaning 'all is explained'); (vii) Grand Inspector Inquisitor Commander: TZEDEKAH (meaning 'Justice'), the reply is MISCHOR (meaning 'Equality'), and then both say together AMEN; (viii) Sublime Prince of the Royal Secret: SALIX, the reply is NONI, and then both say together TENGU (these words are composed of the letters that mark the tents in the Camp of the Princes and are anagrammatic[1]); (ix) Sovereign Grand Inspector General: MICHAMICHAK BEALIM ADONAI (meaning 'who is equal to you, among the great lords?').

Consistory:
34º Knight of Scandinavia: this degree is devoted to the ancient mythology of Scandinavia, emphasizing man's union with God. In particular, this degree is focused on god Odin, whose name means seer and prophet. In Norse mythology, Odin (in Old Saxon, Woden) was associated with healing, death, royalty, the gallows, knowledge, battle, sorcery, poetry, frenzy, and the runic alphabet, and he was the husband of the goddess Frigg. Odin is

---

1 The Key to the anagram is "Lux inens nos agit," meaning 'the light within,' namely, our Royal Secret, 'compels us.'

frequently referred to as a founding figure among various Germanic peoples and in most of Scandinavia. In Anglo-Saxon England, Odin held a prominent position as a euhemerized ancestral figure among royalty.

35º Knight of the Temple: this degree is concerned with the acquisition of knowledge about the Temple of the Universe.

36º Sublime Negociant: this degree is concerned with Geometry and Astronomy, it refers to the consequences resulting from the astronomical observations of the Priests of Babylon, Chaldea, and Sidon, and it quotes a chapter in the Qur'an being the protests of Abraham against star and idol worship.

37º Knight of Shota or Sage of Truth: this degree is focused on the concept of initiation, and it studies ancient initiatory traditions.

38º Sublime Elect of Truth or of the Red Eagle: this degree compares the mysteries of different ancient civilizations which, in effect, represented the contest between Light and Darkness.

39º Grand Elect of the Aeons: in the context of Eastern mystical traditions, 'Aeon' signifies a central point of development and refers to the mystery of divine economy, which is the main subject-matter of this degree.

40º Sage Savaiste or Perfect Sage: this degree considers the fundamental laws of nature and instinct, and it touches upon the existence of a God, who draws us to Himself by eternal chains, whose links are the love of goodness. According to the teachings of this degree, God is the Alpha and the Omega, the beginning and the end of all beings and things.

41º Knight of the Arch of Seven Colors: this degree refers to the Rainbow, which receives its prismatic colors as a reflection from the sun upon the humid atmosphere, and, according to this degree's legends, ancient operative Masons held that the Rainbow was the pattern on which they were building Arches. The scope of this degree is to teach that the Sun is a Well of beneficence and the Regenerator of Nature's beauties, and that the sun symbolizes the deity, the ultimate source of life and beauty. The peculiar symbol of this degree is the Gammadion (i.e., four Greek gammas, or Γ), known also as the swastika, which represents the Great Bear, of seven Stars, in its revolution, round the Pole Star.

At the beginning of His work of creation, "God said, 'Let there be Light,' and there was light."[1] This white glory of the Beginning was soon diversified and reflected by a myriad of rays from the air, the fire, the water, and the earth of the material world as well as by the human being, the crown of the Creation, who became aware of divers colors. The rainbow in the heavens discloses the whole range of colors, of which man is able to distinguish the seven most evident ones, which are known as Red, Orange, Yellow, Green,

---

1 Genesis 1:3.

Blue, Indigo, and Violet. The significance and the symbolism of the most important colors are the following:

White is the combination of all the colors; almost every religion has attributed White and Light to God, and it is an emblem of goodness, innocence, and purity.

Black is the complete absence of light and color, and, thus, it refers to death and loss.

Red is an emblem of God's omnipotence and of man's courage, will, and force.

Yellow is an emblem of God's omniscience and of man's mental functions and knowledge.

Blue is an emblem of God's omnipresence and of the human virtues of honor, love, friendship, fidelity, and prudence. Moreover, blue represents Freemasonic brotherhood, and it implies that, in a Freemason's mind, the aforementioned virtues should be expansive as the blue celestial canopy. From the perspective of English Freemasonry, the light blue that is used in Masonic regalia is derived from the color of the ribbon of the Most Noble Order of the Garter, which was originally light blue. However, in 1831, the color of the ribbon of the Most Noble Order of the Garter was changed to deep blue in order to distinguish it from that which the Stuarts in banishment on the Continent had conferred on their adherents. Thus, in the United Grand Lodge of England, the collars and the aprons of Grand Officers are dark blue.

Green, being the almost universal color of leaves and growing shoots of all vegetation, is an emblem of hope, progress, evolution, and regeneration. In particular, the green used in Masonic regalia of the Grand Lodge of Scotland has been probably taken from the Most Ancient and Most Noble Order of the Thistle.

Purple is associated with imperial rule and dignity, since it is a combination of power (Red) and love (Blue).

Orange is an emblem of zeal, enthusiasm, and man's mental and moral development and self-control.

Violet refers to penitence.

Grey is an emblem of humility.

Brown, being the color of a large part of the planet earth's land, is an emblem of durability, firmness, constancy, and self-abnegation.

42º Prince of Light: this degree teaches purity of heart, unselfishness, and justice.

43º Sublime Hermetic Sage or Hermetic Philosopher: in this degree, the aspirant is encouraged to overrun the twelve Symbolic Houses of the Sun, and this degree teaches that birth and death are represented by the two emblematical columns, Boaz and Jachin, and enclose our earthly destiny. According to this degree, life is the workshop in which is found the hidden treasure-house, where the wise learn to accomplish their destiny with strength, courage, and dignity.

44º Prince of the Zodiac: this degree is concerned with the study of the natural book of Stellar Universe, and with the correspondences between the twelve labors of the Greek divine hero Hercules and the constellations: the first labor is the capture of the man-eating Mares of Diomedes, and it corresponds to the Sign of Aries; the second labor is the capture of the Cretan Bull, and it corresponds to the Sign of Taurus; the third labor is the gathering the Golden Apples of the Hesperides, and it corresponds to the Sign of Gemini; the fourth labor is the capture of the Golden Hind of Artemis, and it corresponds to the Sign of Cancer; the fifth labor is the slain of the Nemean Lion, and it corresponds to the Sign of Leo; the sixth labor is the seizing of the Girdle of Hippolyta, Queen of the Amazons, and it corresponds to the Sign of Virgo; the seventh labor is the capture of the Erymanthian Boar, and it corresponds to the Sign of Libra; the eighth labor is the destruction of the Lernaean Hydra, and it corresponds to the Sign of Scorpio; the ninth labor is the slaying of the Stymphalian Birds, and it corresponds to the Sign of Sagittarius; the tenth labor is the capture and submission of Cerberus, Guardian of Hades, and it corresponds to the Sign of Capricorn; the eleventh labor is the cleansing of Augean Stables, and it corresponds to the Sign of Aquarius; the twelfth labor is the capture of the Red Cattle of Geryon, and it corresponds to the Sign of Pisces.

45º Sublime Sage of the Mysteries: this degree is concerned with the transition from darkness to light and with the mystical meaning of the number three.

46º Sublime Pastor of the Huts: this degree is concerned with the Great Work of alchemy, and it is focused on the encounter with the Green Lion. In alchemical texts, the Green Lion is usually a name for vitriol (the sulfuric acid created by distilling the green crystals of iron sulphate in a flask) or the nitric acid formed from heating saltpeter or niter and iron sulphate. When nitric acid is mixed with the acid that is derived from common salt, hydrochloric acid, produces *aqua regia*, a greenish tinged liquid that could dissolve even gold. Thus, a famous image in alchemy is the Green Lion devouring the sun, and it can be interpreted as *aqua regia* dissolving the solar gold and forming a solution that could tinge metals with gold.

47º Knight of the Seven Stars: this degree is related to the symbolism of the seven Stars of Ursa Major's annual revolution round the Mystery Sun and of the Pleiades. In Hindu mythology, the brightest stars of Ursa Major represent the Seven Sages and the constellation is known as Saptarshi;

these seven sages are Bhrigu, Atri, Angirasa, Vasishta, Pulastya, Pulalaha, and Kratu. In ancient Greek mythology, the Pleiades represent seven divine sisters, whose name was imagined to derive from that of their mother Pleione, effectively meaning 'daughters of Pleione'; Pleione was an Oceanid nymph.

48º Sublime Guardian of the Sacred Mount: this degree is concerned with allegories and symbolisms of the highest mysteries, it teaches constancy and fidelity, and its emblems are the altar of sacrifice and the initiate's combat.

49º Sublime Sage of the Pyramids: this degree urges the aspirant to descent into the depths of his soul and follow the ancient path of initiation, which was the following: the Neophyte was being conducted in front of a marvelous building, and he was arriving at its marble Portico by twenty-one steps of red granite, which resplendent the rays of the setting Sun and indicate to the Neophyte the termination of his journey. The magnificent building had a circle of Crypts that had to be overrun before arrival at the only entrance; those Crypts formed a labyrinth where the Neophyte would have wandered without finding the entrance if he did not have a guide. The Neophyte was entering the first Crypt, and, after retracing his steps several times, he was arriving, by observation and perseverance, at a Vestibule, above which was written, "Gate of the Dead." When the Neophyte was passing through that gate, a Priest was going to his aid he was presenting the Neophyte with the Golden Branch, the Symbol of Initiation. Then the Priest was throwing over the Neophyte's head a black transparent veil, and he was conducting him into a Temple where twenty-one Patriarchs clothed in black tunics were siting. The place was covered with hieroglyphics and painted in lively colors, and all the signs of the Zodiac were represented; in the midst of this Sanctuary, there was a triangular pyramid surmounted by the Sun, and, below it, there was a small richly decorated Altar, upon which laid a book bound in red leather. An Officer of the Temple was opening the book and was asking the aspirant to write his full name and qualities in this book. When this was being done, one of the Patriarchs addressing the aspirant, saying that the Universal Cause acts with one aim, but it acts by different laws, and that the aspirant should examine the chain of love that gathers and unites all below as well as on high.

50º Sublime Philosopher of Samothrace: this degree is devoted to the study of the mysteries of the "Great Gods" (in Greek, *Theoi Megaloi*) of Samothrace (a mountainous island in the northern Aegean). Our evidence for the Samothracian gods and their mysteries imply that there was at least one main female deity, along the lines of a 'Great Mother' (who is depicted on some Samothracian coins), two other male deities that were depicted in statues with the phallus erect,[1] and a fourth attendant figure (Kasmilos). In

---

1 Herodotus, *History*, 2:51.

the first century BC, the ancient Greek historian Diodorus of Sicily wrote about the Mysteries of Samothrace that, even though "the details of the initiatory rite are guarded among the matters not to be divulged and are communicated to the initiates alone," there are rumors about "how these gods appear to mankind and bring unexpected aid to those initiates of theirs who call upon them in the midst of perils," and it is also claimed that "men who have taken part in the mysteries become more pious and more just and better in every respect than they were before."[1]

51º Sublime Titan of the Caucasus: this degree is devoted to the study of the ancient Greek myth of Prometheus, who, according to the ancient Greek mythology, gave fire to mankind.

52º Sage of the Labyrinth: this degree is devoted to the study of Hermeticism.

53º Knight of the Phoenix or Sage of the Phoenix: this degree is devoted to the study of the myth of the Phoenix, which, according to the ancient Greek mythology, was a long-lived bird that was obtaining new life by arising from the ashes of its previous form; the Phoenix "could symbolize renewal in general as well as the sun, Time, the Empire, metempsychosis, consecration, resurrection, life in the heavenly Paradise, Christ, Mary, virginity, the exceptional man, and certain aspects of Christian life."[2]

54º Sublime Skald: the Scandinavian term 'Skald' means poet, and this degree is devoted to the study of the manners in which the different great mythological traditions of the world have addressed the quest for truth.

55º Sublime Orphic Doctor: this degree is devoted to the study of the Orphic Mysteries, associated with literature ascribed to the Greek mythical poet Orpheus, who descended into Hades and returned. According to the ancient Greek mythology, Orpheus founded the Orphic Mysteries. The rites of those mysteries were based on the myth of Dionysus Zagreus, the son of Zeus and Persephone. When Zeus proposed to make Zagreus the ruler of the universe, the Titans disagreed, and they dismembered the boy and devoured him. Athena, the goddess of wisdom, saved Zagreus's heart and gave it to Zeus, who swallowed the heart, from which was born the second Dionysus Zagreus. Moreover, Zeus destroyed the Titans with lightning. From the ashes of the Titans sprang the human race, who were part divine (Dionysus) and part evil (Titan). This double aspect of human nature, the Dionysian and the Titanic, plays a key role in Orphism. The Orphics affirmed the divine origin of the soul, but they believed that the soul could be liberated from its Titanic inheritance and could achieve eternal bliss through initiation

---

1 Diodorus of Sicily, *Library of History*, 49:1–6.
2 Van den Broek, Roelof, *The Myth of the Phoenix: According to Classical and Early Christian Traditions*, Leiden: E. J. Brill, 1971, p. 9.

into the Orphic Mysteries.[1] Plato's theory of ideas transformed Orphism's tradition of mystical cleansing into an integrated philosophical system.

56º Pontiff of Cadmia or Sage of Cadmia: this degree is concerned with the alchemical Great Work, and it urges the aspirant to study the seven musical tones, the seven colors, and the seven vowels. In alchemy, cadmia is an oxide of zinc that collects on the sides of furnaces where copper or brass is smelted and zinc sublimed.

57º Sublime Magus: the word Magus (plural Magi) means a wise man (according to ancient Zoroastrian and Hellenistic traditions and according to the Gospel of Matthew in the New Testament), and this degree is concerned with the derivation of all things from one Almighty Spirit and with the study of the relationship between spirit and matter.

58º Sage Brahmin or Prince Brahmin: this degree is devoted to the study of the spirituality of Brahmanism. Brahmanism was a monotheistic faith in Brahma as Creator, as the Logos/Word of Greek philosophy. The Brahmanic Triad came later, and, in the context of the Brahmanic Triad, we find the acceptance of three Forms of the Deity, that is, three members of the supreme godhead (known as the Trimutri system): Brahma as Creator, Vishnu as Preserver, and Siva as Destroyer. Moreover, in Hinduism, it is generally accepted that each member of the supreme godhead has a *sakti*, that is, a passive or female counterpart or goddess, who are also venerated by the Hindus. According to a notable article of the Hindu faith, Vishnu the Preserver makes occasional descents upon earth to teach mankind and destroy evil forces, and, for this purpose, he takes various animal and human forms; these descents are called Avatars, of which ten principal ones are taught: the most recent was as Krishna, and the last shall be as Khaki riding on a white horse.

59º Sublime Sage of Ogygia or Grand Pontiff of Ogygia: this degree is devoted to the study of Homer's poetic mythology. Odysseus, on leaving Troy, arrives at the island of the beautiful witch-goddess Circe, who, through a magical herb, transformed Odysseus's crew into swine, that is, Circe's magic brought out their male chauvinism from within, and they were brutalized by sensuality. Hermes, the Greek equivalent of the Egyptian god Thoth, protects Odysseus and gives him a sacred plant, called moly, whose root is black, and whose flower is white and milky. Circe's magical arts fail by the spiritual virtue of the plant that Hermes gave to Odysseus, she proposes a union to Odysseus, she swears by dread oaths that tie the powers below, and then she restores her swine to human form. After one year in this state, Odysseus and his crew leave Circe's island, they cross the sea to

---

1 Guthrie, William K. C., *Orpheus and Greek Religion: A Study of the Orphic Movement*, Princeton: Princeton University Press, 1993.

the Cimmerian Cavern, which leads to Tartarus. The necessary sacrifices are made, and then, after visiting the Tartarus, the hero begins his voyage and reaches the island of Ogygia, where he begins a happy life with the nymph Calypso, and he remains seven years with her until Hermes commands his return to his own land.

60º Sublime Guardian of the Three Fires: this degree is concerned with the three principles that constitute the human being: the body, the soul, and the divine spirit that resides in man's mind.

61º Sublime Unknown Philosopher: this degree is devoted to the occult medicine of the alchemists.

62º Sublime Sage of Eleusis: this degree is devoted to the study of the Mysteries of Eleusis, held every year for the cult of Demeter and Persephone based at Eleusis in ancient Greece.

63º Sublime Kawi: the Sanskrit term 'Kawi' means poet and is equivalent to the terms 'Skald' (Scandinavian) and 'Bard' (Celtic). This degree teaches love, union, and labor.

64º Sage of Mithras: this degree is devoted to the study of the Mysteries of Mithras, and it teaches the aspirant that there are mysteries within mysteries, in the sense that there is an exoteric initiation and an esoteric one. Mithras is the Zoroastrian angelic Power of Covenant and Oath as well as a divine Judge, an all-seeing Protector of Truth, and the Guardian of Cattle, of the Harvest, and of the Waters. According to the central premise of Zoroastrianism, which is exposed in the sacred volume called *Avesta* written in the Zend language, Ahura Mazda or Ohrmazd (*Ahura* literally means light, and *Mazda* literally means wisdom), being the highest spirit of worship, and Angra Mainyu or Ahriman, being the destructive spirit, contend with each other upon the earth for the souls of men; man may in this life fall under the evil sway of Ahriman, but Ohrmazd shall be supreme at the end.

Ohrmazd had produced, by his Word, a being called Life, or the Bull (the same word in Zend stands for both). However, Ahriman contrived to harm this being, and Ohrmazd, through the agency of an Amshaspand (spiritual creature) called Saphandomad (Wisdom), formed the first human pair, Meschia and Meschiane. Ahriman managed to corrupt this human couple by a bribe of fruits and milk. As a result an ongoing war broke out between Ohrmazd and Ahriman. The predominant principle of Zoroastrianism is purity symbolized by a sacred flame.

65º Guardian of Sanctuary or Grand Installator: this degree teaches, Faith, Hope, and Charity, and its symbol is a winged egg.

66º Grand Architect of the Mysterious City or Grand Consecrator: this degree is devoted to the concept of spirit or sacred breath, and its symbol is a winged egg on which is a circle with three stars.

67º Guardian of the Incommunicable Name or Grand Eulogist: this degree is devoted to the concept of the divine Son, and its symbol is a winged egg on which is a rayed triangle with the letter G (standing for Gnosis and Geometry) in the center.

68º Patriarch of Truth: this degree concerned with God, intelligence, and the traditions of the ancient Egyptian city Heliopolis. The symbol of this degree is a winged egg on which is a square from which proceed four rays in the middle of the sides; on the center of the square is a delta on the center of which is a star.

69º Knight of the Golden Branch of Eleusis or Sage of the Golden Branch of Eleusis: it explains why the branch is the symbol of initiation. According to Pythagoras's teachings, the path of Virtue and Vice resembles the letter Y; hence, the branch, like the letter Y, symbolizes the double path: the first is narrow and stony, and it leads to Elysium, whereas the second, is broad ad easy, and it leads to Tartarus.

70º Prince of Light or Patriarch of the Planispheres: this degree urges the aspirant to contemplate the divine Orient.

71º Patriarch of the Sacred Vedas: this degree urges the aspirant to contemplate Arjuna's battles at Kurukshetra, mentioned in the *Bhagavad Gita*. As the battle draws close, Arjuna is overcome with self-doubt about the righteousness of the war against his own friends and family. But, after his philosophical dialogue with Krishna, the eighth avatar of the god Vishnu, and with Krishna's help, Arjuna managed to defeat his enemies.

72º Sublime Master of Wisdom: this degree is concerned with the study of the institutions of the mysteries, in general.

73º Patriarch of the Sacred Fire or Doctor of the Sacred Fire: this degree is centered on the occult fire, which is symbolized by the secret ever-burning fire of the temple of Heliopolis, by the serpent issuing from the head of ancient Egyptian King Initiates, by the horns of Isis and of Moses, etc.

74º Sublime Master of the Stoka: in the Sanskrit literature, the *Stoka* is the oldest, simplest, and most popular measure; it consists of a distich of two sixteen-syllable lines divided at the eighth syllable. Thus, in the context of the Memphis–Misraim Rite, a Sublime Master of the Stoka is one who has mastered the occult powers of numbers and rhythm.

75º Knight Commander of the Libyan Chain: this degree is an honorific title, since it is the supreme degree of the Consistory. The title of this degree refers to the chains of gold that were granted by Egyptian and other Oriental kings as a mark of royal favor. The Libyan Sea is the portion of the Mediterranean Sea between the southern coastline of Crete and the coastline of northern Africa. The earliest references to the term 'Libyan' can found in the works of the Greek historians and geographers Polybius (third century BC), Strabo (first century BC), and Plutarch (first century AD).

Sublime Council:

76º Interpreter of Hieroglyphics or Patriarch of Isis: this degree is focused on Isis, and it teaches science, wisdom, and virtue. In the ancient Egyptian mythology, Isis was the wife and sister of Osiris, the mother of Horus, and the first daughter of Geb and Nut. Geb was the Egyptian god of the Earth and a member of the Ennead of Heliopolis.[1] Nut was the Egyptian goddess of the sky in the Ennead of Heliopolis. Isis was chosen by her older brother, Osiris, to share the throne. She instituted marriage, she taught women to grow corn and wear clothes, and she taught men to cure disease. When Osiris was killed by their brother Set, who usurped the throne, Isis searched the Nile for her husband's body. Upon finding Osiris's coffin, she bathed it in tears and brought it back to Egypt, where she restored it, allowing Osiris to posthumously conceive a son, called Horus, with her. In order to achieve the permanent annihilation of Osiris, Set cut Osiris's body into fourteen pieces, which he then scattered throughout Egypt. Isis searched and recovered every piece of Osiris's body, except for the phallus, which had been devoured by a crab, and then she performed for the first time in Egyptian history the rites of embalmment, which gave Osiris eternal life. Isis was helped by Anubis, Thoth, and her son, Horus. Moreover, Thoth became the judge of Horus and Set, and he sentenced Set to return the Kingdom of Egypt to Horus. Isis represents the Kabbalistic Sefira of Binah.

77º Sublime Knight or Sage Theosopher: this degree is concerned with comparative mythology. In this context, the Kabbalistic Tree of Life can be used as a system of comparative religion/mythology in the context of which one draws correspondences between divine figures and the Sefirot of the Kabbalistic Tree of Life. For instance, one can draw the following correspondences:

1. Kether: Ptah, the Egyptian god of Memphis and defender of craftsmen and artists

2. Hokhmah: Thoth

3. Binah: Isis

---

1 According to the Ennead of Heliopolis, in the beginning there was nothing (Nun), a mound of earth rose from Nun, and upon it Atum (later Amun or Ra) emerged as the cause of himself. He did not want to be alone, and, thus, he spoke the Great Word (according to the Memphite theology), or he masturbated (according to the Helipolitan system), producing air (Shu), and moisture (Tefnut). Shu and Tefnut gave birth to the earth (Geb) and the sky (Nut). Geb and Nut were separated by Shu, creating our world. The children of Nut and Geb were Osiris, Horus the elder, Set, Isis, and Nephthys.

4. Hesed: Amoun, known also as "Little king of the gods," he was the god of expedition and discovery

5. Gevurah: Horus

6. Tifereth: Ra

7. Netsah: Hathoor, the goddess of joy, love, dance, music, song, and weaving

8. Hod: Anubis, the god of embalming and the companion of souls

9. Yesod: Shu, the god of light and air and as such personified the wind and the earth's atmosphere

10. Malkuth: Osiris.

78º Grand Pontiff of the Thebais: this degree is concerned with the mythological and scientific traditions of Thebes. Thebes was the most ancient part of Egypt, and Osiris was born in Thebes. According to Diodorus of Sicily, the Thebans were the most ancient of people, and, according to Lucian, the Egyptians were the first who erected temples. Moreover, according to Lucian, the Ethiopians and the Thebans invented the Science of the Stars and named the planets.

79º Knight of the Formidable Sada or Sage of the Formidable Sada: in Sanskrit, *Sada* means ever, always, or constantly, and, thus, this degree emphasizes that constancy which the members of the Memphis–Misraim Rite must observe in delving into the mysteries of nature and science.

80º Sublime Elect of the Sanctuary of Heliopolis or of Mazias: the ancient Egyptian cult center Iunu, named "On" in the Hebrew Bible, was renamed Heliopolis by the Greeks, because the sun-god Ra (in Greek, *Helios*) presided there. Iunu is mentioned in the *Pyramid Text* as the "House of Ra," and Ra means creator. According to the ancient Egyptian mythology, Ra, before manifesting in Heliopolis, rested under the name Atum in the ocean. However, one day, Ra rose out from the abyss enclosed within a lotus, and he shined in the Egyptian sky. From Ra came Shu and Tefnut, from whom came Geb and Nut, from whom came Osiris and Isis. Sometimes, Ra is personified as a man with a head of a falcon under the name Ra-Harakhty (i.e., the god of Heliopolis).

Moreover, according to the ancient Egyptian mythology, Ra sprang from the Cosmic Egg. In particular, in the Egyptian *Book of the Dead*, Ra is shown beaming in his egg (precisely, the Sun), and he started off when the god Shoo (i.e., the Solar energy) awakened and gave him the impulse. According to the Egyptian Book of the Dead, 85, Ra exclaims: "I am the creative soul of the celestial abyss. None sees my nest, none can break my egg, I am the Lord!" In general, the first manifestation of the cosmos in the form of an egg (i.e., the primordial, unnamed 'First Cause') was a widely diffused tradition of antiquity. For instance, according to the ancient Egyptian mythology, Seb, who was the god of Time and of the Earth, laid an egg, precisely the universe. Similarly, according to the *Brahmanda Purana*[1] and the "Nasadiya Sukta,"[2] the 'First Cause' created the cosmos from the monistic *Hiranyagarbha* or Golden Egg. In addition, in the ancient Greek Orphic tradition, the Orphic Egg is the cosmic egg from which hatched the primordial hermaphroditic deity Phanes/Protogonos, who, in turn, gave birth to the other gods.[3]

81° Intendant Regulator or Patriarch of Memphis: this degree is focused on Horus, and it is concerned with the concepts of the divine Son, the divine mediator, fatherhood, meekness, and justice. Our knowledge of the Memphite 'school' is based on an inscription on the right-hand side of the Shabaka Stone, the so-called Memphis Theology. The Shabaka Stone is a heavy, near black block or slab of "Green breccia" from Wadi Hammamat named after Pharaoh Shabaka, who ruled in the XXVth Dynasty (eighth century BC).[4]

The Shabaka Stone (lines 1 and 2) includes the following text:

> The living Horus: excellent Two Lands; the Two Ladies: excellent Two Lands; the Golden Horus: excellent Two Lands; King of Upper and Lower Egypt: Neferkare, the son of Ra, [Shabaka], beloved of Ptah-South-of-his-Wall, who lives like Ra forever.

According to the Shabaka Stone and the Pyramid Texts, creation emerges as "the risen land," or "ta-Tenen," out of Nun, the primordial chaos (a chaotic state before creation). Atum-Ra, the creator-god manifesting as the Sun, rested upon the sacred hill of Heliopolis when he rose for the first time. Whereas Nun is the inert primordial ocean, the primordial hill, namely, Heliopolis, is the mount of creation. This pictorial representation refers to the ancient Egyptian mythological cosmogony: in this context, the "risen land" was a metaphor of the emergence of creation and light out of the undifferentiated 'waters,' in which inert chaos lay dormant and hidden by darkness, and in which the creative cause, precisely, Atum (i.e., the *ba* or 'soul' of chaos) 'floated.'

1 The *Brahmanda Purana* (The History of the Universe), is one of the eighteen *Mahapuranas*, that is, eighteen Hindu religious texts. The Sanskrit term 'Brahmanda' is derived from the Sanskrit terms 'Brahma' and 'anda': 'Brahma' is regarded as a manifestation of 'Brahman' as the creator deity, and, by extension, it refers to the universe coming from the root *brith*, meaning expansion; the word 'anda' means egg.
2 The "Nasadiya Sukta," also known as the "Hymn of Creation," is the 129th hymn of the 10th Mandala of the *Rigveda*.
3 West, Martin L., *The Orphic Poems*, Oxford: Oxford University Press, 1983. In Greek, 'Protogonos' means First-Born, and 'Phanes' means 'Manifestor' or 'Revealer,' and it is related to the Greek words 'light' and 'to shine forth.'
4 Frankfort, Henri, *Kingship and the Gods*, Chicago: University of Chicago Press, 1979, chapter 2; *Ancient Egyptian Religion: An Interpretation*, New York: Dover, 2000.

82º Grand Elect of the Temple of Midgard: in Norse cosmology, Midgard (in Old Saxon, Middilgard) is the name for the world inhabited by and known to humans, that is, it is synonymous with the Greek term *ecumene*. Obviously, this degree is concerned with philosophy of religion and comparative religion.

83º Sublime Elect of the Valley of Oddy: this degree is concerned with the symbolical significance of the Ennead of Heliopolis. According to the Memphite theological system, Ptah is the speaking Atum-Ra: he is all-encompassing, and, by speaking the Great Word, he created the Ennead of Heliopolis.[1] In other word's Atum's Great Word, or Logos, is the first cause of the created universe. According to the Shabaka Stone and the Pyramid Texts, the principle of mind whose essence is the heart and the principle of creative speech whose essence is the tongue are, respectively, the 'semen' and the 'hands' of Atum. In particular, according to the Shabaka Stone (lines 53 and 54), Horus is a power or an epiphany of Ptah's mind (heart), and Thoth is a power or an epiphany of Ptah's tongue (speech):

> There comes into being in the heart. There comes into being by the tongue. (It is) as the image of Atum. Ptah is the very great, who gives life to all the gods and their vital essence (*ka*). It all in this heart and by this tongue. Horus came into being in him; Thoth came into being in him as Ptah.

84º Patriarch of the Izeds or Doctor of the Izeds: according to Zoroastrianism, Ohrmazd created spirits ranged in a certain hierarchical order; the Amshaspands occupy the first rank, the Izeds the second, and the Fervers the third. Moreover, according to Zoroastrianism, there are twenty-eight Izeds, of whom Mithras is the chief.

85º Sublime Sage or Knight of Kneph: in ancient Egyptian religious art, *Kneph* is a motif consisting in a winged egg, which symbolizes universal spirit acting on primordial matter, and, generally, it represents the productive world.

86º Sublime Philosopher of the Valley of Kab: this degree refers to the Sublime Rose of the Valley of Kab. In particular, the priests of Memphis used to consecrate a Rose bush to Isis, who was called the Queen of Roses. Kab is the name of the sacred site of Memphis where the symbolic rose was found.

87º Sublime Prince of Masonry: this degree reviews all previous ones.

88º Grand Elect of the Sacred Curtain: Clement of Alexandria has said that, in the temples of Egypt, an immense curtain separated the Congregation from the Sanctuary. That curtain was drawn over five pillars, which symbolize the five senses, and was made of four colors symbolizing

---

1 Ibid.

both the four elements and the four Cardinal Points. In the context of the Memphis–Misraim Rite, the Sacred Curtain is an emblem of the completion of Initiation, and it represents the esoteric teaching of Masonry as distinct from the exoteric one.

89º Patriarch of the Mystical City: this degree urges the candidate to contemplate Truth, Hope, Life, and Death.

90º Sublime Master of the Great Work: this degree is an honorific title, since it is the supreme degree of the Sublime Council.

Grand Tribunal:

91º Grand Defender: the active members of this degree constitute a body of Nine Dignitaries entitled the Grand Tribunal of Defenders of the Order, and their Chief Magistrate is called the Grand Shofet (in Hebrew, *Shofet* means judge). This degree is concerned with the administration of justice within the Order.

92º Grand Catechist: the active members of this degree constitute a body of Seven Dignitary Officers entitled the Grand Liturgical College of Sublime Catechists of the Order. Their duty is to inspect the labors of the subordinate bodies.

93º Regulator General: the active members of this degree constitute a body of Nine Dignitaries entitled the Grand Consistory of Inspector Regulators General of the Order, subordinate to G.C. of 94°.

94º Prince of Memphis or Grand Administrator: the active members of this degree constitute a body of Seven Dignitary Officers entitled the Grand Council General of Administrators of the Order, Princes of Memphis.

95º Grand Conservator: the active members of this degree constitute a body of Seven Dignitary Officers entitled the Sovereign Sanctuary of Patriarchs and Matriarchs Grand Conservators of the Order.

96º Grand and Puissant Sovereign of the Order: the active members of this degree constitute a body of six Sublime Magi, 96°, presided over by a Grand Hierophant, 97°, and the Assembly is entitled Grand Areopagus of the Celestial Empire of the Sublime Magi 96°, Grand and Puissant Sovereigns of the Order.

97º Grand Hierophant: The Supreme Head of a Sovereign Grand Sanctuary of the Order.

6. The United Traditionalist Grand Sanctuaries Of The Ancient And Primitive Rite Memphis–Misraim

97

✠

33

Preamble

"Blessed are those who hear the word of God and keep it!"[1]

Let it be known that there exists, unknown to many people, a very ancient fraternity of divine wisdom whose object is the amelioration and spiritual evolution of humanity by helping humanity to participate in the real truth. This fraternity was already in existence in the most remote times, and it has manifested its activity secretly and openly in the world under different names and in various forms: it has always struggled for the deification of humanity through philosophical, theological, and political means.

This fraternity is 'secret' (in Greek, *mystikē*), in the sense that it consists in an ontologically founded mystical experience of man's deification: the experience of man's participation in the deity transcends any kind of propositional language. To this 'secret fraternity' every wise and spiritually enlightened person belongs by right of his or her ethos: they all, even if they are personally unknown to each other, are *de facto* members of a spiritual nobility, since they are rich enough to be psychically open and unselfishly giving, and they are wise enough to live a life that is always united with its transcendent meaning, or *telos*. Into this fraternity no one can be really admitted by another unless he has the power to enter it by virtue of his spiritual freedom, that is, by virtue of his

---

1 Luke 11:28.

freedom from the logic of physical and historical necessities and by virtue of his communion with the ultimate source of the meaning of beings and things in the world; neither can anyone after he has once entered this sacred society be expelled unless he should expel himself by following a spiritually errant course and falling short of his ontological potential.

Every enlightened person is aware of the aforementioned truths. But rather few persons are aware that there exists also an external, historically existent organization of such men and women, who, having adopted the aforementioned 'noble' mode of existence, are willing to share their Royal Secret with others, desirous of adopting that mode of existence, and to bestow the aforementioned type of nobility on those who seek spiritual nobility.

This organization is known at the present time as the United Traditionalist Grand Sanctuaries of the Ancient and Primitive Rite Memphis–Misraim (henceforth, referred to, for the sake of brevity, as the UTGS). It is a traditionalist, lay, Freemasonic fraternity working the degrees of the Ancient and Primitive Rite Memphis–Misraim, investigating the spiritual quests of humanity throughout the history of civilization, studying comparative religion, mythology, and political philosophy, and endorsing the spiritual heritage of Plato's metaphysics and of the mystical theologians of the Greek East, known also as the Hesychasts or Neptic fathers, with regard to the deification of humanity. The UTGS is international, and it has connections in every civilized country in the world. Every man or woman who becomes a member of the UTGS has an indefeasible right to Symbolic Masonry.

CONSTITUTION

Article I

SECTION 1: Under the style and title "United Traditionalist Grand Sanctuaries of the Ancient and Primitive Rite Memphis–Misraim," an organization, formerly known as the Ancient and Primitive Rite Memphis–Misraim, has been reorganized and reconstituted. This reconstituted Order is an international organization and is hereinafter referred to as the UTGS.

Article II

SECTION 1: The UTGS declares the following: sovereignty naturally belongs only to the Great Architect of the Universe, the created human being has potential access to the uncreated energies of the ontologically sovereign Great Architect of the Universe, and, to the extent that the human being actualizes this potential, humanity is deified.

SECTION 2: The principle purpose of the UTGS is to teach true fraternal relations, to make people aware that the human being is potentially a god-in-the-making, and to act as a civilizing force in the life of humanity.

SECTION 3: The subsidiary aims of the UTGS are:

(a) to develop a traditionalist, activist, interventionist, and scholarly rigorous Masonic movement, and to initiate its members into the principles of transcendental mysticism, for which purpose its members are, first of all, perfected in Symbolic Masonry;

(b) to establish and administer Lodges, Colleges, Chapters, Senates, Areopaguses, Tribunals, Consistories, Supreme Councils, Grand Tribunals, and Grand Sanctuaries were the degrees of the Ancient and Primitive Rite Memphis–Misraim are worked according to rituals officially compiled and approved by the authorities of the UTGS;

(c) to organize conferences, workshops, seminars, and cultural events and to publish special editions and executive reports related to the ethos and the aims of the UTGS.

SECTION 4: An official banquet, called *Agápe*, takes place after every official meeting of Colleges, Chapters, Senates, Areopaguses and Tribunals, Consistories, and Sublime Councils. Each *Agápe* has at least one Chaplain appointed by the Order's Grand-Hierophant General, who is the President of the Order's Council of Chaplains. In order to be eligible to be appointed as a Chaplain of an *Agápe*, one must be in possession of at least the ninetieth degree of the Order.

SECTION 5: During an *Agápe*, before the meal, the following prayer is read by the Chaplain: "In the Name of the Holy Nous, or God the Father, and of the Holy Logos, or God the Son, and of the Holy Spirit, three Persons one Nature. May the Most High enlighten us with the knowledge of His truth, and grant that we may be endued with wisdom to understand and explain the mysteries of the Holy Faith. May He be with us in all our assemblies, guide us in the paths of rectitude, enable us to keep all His statutes while this life shall last, and, finally, bring us to the perfect knowledge of His holy Name."

After the previous prayer, the Chaplain serves bread, saying the following: "Let us now eat this bread which we receive at the point of the sword, which symbolizes our willingness to divide our last loaf with our Brothers and Sisters, our generosity in giving, our respect and pity for all weakness and steadfastness in defending them, our loyalty to truth and to the pledged word, our determination to fight against injustice, our refusal to retreat before the enemy, and our championship of the right and good in every place and at all times, against the forces of evil." In the sequel, the Chaplain serves red wine, saying the following: "Brothers and Sisters, we shall now refresh ourselves with wine, which, in the Holy Bible, symbolizes love toward the neighbor and the good of faith.[1] We shall receive this wine over the sword, to teach us that we should ever be ready to divide the luxuries as well as the necessities of life with our Brothers and Sisters, and, generally, to succor, protect, and defend our neighbor. If he hunger, feed him; if he thirst, give him to drink; if he be naked, clothe him; if he be sick or afflicted, visit him and take good care of him; if he be depressed, offer him spiritual guidance."

After the aforementioned ceremony, the meal will be served. At the end of the meal, the Chaplain will say the following prayer: "In the Name of the Father, and of the Son, and of the Holy Spirit. 'Every good and perfect gift is from above, coming down from the Father of the heavenly lights, who does not change like shifting shadows.'[2] Blessed be God, eternal King, for these and all His good gifts to us. Amen."

Article III

SECTION 1: The UTGS is part of the general Freemasonic institution, but it maintains its own doctrines, ethos, and aims. Additionally, the UTGS is part of the great and universal quest for the real truth.

SECTION 2: The jurisdiction of the UTGS extends worldwide. For administrative reasons, the international jurisdiction of the UTGS is divided into local Grand Sanctuaries, each of which is presided by a Grand and Puissant Sovereign of the Order (96th Degree).

SECTION 3: The Grand and Puissant Sovereigns of the Order's Grand Sanctuaries are appointed and overseen by the Grand Hierophant-General of the UTGS, and they serve in their offices for as long as the Grand Hierophant-General of the UTGS pleases.

SECTION 4: Organizations throughout the world adopting this Constitution become integral parts of the UTGS upon receipt of official notification of their acceptance as such. All such joining organizations have to comply with whatever conditions the authorities of the UTGS may impose.

SECTION 5: The Central Office of the UTGS is wherever its supreme administrative authorities may decide at any time.

Article IV

SECTION 1: There shall be One Supreme Office in which shall be vested paramount authority regarding all matters that concern the welfare and administration of the UTGS.

---

1 Isaiah 55:1, Hosea 9:2–4, Jeremiah 48:32–33, Matthew 26:29, Luke 22:17–18, and Revelation 6:6.
2 James 1:17.

SECTION 2: The title of the person filling this office shall be Grand Hierophant-General of the United Traditionalist Grand Sanctuaries of the Ancient and Primitive Rite Memphis–Misraim, and he or she shall be addressed as Most Illustrious Brother/Sister.

SECTION 3: The person (male or female) filling this office shall serve for life, or until his or her resignation.

SECTION 4: The person filling this office shall officially and in writing appoint his or her successor.

Article V

SECTION 1: The Grand Hierophant-General of the UTGS shall be the sole executive officer of the UTGS; he or she has to act as the first servant of the Order's principles and aims; he or she shall cultivate the principles of love and labor throughout the Order; he or she shall be the ultimate guarantor and defender of the Order's ethos and goals; he or she shall be the Custodian of the Archives and the Library of the UTGS.

SECTION 2: The Grand Hierophant-General of the UTGS shall have the sole power of filling all general offices by appointing persons to occupy the same, with the exception of the offices that are subject to Article VII, and he or she shall have the power of removing any general officer at will. Moreover, the Grand Hierophant-General of the UTGS shall have exclusive jurisdiction to hear and resolve disputes involving members who hold degrees higher than the 90th.

SECTION 3: The Grand Hierophant-General of the UTGS shall have power to declare the policy of the UTGS and to direct and manage the affairs of the UTGS in accordance with the Order's Ritual and ethos.

SECTION 4: The Grand Hierophant-General of the UTGS shall have the right to cancel or suspend the Charter of any subordinate organization (Lodge, College, Chapter, Senate, Areopagus and Tribunal, Consistory, Sublime Council, Grand Tribunal, and Grand Sanctuary) and shall also have the right to suspend or dissolve the membership of any person whenever such action is, in his or her opinion, for the interest of the UTGS.

Article VI

SECTION 1: All general business of the UTGS is transacted in assemblies described as Symbolic Lodges. Each Symbolic Lodge confers the following degrees: 1º Apprentice; 2º Companion; and 3º Master.

SECTION 2: The Officers of a Symbolic Lodge of the UTGS are the following:

Worshipful Master: he/she is the presiding officer, and he/she is responsible for every single thing within his/her Lodge. His/her Jewel is a Square, and he/she sits in the East of the Lodge room. In case the Lodge Master is a Grand Hierophant, his/her jewel consists of a Square and a diagram of the Pythagorean Theorem.

Senior Warden: He/she is the second in command of the Lodge, and, in the absence of the Worshipful Master, the Senior Warden assumes the Worshipful Master's duties. His/her Jewel is a Level, and he/she sits in the West of the Lodge room. It is the Senior Warden's duty to oversee the Brothers' and the Sisters' morals while the Lodge is in session.

Junior Warden: He/she is the third in command of the Lodge, and, he/she, too, may open the Lodge if the Worshipful Master is unable to attend the meeting. His/her Jewel is a Plumb, and he/she sits in the South of the Lodge room. It is the Junior Warden's duty to oversee the Brothers' and the Sisters' morals while the Lodge is at ease or refreshment.

Orator: His/her duty is to oversee and promote Masonic education and research. His/her Jewel is a Double Scroll or an Open Book, and he/she sits to the right of the Senior Warden.

Secretary: He/she is the Lodge's Recorder, chief communication officer, and chief advisor to the Worshipful Master. His/her duties require a high degree of Masonic knowledge and experience combined with diplomacy, knowledge of human resources management, and detailed paperwork skills, since the Secretary is the Lodge's backbone and communication center. His/her Jewel is a Pair of Crossed Quill Pens, and he/she sits in the North.

Treasurer: He/she is the Chief Financial Officer of the Lodge. His/her Jewel is a Pair of Crossed Keys, signifying that he/she is the Collector and the Distributor of all Lodge Monies in accordance with the Worshipful Master's commands. He/she sits to the right of the Secretary.

Director of Ceremonies: His/her duties and principle role consist in the organization of processions and ensuring the correct precedence and etiquette in formal proceedings. He/she is responsible to formally conduct visitors into the Lodge and introduce them to the members when the Lodge is in session. His/her Jewel is a Pair of Crossed Batons, and he/she sits to the right of the Junior Warden. During the opening and the closing ceremonies, the Director of Ceremonies opens the Bible to the correct passage of the degree being worked and closes it after the Lodge is adjourned. Moreover, he/she lights and extinguishes the candles in the Lodge and displays the appropriate Tracing Board.

Mystagogue: His/her Jewel is the Set of Compasses, and his/her position is on the lower level, to the right of the Worshipful Master in the East (the Mystagogue's roles and duties are those that, according to the United Grand Lodge of England's Emulation Ritual, are ascribed to the Senior and the Junior Deacons of an English Lodge). He/she is the messenger of the Worshipful Master, and he/she carries a long staff (or rod), which is symbolic of the caduceus (or wand) of the ancient Greek god Hermes. It is his/her duty to assist the Worshipful Master and carry orders between the Worshipful Master and the Senior Warden. During degree rituals, he/she guides the candidate and conducts him/her around the Lodge room.

Assistant Secretary: He/she is the Secretary's deputy and general assistant. It is his/her duty to keep accurate Lodge Minutes. His/her Jewel is similar to that of the Secretary, but it bears the inscription "ASSISTANT," and he/she sits to the right of the Secretary.

Assistant Director of Ceremonies: He/she is the Director of Ceremonies' deputy and general assistant. His/her Jewel is similar to that of the Director of Ceremonies, but it bears the inscription "ASSISTANT," and he/she sits to the left of the Junior Warden.

Inner Guard: He/she is the Lodge's Chief Security Officer, and it is his/her duty to ascertain at all times whether the Tyler is guarding the door and only allowing visitors to enter after they have been properly vouched for. His/her Jewel is a Pair of Crossed Swords, and he/she sits to the right of the Senior Warden, to whom he/she is accountable.

Tyler/Outer Guard: Hs/her duties and principle role consist in ensuring that only those who are duly qualified are allowed to enter the Lodge room. His/her Jewel is a Sword, and his/her position is outside the closed door of the Lodge room, armed with a sword. Additionally, it is his/her duty to make sure that each visitor is "properly clothed" and in possession of the proper Masonic secrets (according to the degree being worked) before entrance into the Lodge room. After the Lodge members are inside the Lodge room, the door is "closed tyled," and the Tyler sits to the right of the Senior Warden. However, during initiation/promotion ceremonies, the Tyler remains outside the Lodge room and acts according to the corresponding degree's ritual. The Inner Guard and the Tyler communicate with each other by knocking on the door: the Tyler from the outside, and the Inner Guard from the inside.

SECTION 3: The degrees beyond the 3rd one are conferred in special assemblies described as follows:

Colleges: they confer the degrees $4^{\underline{o}}$–$14^{\underline{o}}$,

Chapters: they confer the degrees $15^{\underline{o}}$–$18^{\underline{o}}$,

Senates: they confer the degrees $19^{\underline{o}}$–$29^{\underline{o}}$,

Areopaguses and Tribunals: they confer the degrees $30^{\underline{o}}$–$33^{\underline{o}}$,

Consistories: they confer the degrees $34^{\underline{o}}$–$75^{\underline{o}}$,

Sublime Councils: they confer the degrees $76^{\underline{o}}$–$90^{\underline{o}}$,

Grand Tribunals: they confer the degrees $91^{\underline{o}}$–$96^{\underline{o}}$.

Every assembly of higher degrees must be allied directly to a Symbolic Lodge and bear the same number and distinctive name as the corresponding Symbolic Lodge.

SECTION 4: The 97th and *ne plus ultra* Degree of the Order is purely administrative, and it is only held by the Grand Hierophant-General of the UTGS. However, the Degree of Grand Hierophant (Honoris Causa) 97° may be conferred by the Grand Hierophant-General of the UTGS on a Brother or a Sister who has shown outstanding devotion to the aims of the Order, in general, and outstanding administrative skills in the context of the UTGS, in particular.

SECTION 5: When a Symbolic Lodge has a College, a Chapter, a Senate, an Areopagus and Tribunal, a Consistory, a Sublime Council, and a Grand Tribunal attached to it, it may apply for a Charter to form a Grand Sanctuary. Each and every Grand Sanctuary shall be established by, and operate according to a relevant Charter issued, signed, and sealed by the Grand Hierophant-General of the UTGS, bearing both the Seal of the UTGS and the personal Seal of the Grand Hierophant-General of the UTGS.

Article VII

SECTION 1: There shall be a First-Degree Judicial Body, called the Grand Tribunal of Defenders of the Order, consisting of nine active members of the 91st Degree, inclusive of their Chief Magistrate, called the Grand Shofet. This is the Order's Court of First Instance, and its jurisdiction is limited to cases involving members of up to and including the 90th Degree. Its members and Chief Magistrate are appointed and overseen by the Grand Council General of Administrators of the Order every four years. Its decisions are made by majority rule.

SECTION 2: There shall be an Educational and Supervisory Body, called the Grand Liturgical College of Sublime Catechists of the Order, consisting of seven active members of the 92nd Degree, inclusive of their Chief Magistrate, called the Supreme Grand Catechist, and its duties are to protect the Order's Rituals and Constitution, to execute commands issued by the Grand Hierophant-General of the UTGS, to inspect the labors of the subordinate bodies, and to organize educational seminars for the Order's members. Its members and Chief Magistrate are appointed and overseen by the Grand Council General of Administrators of the Order every four years.

SECTION 3: There shall be a Second-Degree Judicial Body, called the Grand Consistory of Inspector Regulators General of the Order, consisting of nine active members of the 93rd Degree, inclusive of their Chief Magistrate, called the Supreme Regulator General. This is the Order's Court of Appeal, and its jurisdiction is limited to cases involving members of up to and including the 90th Degree. Its members and Chief Magistrate are appointed and overseen by the Grand Council General of Administrators of the Order every four years. Its decisions are made by majority rule.

Article VIII

SECTION 1: There shall be a General Administrative Body, called the Grand Council General of Administrators of the Order, consisting of seven active members of the 94th Degree, entitled Princes of Memphis, inclusive of their Chief Magistrate, called the Supreme Prince. Its decisions are made by majority rule. Its members are appointed and overseen by the Grand Hierophant-General of the UTGS, and they serve in their offices for as long as the Grand Hierophant-General of the UTGS pleases.

SECTION 2: There shall be a Supreme Overseeing Body, called the Sovereign Sanctuary of Patriarchs and Matriarchs Grand Conservators of the Order, consisting of seven active members of the 95th Degree of the Order, appointed and presided by the Grand Hierophant-General of the UTGS; they serve in their offices for as long as the Grand Hierophant-General of the UTGS pleases. The duties of the members of the Sovereign Sanctuary of Patriarchs and Matriarchs Grand Conservators of the Order shall be to aid the Grand Hierophant-General of the UTGS in safeguarding compliance with and strict observance of the Order's Constitution and Ritual throughout the Order's assemblies.

SECTION 3: There shall be an Advisory Body, called the Grand Areopagus of the Celestial Empire of the Sublime Magi 96°, consisting of six active members of the 96th Degree of the Order, appointed and presided by the Grand Hierophant-General of the UTGS; they serve in their offices for as long as the Grand Hierophant-General of the UTGS pleases. Moreover, every active member of the 96th Degree who has not been appointed by the Grand Hierophant-General of the UTGS as an active member of the Grand Areopagus of the Celestial Empire, but he/she happens to be the Grand Hierophant of one of the Grand Sanctuaries of the UTGS, participates in the Grand Areopagus of the Celestial Empire ex officio as a supernumerary member. The duties of the members of the Grand Areopagus of the Celestial Empire of the Sublime Magi 96° shall be to aid the Grand Hierophant-General of the UTGS in promulgating and establishing the measures emanating from that office. It shall be the duty of the Grand Areopagus of the Celestial Empire of the Sublime Magi 96° to provide bye-laws for the UTGS and its subordinate organizations; no bye-laws shall become operative until approved by the Grand Hierophant-General of the UTGS.

SECTION 4: Within the UTGS, there is an Inner Circle, which, in essence, is an elitist fraternity within the fraternity of the UTGS.

SECTION 5: The Inner Circle of the UTGS is called the "Venerable Order of the Illuminati Princes, Knights of the Hellenic Gnosis, York, Constantinople, the Kievan Realm, and Moscow" (for simplicity often referred to as the Venerable Order of the Illuminati Princes), and its members are the spiritual and political soldiers of the UTGS. This Order is concerned with the study and the promotion of the idea of the Constantinian Arc, a geocultural space whose strategic pivots are the following: the historical Greek space in the Haemus Peninsula (known also as the Balkan Peninsula), being the geographical cradle of the Greek culture (which was also the cultural underpinning of the Roman Empire); the English city of York (whose Roman name was Eboracum), where Constantine the Great was proclaimed Roman Emperor in 306 AD; Constantinople (known also as the New Rome), the over-millenary capital of the Eastern Roman Empire (from 330 AD until 1453); the Kievan Realm, where Vladimir Sviatoslavich the Great converted to Byzantine Christianity in 988 and Christianized the Kievan Rus; and Moscow (known also as the Third Rome), which became the administrative center of the Russian Orthodox Church in 1589, when the See of Moscow was elevated to a Patriarchate.

SECTION 6: The authority of inviting members of the UTGS to join the Venerable Order of the Illuminati Princes lies exclusively in the hands of the Grand Hierophant-General of the UTGS, who is the *ex officio* head and sole executive officer of the Venerable Order of the Illuminati Princes. The active members of the Grand Areopagus of the Celestial Empire of the Sublime Magi 96° are *ex officio* members of the Inner Circle of the UTGS. Every year, the active members of the Grand Areopagus of the Celestial Empire of the Sublime Magi 96° propose to the Grand Hierophant-General of the UTGS a list of members of the UTGS whom, in their opinion, the Grand Hierophant-General of the UTGS should invite to join the Venerable Order of the Illuminati Princes.

SECTION 7: The candidates for the Inner Circle of the UTGS must be in possession of at least the 32nd Degree of the UTGS, they must have outstanding intellectual and moral qualifications, and they must have fully understood and endorsed the philosophy and the goals of the UTGS. The activities of the Venerable Order of the Illuminati Princes are very rarely, if ever, mentioned outside the circle of its members.

Article IX

SECTION 1: There shall be an Executive Committee of Three, whose duty shall be to administer the affairs of the UTGS under the general supervision of the Grand Hierophant-General of the UTGS. All official acts and decisions of the Executive Committee are subject to the approval of the

Grand Hierophant-General of the UTGS and are null and void if disapproved by the Grand Hierophant-General of the UTGS.

SECTION 2: The Grand Treasurer of the Celestial Empire, the Grand Secretary of the Celestial Empire, and the Grand Hierophant-General of the UTGS are the three members of the Executive Committee. The Executive Committee consists of two Subcommittees: the Financial Subcommittee and the Doctrinal and Protocol Subcommittee. The Grand Hierophant-General of the UTGS and the Grand Treasurer of the Celestial Empire constitute the Financial Subcommittee of the UTGS, while the Grand Hierophant-General of the UTGS and the Grand Secretary of the Celestial Empire constitute the Doctrinal and Protocol Subcommittee of the UTGS.

SECTION 3: The Grand Treasurer of the Celestial Empire and the Grand Secretary of the Celestial Empire must be in possession of the 95th Degree of the Order, they shall be appointed by the Grand Hierophant-General of the UTGS, and they shall serve in their offices for as long as the Grand Hierophant-General of the UTGS pleases.

Article X

SECTION 1: Should any vacancy occur in the office of the Grand Hierophant-General of the UTGS, the Grand Areopagus of the Celestial Empire of the Sublime Magi 96° presided by its most senior active member shall have power to perform the duties of that office until the successor to that office takes possession of the same. In this case, 'seniority' is determined by the length of continuous membership in the Grand Areopagus of the Celestial Empire of the Sublime Magi 96°; if two or more members of the Grand Areopagus of the Celestial Empire of the Sublime Magi 96° have the same length of continuous membership in it, then the temporary presiding officer of the Grand Areopagus of the Celestial Empire shall be selected by lottery from among them.

Article XI

SECTION 1: The Grand Hierophant-General of the UTGS may appoint agents and establish *ad hoc* committees for any purpose and endow them with whatever powers he or she may elect to delegate under his or her hand and seal.

Article XII

SECTION 1: Any person, male or female, at least 21 years of age, who has signed the preliminary pledge form may become a member of the UTGS if his or her application has been approved by the Worshipful Master of the Lodge to which he or she has applied, by the Grand Hierophant to whose

Grand Sanctuary that Lodge belongs, and by the Grand Hierophant-General of the UTGS.

SECTION 2: For promotion beyond the 14th Degree, it is required that every candidate must profess the Trinitarian Christian faith and write a paper clarifying his or her thoughts and intentions about his or her role and work within the UTGS.

SECTION 3: Every application for admission must be sent in writing to the Central Office or to one of the authorized local organizations. Upon receipt of one's enquiry, he or she will be put in touch with a representative of the corresponding Lodge who will be able to give one further information about joining and will make a preliminary evaluation of one's potential for admission.

SECTION 4: All diplomas and charters must be issued under the hand and seal of the Grand Hierophant-General of the UTGS.

SECTION 5: Eleven or more members of the Order may apply for a Charter to form a subordinate Lodge or organization (i.e., a College, a Chapter, a Senate, an Areopagus and Tribunal, a Consistory, a Sublime Council, a Grand Tribunal, or a Grand Sanctuary). For the creation of a Grand Sanctuary, in particular, at least thirty-three members are necessary. No person may be an active member of two Lodges at the same time. However, a person may be an honorary member of several Lodges.

Article XIII

SECTION 1: Every subordinate Lodge or organization shall have the right to conduct its own affairs according to its own wishes and bye-laws, provided that its acts and bye-laws are not contrary to the letter or spirit of this Constitution, and that they have been officially approved by the Executive Committee. The bye-laws of subordinate Lodges or organizations must bear the signature of the Grand Hierophant-General of the UTGS.

Article XIV

SECTION 1: A Congress of the UTGS may be called by the Grand Hierophant-General of the UTGS to assemble at such place and time as that officer may designate.

SECTION 2: Each subordinate Lodge or organization shall be entitled to one vote in the Congress for its first seven members, and one additional vote for each succeeding three members.

SECTION 3: The Executive Committee shall have power to prevent the discussion of, or action on, any subject which in the judgment of that committee is against the welfare of the UTGS.

SECTION 4: This Constitution may be amended by a three-fourth vote of a Congress. But no amendment shall take effect and become law until approved by the Grand Hierophant-General of the UTGS. In case of emergency, the Grand Hierophant-General of the UTGS has supreme power to amend this Constitution by 'Edict' under his/her hand and seal, which is to be recorded in the Golden Book of the UTGS.

GLOSSARY

Soul (Psyche): it is the totality of the faculties and the attributes of the human being that transcend pure biology. Moreover, the term 'soul' refers to the *personal* manner in which each human being manifests life.

Consciousness: it is that state of being which enables us to develop the functions that are necessary in order to know our environment as well as the events that happen around us and within ourselves.

Conscience (moral consciousness): it is the consciousness of existence, or, more broadly, a soul, that judges. In other words, when the consciousness of existence operates as a judge, it is called conscience.

Human Individual: this term may refer to two things: first, it may refer to a physical sample of the human species; secondly, it may refer to a particular moral agent and to a particular actor who has intrinsic (*a priori*) value, and, hence, he is a morally autonomous and responsible human being.

Person: an existential otherness (individuality) in communion, that is, endowed with sociality.

Civilization: it is a structure that consists of technology and institutions. In other words, 'civilization' refers to both the means by which a conscious community attempts to improve the terms of its adaptation to the world and the results of a conscious community's attempt to improve the terms of its adaptation to the world.

Culture: it is the result of man's reflection on his life. In other words, 'culture' is a reflective attitude toward institutions and technology as well as an attempt to transcend institutions and technology through myth, whose complex structure, however, is dialectically related to the structure of institutions and technology. The concepts of 'civilization' and 'culture' do not contradict each other. Even though civilization corresponds to 'technical construction,' and culture corresponds to 'spiritual creation,' culture is embodied in civilization and underpins civilization, which, in turn, underpins the integration of culture into history.

Individualism vs. Collectivism vs. Personalism: 'Individualism' refers to a culture that emphasizes individuality, that is, the existential otherness, of conscious beings. In the context of individualism, one's identity is primarily subjective. 'Collectivism' is a culture that emphasizes the sociality of conscious beings. In the context of collectivism, one's identity primarily stems from the group. 'Personalism' refers to a culture that emphasizes personhood, that is, it treats humans as persons. In the context of personalism, the individuals (that is, the existential othernesses) are in communion with a common, transindividual principle, which underpins the socialization of the individual. My theory of transcendental mysticism is personalistic, that is, it gives rise to personalism.

Orientalism: it refers to the family of civilizations that constitute the historical and geocultural entity which is called the 'Orient.' The major constituent parts of Orientalism are the Hindu civilization zone, the Chinese civilization zone, and the Islamic civilization zone. Orientalism has two complementary distinctive characteristics: in the context of Orientalism, society imposes relations of tight interdependence among its members, and, from this perspective, it contradicts individualism and gives rise to collectivism (holism), but, on the other hand, Oriental systems of mysticism allow and, indeed, encourage a mystic to pursue his independence from his social environment through the renunciation of the world. Thus, pursuing their individuation outside this world, Oriental mystics can be characterized as 'otherworldly individuals,' in order to be distinguished from Western 'worldly individuals,' who pursue their individuation within this world. However, due to their essentially individualistic character, many 'schools' of Oriental mysticism, especially those associated with Buddhism and Sufism, are popular in the West.

For instance, in the context of Hinduism, collectivism (holism) is founded on the concepts of *dharma* (right, duty) and *danda* (force, punishment). According to Hindu political thought, human society reproduces the cosmic order (*rta*), and the essence of political government consists in using *danda* to maintain *dharma*; the major sources of *dharma* being the *Vedas*, the *Smritis*, and *Vyavahara* (custom). Nevertheless, Hindu mystics may follow an individualistic path which is *samnyasa*, meaning renunciation or abandonment. Of the 108 Upanisads which are contained in the *Muktika*, 23 are focused on *samnyasa* as the path to *moksa*, meaning liberation. Moreover, Buddhism has invigorated the individualistic traits of Hindu civilization by

172

rejecting the caste system, by founding monasteries, by articulating a non-theological religion, and by enjoying the support of inferior social classes (e.g., traders, craftsmen, merchants, and foreign settlers).

In the context of Islamic political thought, collectivism (holism) is founded on the concept of the Caliphate, which is an organic perception of society founded on the *Sharia* (religious law). Sunni Islam holds that political and religious authority should be vested in the person of an imam-caliph elected by the *Ummah* (community), while Shia Islam (whose main groupings are the Twelvers, the Ismailis, and the Zaidis) limits the legitimacy to Mohammed's son-in-law and cousin Ali, who was ruling over the Islamic Caliphate from 665–61 AD. However, both the Sunni and the Shia emphasize the maintenance of the *Sharia*. On the other hand, Muslim mystics may follow an individualistic path. In particular, the Sufi Orders (e.g., Alevi, Bektashi, Mevlevi, Ba'Alawi tariqa, Rifa'i, Chisti, Naqshbandi, Shadhili tariqa, etc.) follow an individualistic approach to Islam, emphasizing the transmission of the divine light from the teacher's heart to the heart of the student, independently of the worldly society and its values. In the eighth and the ninth centuries AD, great Sufi masters argued that they achieved the illumination of their individual souls by individual exertion, mortification, and austerity. Moreover, despite the Islamic tradition's general discomfort with parable, allegory, and metaphor, many Sufi masters make extensive use of parable, allegory, and metaphor.

In contrast to both Orientalism and Western individualism, the Greek East, being founded on Hesychasm, maintains that the world is neither a morally 'neutral' object to be exploited by *homo economicus* nor something that must be renounced. Thus, Hesychast asceticism is substantially different from an Oriental mystic's path of renunciation. A Hesychast affirms the goodness of Creation (in accordance with Genesis 1:31), prays for the entire world, participates in the communal life of the Church, and, far from pursuing his individuation outside this world, he participates in the afflictions of the world through Christocentric love and prayer, and he aims at directly socializing with God, Whom he understands as the source of the significance of all beings and things. The Hesychasts understand the world as a structure of *logoi*, and, therefore, they do not fight against the body, but they aim at liberating the body from the law of sin (precisely, from impersonal, uncontrolled impulses and instincts and from selfishness) and at establishing there the mind as an overseer. Moreover, the Hesychasts emphasize the difference between the terms 'mind' (in Greek, *nous*), which they conceive as the repository of God's uncreated energies (grace) within the human being, and 'intellect' (rational faculty), and, therefore, in contrast to Oriental mystical systems of meditation, the Hesychasts' notion of stillness implies that it is the mind, and not the intellect, that must be detached from the world of the senses.

Science, models, and concepts: The description of objects is called modeling, and it can be achieved through various different means, the most important of which is language. A model is an abstraction, that is, it describes only some of the corresponding object's properties. However, every model is an object itself, and, thus, it can be further described (that is, modeled) by intellectually ascending to a higher level of abstraction. Thus, in the context of scientific modeling, by the term 'object,' we refer to the following things: (i) material objects and phenomena of the physical world, (ii) models that have been created by the scientific consciousness at different levels of abstraction, and (iii) syntheses (i.e., synthetic judgments) that are derived from models.

In the context of science, the scientific consciousness creates objects from the scientific world by using a universal language. In each different scientific field, scientists may use only particular segments of , which, however, are subject to change (e.g., they can be enriched by other scientists in the context of 'scientific progress'), and, therefore, they are open systems of models. Models are usually symbolized by terms of (the universal language of modeling), and phenomena are characterized through judgments.

Specific models of phenomena are called relations. The basic relations (i.e., models of phenomena) are the following: 'segment' or 'subset' , 'if then' , 'a, not a' , 'or' , 'and' . In the context of science, the models (relations) of the previous five basic relations are formulated through the judgments, , of formal logic, and they give rise to the axiomatic system, , of formal logic. The models that satisfy the axiomatic system of formal logic are called concepts. In other words, the axiomatic system of formal logic determines a type of model that is called concept. Science is concerned with the study of objects whose models are concepts. The objective of a 'formal theory,' in particular, is the creation of models of concepts.

Idea, idealism, and (philosophical) realism: In the context of Plato's philosophy, 'ideas' are eternal cosmic energies, and, in a sense, they correspond to what the Hesychasts (Orthodox Christian mystics) call God's uncreated energies and wills. In other words, according to Plato and the Hesychasts, ideas exist independently of human consciousness, and, therefore, they are not concepts (concepts were discovered by Aristotle). Given that the reality of Plato's ideas is independent of human consciousness, Plato's theory of ideas is a variant of philosophical realism. On the other hand, in the context of modern philosophy, idealism is founded on the argument that ideas are concepts, and, therefore, reality is primarily a system of abstractions. The development of modern idealism took different forms in the eighteenth, the nineteenth, and the twentieth centuries. The most radical form of idealism is solipsism, according to which the only reality is one's own consciousness, and, therefore, knowledge of anything outside of one's own consciousness is unjustified. Moreover, idealism (in the modern sense of the term) coupled with collectivism underpins the most dangerous forms of fascism and autocratic totalitarianism.

In the history of philosophy and philosophical theology, the most important variants of (philosophical) realism are the following: (i) Platonic realism: ideas are eternal cosmic energies, which underpin the order of the world, and to which the human soul has partial access, according to the degree of one's intellectual and moral progress. (ii) Hesychast realism: ideas are divine wills, or God's uncreated energies, of which man can partake (thus, becoming god by grace) by transcending both logic and morality and by offering his mind, empty from every type of intellectual, sentimental, and volitional egoism, to the Absolute (i.e., the deity) in order to be mystically filled with God's uncreated energy, or grace. (iii) Scholastic realism: ideas are logical substances in the mind of God, which underpin theologia naturalis, that is, theological rationalism. Two important secular (atheistic) variants of scholastic realism are Hegel's philosophy of history and Marx's philosophy of history, which, in essence, is an inversion of Hegel's dialectic.

Bibliography

In addition to the sources mentioned in the text, I have used: Oxford's scholarly editions and Penguin Classics for the study of classical Greek and Latin philosophers; J. P. Migne's *Patrologia Graeca* for the study of the Greek Church fathers; J. P. Migne's *Patrologia Latina* for the study of the Latin Church fathers; Ph. Schaff's and H. Wace's *A Select Library of Nicene and Post-Nicene Fathers of the Christian Church*; the collection *Sources Chrétiennes* (a bilingual collection of patristic texts founded in Lyon in 1942 by the Jesuits Jean Daniélou, Claude Mondésert, and Henri de Lubac); the Nestle–Aland edition of the New Testament; the *Septuagint* and the *Biblia Hebraica Stuttgartensia* for the study of the Old Testament; the World English Bible (WEB) public domain (http://ebible.org/web/); the *Philokalia* editions by Perivoli tis Panagias Publications (Thessaloniki, Greece) and by "Aster" Publishing (Athens, Greece) for the study of the Hesychasts (Neptic fathers); the *Little Russian Philokalia*, published by St Herman Press (Saint Herman of Alaska Monastery, Platina, California); *To Gerontikon* (a Greek collection of sayings of Eastern Orthodox monks), edited by Monk Pavlos, published by the Orthodox Foundation "Apostle Barnabas" (Athens, Greece); the *Sacred Books of the East* (a 50-volume set of English translations of Asian religious writings), edited by Max Müller and published by the Oxford University Press between 1879 and 1910, for the study of Hinduism, Buddhism, Taoism, Confucianism, Zoroastrianism, Jainism, and Islam.

In the context of my research in Freemasonry, I have studied several rituals of the following Masonic Orders:

Symbolic Masonry (the 'Craft'),

Holy Order of the Royal Arch of Jerusalem,

Ancient and Accepted Scottish Rite (33 Degrees),
Ancient and Primitive Rite Memphis–Misraim (97 Degrees),
Order of the Mark Master Masons,
Order of the Royal Ark Mariners,
Order of the Royal and Select Masters,
United Religious, Military, and Masonic Orders of the Temple and of St.
John of Jerusalem, Palestine, Rhodes, and Malta,
Rectified Scottish Rite (Order of the Knights Beneficent of the Holy City),
Order of Strict Observance,
Order of the Holy Royal Arch Knight Templar Priests,
Royal Order of Scotland, and
Societas Rosicruciana in Anglia.

References

Antoine Faivre, *Access to Western Esotericism*, New York: State University of New York Press, 1994.

Bamford, Christopher, *An Endless Trace: The Passionate Pursuit of Wisdom in the West*, New York: Codhill Press, 2003.

Barnstone, Willis, ed., *The Other Bible: Jewish Pseudepigrapha, Christian Apocrypha, Gnostic Scriptures, Kabbalah, Dead Sea Scrolls*, San Francisco: Harper, 2005.

Bauer, Walter, *Orthodoxy and Heresy in Earliest Christianity*, Philadelphia: Fortress Press, 1971.

Braudel, Fernand, "Histoire et sciences socials: la langue durée", *Annales*, Vol. 4, 1958

Carr, Edward H., *What Is History?*, London: Penguin, 1961.

Carr, Harry, *The Freemason at Work: The Definitive Guide to Craft*, 7th edition, revised by Frederick Smyth, London: Ian Allen, 2007.

Cassirer, Ernst, *The Philosophy of Symbolic Forms*, Volume One: Language, Volume Two: Mythical Thought, trans. R. Manheim, New Haven: Yale University Press, 1955.

Dobbs, B. J. T., "Newton's Commentary on the Emerald Tablet of Hermes Trismegistus," in *Hermeticism and the Renaissance*, edited by I. Merkel and A. G. Debus, Washington: Folger Shakespeare Library; London : Associated University Presses, 1988.

Durand, Gilbert, *Les Structures Anthropologiques de l'Imaginaire: Introduction à l'Archétypologie Générale*, Paris: P.U.F., 1963.

Dwor, Mark S., "The Tracing Boards," presented at the Vancouver Grand Masonic Day, October 16, 1999, Centennial-King George Lodge No. 171. See: http://freemasonry.bcy.ca/texts/gmd1999/tb_history03.html

Edinburgh Encyclopedia, Vol. 17, Philadelphia: Joseph Parker, 1832.

Ellul, Max Joseph, *The Green Eight Pointed Cross*, Malta: Watermelon/Saint Lazarus Hospice Foundation, 2004.

Farina, Salvatore, *Il Libro Completo dei Riti Massonici*, Milan: Gherardo Casini Editore, 2009.

Faulks, Ph., and Cooper, R. L. D., *The Masonic Magician: The Life and Death of Count Cagliostro and His Egyptian Rite*, London: Watkins, 2008.

Findel, J. G., *The History of Freemasonry: From Its Origin Down to the Present Day*, 2nd revised edition, London: George Kenning, 1869.

Flowers, S. E., and Moynihan, M., *The Secret King: The Myth and Reality of Nazi Occultism*, revised and expanded edition, Port Townsend, WA: Feral House, 2007.

Frankfort, Henri, *Kingship and the Gods*, Chicago: University of Chicago Press, 1979.

Friedman, David D., *The Machinery of Freedom*, La Salle, Illinois: Open Court, 1995.

Gabb, Sean, "Must Libertarians Believe in Open Borders?", 12 August 2015; see: http://thelibertarianalliance.com/2015/08/12/must-libertarians-believe-in-open-borders/

Ganser, Daniele, *NATO's Secret Armies*, Oxford: Frank Cass, 2005.

Garnier, John, *Israel in Britain*, London: Robert Banks & Son, 1890.

Gaza, Enea di, *Teofrasto*, Napoli: Salvatore Iodice, 1958.

Gibb, H. A. R., *The Damascus Chronicle of the Crusades: Extracted and Translated from the Chronicle of Ibn Al-Qalanisi*, New York: Dover, 2003.

Goodrick-Clarke, Nicholas, *The Occult Roots of Nazism: Secret Aryan Cults and Their Influence on Nazi Ideology*, London: I. B. Tauris & Co., 2004.

Gould, Robert F., *The History of Freemasonry*, Vol. V, London: Caxton, 1931.

Guthrie, William K. C., *Orpheus and Greek Religion: A Study of the Orphic Movement*, Princeton: Princeton University Press, 1993.

Halliday, Frank E., *An Illustrated Cultural History of England*, London: Thames & Hudson, 1967.

Hamill, John, *The Craft: History of English Freemasonry*, London: Aquarian Press,

Hoyos, Arturo de, "On the Origins of the Prince Hall Scottish Rite Rituals," in *Freemasonry in Context: History, Ritual, Controversy*, edited by A. de Hoyos and S. B. Morris, Lanham, Maryland: Lexington Books, 2004.

Hunger, Herbert, *Die Hochsprachliche Profane Literatur der Byzantiner*, Vol. 2, München: Beck, 1978.

Jung, Carl G., "The Relations Between the Ego and the Unconscious", in *The Portable Jung*, edited by J. Campbell, New York: Penguin Books, 1971.

Laos, Nicolas, *Methexiology: Philosophical Theology and Theological Philosophy for the Deification of Humanity*, Eugene, Oregon: Wipf and Stock Publishers, 2016.

Lévi-Strauss, Claude, *The Raw and the Cooked*, trans. John and Doreen Weightman, Chicago: The University of Chicago Press, 1969.

Ligou, Daniel, *Histoire des francs-maçons en France*, France, private publisher, 2000, Tome 1.

Livingstone, David, *Black Terror White Soldiers: Islam, Fascism, and the New Age*, U.S.A.: Sabilillah Publications, 2013 .

Mackey, A. G., *Encyclopedia of Freemasonry*, new and revised edition, New York and London: The Masonic History Company, 1914.

Marcel, Gabriel, *Being and Having*, trans. K. Farrer, Westminister: Dacre Press, 1949.

Mémoire historique sur la maçonnerie, supplément de l'Encyclopédie, 1773.

Mendoza, Harry, *Fifty Royal Arch Questions Answered*, England, private publication, 1994.

Oliver, Rev. George, *The Antiquities of Free-Masonry*, new edition, London: Richard Spencer, 1843.

Parfitt, Tudor, *The Lost Tribes of Israel: The History of a Myth*, London: Phoenix, 2003.

Pirenne, Henri, *Medieval Cities: Their Origins and the Revival of Trade*, updated edition, Princeton, NJ: Princeton University Press, 2014.

Poole, Rev. W. H., *Anglo-Israel*, Toronto: Bengough Bros., 1879.

Pritchard, James B., *Archaeology of the Old Testament*, edited by K. C. Hanson, Eugene, Oregon: Wipf and Stock, 2008.

Purver, Margery, *The Royal Society: Concept and Creation*, Cambridge: M.I.T Press, 1967.

Ralls, Karen, *Knights Templar Encyclopedia*, Franklin Lakes, NJ: Career, 2007.

Riley, J. R., "Masonic Certificates," *Quatuor Coronati Antigrapha*, Vol. VIII, 1891.

Sabine, G. H., and Thorson, T. L., *A History of Political Theory*, 4th edition, Fort Worth: Holt, Rinehart and Winston, 1973.

Saussy, F. Tupper, *Rulers of Evil: Useful Knowledge about Governing Bodies*, HarperCollins, 2001.

Sharp, David, *Oliver Cromwell*, Oxford: Heinemann, 2003.

Tharoor, Ishaan, "The Aryan Race: Time to Forget It?" *Time*, December 15, 2011; see: http://world.time.com/2011/12/15/the-aryan-race-time-to-forget-about-it/

Tomlinson, Richard, *The Big Breach: From Top Secret to Maximum Security*, Moscow: Narodny Variant Publishers, 2001. See: http://www.telegraph.co.uk/news/worldnews/1319316/Tomlinson-spy-memoir-plot-thickens.html

Van den Broek, Roelof, *The Myth of the Phoenix: According to Classical and Early Christian Traditions*, Leiden: E. J. Brill, 1971.

Van Olst, Bas Rijken, "Max Müller and H. P. Blavatsky," *Sunrise: Theosophical Perspectives*, June/July 2006 (Theosophical University Press); see: http://www.theosophy-nw.org/theosnw/world/general/ge-bas2.htm

Warren, Marcus, "Tomlinson Spy Memoir Plot Thickens," *The Telegraph*, January 24, 2001; see: http://www.telegraph.co.uk/news/worldnews/1319316/Tomlinson-spy-memoir-plot-thickens.html

Waterfield, Robin, *René Guénon and the Future of the West*, 2nd edition, Hillsdale, NY: Sophia Perennis, 2002.

West, Martin L., *The Orphic Poems*, Oxford: Oxford University Press, 1983

Willan, Philip, "Terrorists 'Helped by CIA' to Stop Rise of Left in Italy," *The Guardian*, March 26, 2001; see: http://www.theguardian.com/world/2001/mar/26/terrorism

Ziegler, Günter M., *Do I Count?: Stories from Mathematics*, Boca Raton, FL: CRC Press/Taylor & Francis Group, 2014.

"*... too high-minded to endure the degradations of the others...*"
Thomas Jefferson
First Inaugural Address, March 4, 1801

"*... The simplest and most accessible key to our self-neglected liberation lies right here: Personal non-participation in lies...*"
Alexander Solzhenitsyn
"Live Not By Lies," February 12, 1974

About the Author

Dr. Nicolas Laos was born in Athens, Greece, on July 2, 1974. His father, Kyriakos Laos, an officer of the Greek Gendarmery, and his mother, Eleftheria née Karaouli, a government employee at the Greek Ministry of Public Order, ensured a comfortable youth and a sound education for him. Dr. Nicolas Laos is a philosopher, politologist, and political consultant. His primary areas of expertise are ontology, epistemology, ethics, philosophical theology, political philosophy, noopolitics, netwar, and cultural diplomacy; his secondary areas of expertise are geopolitics, geoeconomics, political economy, organizational behavior, hypergame theory, monotonic and non-monotonic logics, and history of intelligence.

Dr. Laos has a versatile academic and research background. He has studied Mathematics, Politics, and Humanities. He graduated from the University of La Verne (California) with Honors and awards from the same University's Department of Mathematics. At the University of La Verne, under the supervision of Professor Themistocles M. Rassias (Fellow of the Royal Astronomical Society, London, UK), he conducted advanced research in mathematical analysis, differential geometry, mathematical logic, and the history of science, and he authored the book *Topics in Mathematical Analysis and Differential Geometry*, which was published in 1998 by World Scientific Publ. Co. as Volume 24 in their prestigious research Series of Pure Mathematics. During his mathematical studies at the University of La Verne, he also completed the courses "Intellectual History of the U.S. Since 1865," "Development of American Democracy," "World Civilizations," "Principles of Sociology," "Classical Political Philosophy," "American Government & Politics," "Political Behavior," and "European Government & Politics", and he conducted research in the applications of logic and mathematics in the study of internationalpolitical affairs. In this context, he authored the book *Theory Construction and Empirical Relevance in International Relations*, which was published in 2000, in English, by the Greek academic publisher Ant. N. Sakkoulas Publications. He expanded the previous research work in his books *Foundations of Cultural Diplomacy* (New York: Algora Publishing) and *The Metaphysics of World Order* (Eugene, Oregon: Wipf and Stock Publishers).

Dr. Laos has earned a Doctoral Degree in Christian Philosophy (*Summa cum laude*) from the Academia Theológica de San Andrés, Mexico (Ukrainian Orthodox Church in Mexico). His Doctoral Degree Program in Christian Philosophy included the following courses: Methodology of Philosophical Research I–IV, Theology and Philosophy I–IV, Selected Topics in Christian Philosophy I–IV, Research in Christian Philosophy I–IV, and Interpretation of Philosophical Texts I–IV, in all of which he achieved an A grade.

He has taught theory of international politics and political philosophy at the University of Indianapolis (Athens Campus). On August 20, 2013, the then Vice Chancellor for Academic Affairs of the University of Indianapolis Athens Campus, Professor Susie Michailidis, issued an evaluation report on Dr. Nicolas Laos's scholarly work, mentioning the following: "The quality of his academic preparation, curricular design and implementation skills, as well as his rapport with the students surely places him at the top 5% of his peers." Moreover, he has consulted in noopolitics, geopolitics, geoeconomics, and world security with the R-Techno private intelligence company (Moscow), with shipping, energy, and construction corporations, and with the Research Institute for European and American Studies (Athens, Greece).

He has authored several books and articles in philosophy (including philosophical theology), politics, and the foundations of mathematics that have been published in English and Greek. Between 2012 and 2015, he authored more than four hundred investigative articles on world affairs that were published in authoritative Greek newspapers and magazines as well as on informative websites and blogs. In 2014, he developed and launched a successful weekly investigative documentary program called "Geopolitiki kai Noopolitiki" (Geopolitics and Noopolitics) on the Greek web TV channel Vmedia.

At the 26th Investiture Ceremony of the Grand Priory of England, Wales, Isle of Man and Channel Islands of the Hospitaller Order of Saint Lazarus of Jerusalem, held on September 27, 2008 in the Priory Church of Saint Bartholomew the Great in the City of London, Dr. Nicolas Laos was awarded the title of Knight of Saint Lazarus of Jerusalem by the Master-General of the United Grand Priories of the Hospitaller Order of Saint Lazarus of Jerusalem, Frà John Baron Dudley von Sydow von Hoff (under the Patronage of Lord Robert Balchin, Baron Lingfield, Kt, DL, a Conservative member of the UK House of Lords and Pro-Chancellor of Brunel University). In 2013, on Saint Theodosius of Kiev's feast day, Dr. Nicolas Laos was awarded the title of Chevalier-Grand Profès de l' Ordre des Pauvres Chevaliers du Christ et des Saints Cyrille et Méthodie by His Beatitude Dr. Daniel de Jesús Ruiz Flores, First Hierarch of the Ukrainian Orthodox Church in Mexico (Iglesia Ortodoxa Ucraniana en México). Moreover, on May 8, 2013, the Most Rev'd Dr. Norman S. Dutton, Metropolitan Archbishop of the Anglican Episcopal Church International, bestowed upon Dr. Nicolas Laos the title of Ecclesiastical Duke of Bethphage.

Dr. Laos is the Founder and Grand Hierophant-General of the "United Traditionalist Grand Sanctuaries of the Ancient and Primitive Rite Memphis–Misraim," an international Freemasonic and scholarly organization founded in 2015 on his theory of transcendental mysticism and noopolitical research work.

APPENDIX: PERSONAL DOCUMENTS

Document 1

Above: Dr Nicolas Laos, 97° (in the back row, the fourth from the left), in his full Masonic regalia as the Grand Hierophant-General of the United Traditionalist Grand Sanctuaries of the Ancient and Primitive Rite Memphis-Misraim (U.T.G.S.), among officers of the "Solon" Lodge of the A.P.R.M.M., Athens, Greece, after the Installation Ceremony on December 14, 2015.

Document 2:

Right, the Most Illustrious: Brother Dr Nicolas Laos, 97°, Grand Hierophant-General of the United Traditionalist Grand Sanctuaries of the Ancient and Primitive Rite Memphis-Misraim (U.T.G.S.), with (Left) the Most Puissant Brother Angelos Bavellas, 33°, Grand Commander of the Supreme Council of the Regular Grand Orient of Rites for Greece (Past Master of the "Ionia" Lodge No. 7 of the National Grand Lodge of Greece and Past Grand Secretary of the Supreme Council of the AASR for Greece under former Grand Commander M. P. Bro. Raul De Sigura), at the "Solon" Lodge of the A.P.R.M.M., Athens, Greece, 2015.

Document 3

Left, Dr Nicolas Laos's Certificate of elevation to the 33rd Degree of the AASR signed and sealed by Bro. Angelos Bavellas.

Document 4

The major emblem of the United Traditionalist Grand Sanctuaries of the Ancient and Primitive Rite Memphis-Misraim: the Cosmic Egg with stretched wings, the letter Yod in the center of the Cosmic Egg (since Yod refers to the primal vibration of the universe, and it is the first letter of the Holy Tetragrammaton), nine stars (seven plus two) surrounding the Cosmic Egg (nine is called thin Triple Ternary and refers to the perfection of the spheres; seven is the perfect number, also termed the most venerable, since it refers to the creation of the World; two refers to the active and the passive qualities of Nature), and the eye of Horus in a radiant equilateral triangle (Sacred Delta) superimposed on the Cosmic Egg. This symbol is embroidered on every sash worn by members of the Ancient and Primitive Rite Memphis-Misraim from the ninetieth degree to the ninety-seventh degree inclusive.

Document 5

From left to right: The Ankh, also known as breath of life, the key of the Nile, or *crux ansata* (Latin meaning 'cross with a handle'): it is an ancient Egyptian symbol (hieroglyphic character)

meaning life. All members of the United Traditionalist Grand Sanctuaries of the Ancient and Primitive Rite Memphis-Misraim from the third degree to the eighty-ninth degree inclusive wear a collar on which are embroidered an Ankh (on the left-hand side), the Eye of Horus within an equilateral triangle (in the middle), as well as a square and a set of compasses joined together and superimposed by a cross pattée (on the right-hand side). The Pythagorean Tetractys with the four letters of the Holy Tetragrammaton (Yod-He-Vav-He), the Ineffable Name of God according to the Hebrews' Bible and the Kabbalah: this symbol is embroidered on the ninety-seventh degree's sash together with other ancient Egyptian and Masonic symbols.

Document 6

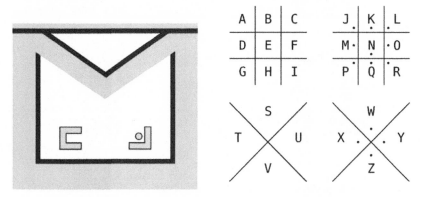

Above: On the left, the Companion Apron of the United Traditionalist Grand Sanctuaries of the Ancient and Primitive Rite Memphis-Misraim (this apron is worn by all members of the Order from the second degree to the eighty-ninth degree inclusive): it is of white satin bordered with a moiré ribbon of light sky-blue and crimson overlaid with gold fringe and having a triangular flap with a matching fringe; in the white satin area of the apron, are two embroided ciphered letters of light sky-blue and crimson that, according to the aforementioned key of the Freemason's cipher, stand for the letters F and J respectively meaning 'Freemasonry' and 'Jachin' (the Companion Degree Word).

On the right, the pigpen cipher (sometimes referred to as the Freemason's cipher) that is used by the United Traditionalist Grand Sanctuaries of the Ancient and Primitive Rite Memphis-Misraim, precisely, a geometric simple substitution cipher, which exchanges letters for symbols that are fragments of a grid.

Document 7

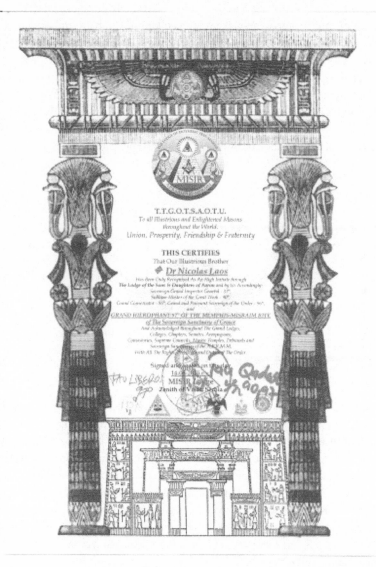

Above: Dr Nicolas Laos's Certificate of elevation to the 97th Degree of the Ancient and Primitive Rite Memphis-Misraim and of installation as Grand Hierophant of the Sovereign Grand Sanctuary of Greece of the Ancient and Primitive Rite Memphis-Misraim; issued and signed in 2015 by the Sovereign Grand Sanctuaries of Serbia (Orient of Vršak) and of the State of Georgia, U.S.A. (Orient of Atlanta) of the Ancient and Primitive Rite Memphis-Misraim.

Document 8:

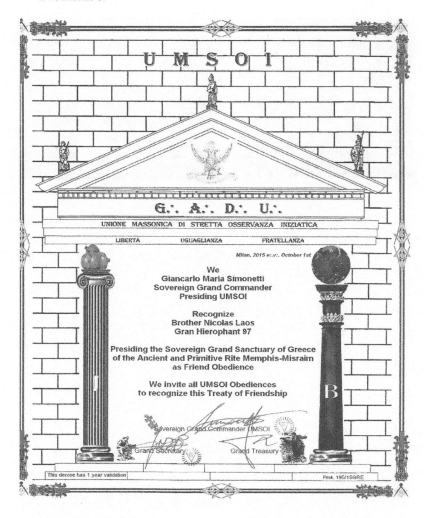

Above: The Official Statement and Masonic Treaty with which, in 2015, the Italian Freemasonic organization Unione Massonica di Stretta Osservanza Iniziatica (U.M.S.O.I.) recognized the Sovereign Grand Sanctuary of Greece of the Ancient and Primitive Rite Memphis-Misraim and Dr Nicolas Laos as the Grand Hierophant, 97o, of it. Moreover, on October 1, 2015, the Sovereign Grand Commander and President of the U.M.S.O.I., Most Puissant Bro. Giancarlo M. Simonetti, signed and sent an official letter to the Grand Hierophant of the Sovereign Grand Sanctuary of Greece of the Ancient and Primitive Rite Memphis-Misraim, Most Illustrious Bro. Dr Nicolas Laos, expressing the first's Masonic recognition, solidarity, and wishes to the second.

Document 8:

Above: On the left, Chev. Dr Nicolas Laos, wearing the distinctive chain collar of a Knight of Saint Lazarus of Jerusalem, between Lord Robert Balchin, Baron Lingfield, Kt, DL (on his right) and Lady Balchin (on his left) at the 26th Investiture Ceremony of the Grand Priory of England, Wales, Isle of Man and Channel Islands of the Hospitaller Order of Saint Lazarus of Jerusalem, held on September 27, 2008 in the Priory Church of Saint Bartholomew the Great in the City of London.

On the right, Chev. Dr Nicolas Laos, with the insignia of a Knight of Saint Lazarus of Jerusalem, with the Master-General of the United Grand Priories of the Hospitaller Order of Saint Lazarus of Jerusalem, Frà John Baron Dudley von Sydow von Hoff, who has also served as a senior officer of the Grand Lodge of Mark Master Masons of England.

Document 9:

Above: On the left, the cetificate that proclaims that Chev. Dr Nicolas Laos was knighted and appointed as Grand Commander of the Ordre des Pauvres Chevaliers du Christ et des Saints Cyrille et Méthodie by His Beatitude Dr Daniel de Jesús Ruiz Flores, First Hierarch of the Ukrainian Orthodox Church in Mexico, in 2013.

On the right, the cetificate that proclaims that His Grace Dr Nicolas Laos was awarded the title of Ecclesiastical Duke of Bethphage by the Most Rev'd Dr Norman S. Dutton, Metropolitan Archbishop of the Anglican Episcopal Church International, in 2013.

Document 10:

Above: On the left, Dr Nicolas Laos lecturing on *Pax Christiana* at an international gathering of his Order.

On the right, an evaluation report on Dr Nicolas Laos's scholarly work at the University of Indianapolis Athens Campus, issued and signed by the then Vice Chancellor for Academic Affairs of the University of Indianapolis Athens Campus, Professor Susie Michailidis, on August 20, 2013, mentioning the following: "This letter . . . is based in part on Dr Nicolas Laos's assessment of instructional materials while teaching courses: IREL 545 International Relations Theory, IREL 345 International Relations Theory. More particularly, Dr Nicolas Laos had an excellent students' evaluation of the courses he taught and demonstrated his professional and intellectual leadership in class . . . The quality of his academic preparation, curricular design and implementation skills, as well as his rapport with the students surely places him at the top 5% of his peers."

Document 11:

 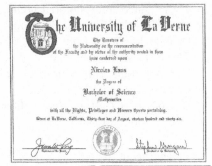

Above: On the left, Dr Nicolas Laos with Professor Themistocles M. Rassias (right) at the University of La Verne (California), in 1996, when Dr Laos received his B.Sc. in Mathematics, shown on the right. In the 1990s, at the University of La Verne, under the supervision of Professor Themistocles M. Rassias (the then Chairman of the University of La Verne's Department of Mathematics) and Professor Rehavia U. Yakovee (a faculty member of the University of La Verne's Department of Politics and International Relations), Dr Laos conducted advanced postgraduate research in the application of differential dynamics and hypergames in the study of arms races, arms transfer control policies, and diplomatic negotiations.

Document 12:

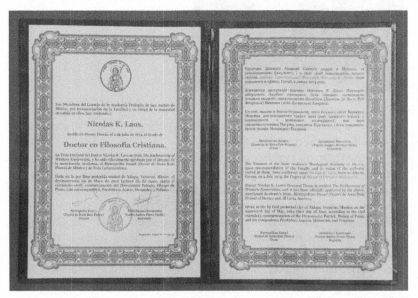

Above: Dr Nicolas Laos's Doctoral Degree in Christian Philosophy from the Saint Andrew's Theological Academy of Mexico (Ukrainian Orthodox Church).